Poet, writer, translator, Aileen Palmer – eldest daughter of Vance and Nettie Palmer, sister of Helen – volunteered for service in the Spanish Civil War and for Ambulance work in London during the second World War. This vivid study highlights her courageous struggle for freedom and self-definition as a writer and political activist in Melbourne's post war literary and arts community.

Sylvia Martin, author of the classic study of Ida Leeson, the Mitchell Librarian, has had unrivalled access to hitherto unexplored archives, and presents a memorable group portrait of interwoven lives.

Vivian Smith, poet and writer.

INK IN HER VEINS

Sylvia Martin is a scholar based at the University of Tasmania. Her previous publications include *Passionate Friends: Mary Fullerton, Mabel Singleton and Miles Franklin* (Onlywomen Press 2001), and *Ida Leeson: a life. Not a bluestocking lady* (Allen & Unwin 2006).

INK IN HER VEINS

THE TROUBLED LIFE OF AILEEN PALMER

SYLVIA MARTIN

UWA PUBLISHING

First published in 2016 by
UWA Publishing
Crawley, Western Australia 6009
www.uwap.uwa.edu.au

UWAP is an imprint of UWA Publishing
a division of The University of Western Australia

National Library of Australia
Cataloguing-in-Publication entry:
Martin, Sylvia, author.
Ink in her veins: the troubled life of Aileen Palmer / Sylvia Martin.
ISBN: 9781742588254 (paperback)
Includes bibliographical references and index.
Palmer, Aileen, 1915–1988
Women poets, Australian—20th century—Biography.
Women political activists—Australia—Biography.
Translators—Australia—Biography.
Women communists—Australia—Biography.
Spain—History—Civil War, 1936–1939.
A821.3

Cover design by Upside Creative
Cover photograph: Aileen Palmer, London, 1939.
Photographer: A. Furness. National Library of Australia.
Typeset in Bembo by Lasertype
Printed by Lightning Source

Contents

Nettie Palmer with baby Aileen, London, August 1915. Photographer: Harold Moyse. National Library of Australia Pictures Collection, pic-vn3584575.

Palmer family at Killenna, Melbourne, 1918. Nettie, Helen, Vance and Aileen. National Library of Australia Pictures Collection, pic- vn3579985.

Palmer family, Killenna, Victoria, 1918. National Library of Australia Pictures Collection, pic-vn11817.

Aileen and Helen Palmer at Ardmore, Kew, Melbourne, 1932. National Library of Australia Pictures Collection, pic-vn556901.

Vance Palmer at work on Green Island, Queensland, 1932. National Library of Australia Pictures Collection, PIC778/89 LOC Album885/1.

Thora Silverthorne and Aileen Palmer, Grañen, Aragon Front, Spain, caOctober 1936. Working Class Movement Library, Salford, UK.

Medical unit at Grañen, Aragon Front, Spain, caOctober 1936. National Library of Australia Manuscripts Collection, MS6759/5/1.

Australasian Supporters of the Spanish Govt Meet in Barcelona (Aileen Palmer second from left), December 1936. National Library of Australia Manuscripts Collection, MS6759/5/1.

Aileen Palmer, Torrelodones, Spain, 1937. National Library of Australia Manuscripts Collection, MS6759/5/1.

Sunbathing at Our Last Hospital: Our Chief Spanish Surgeon (Aileen Palmer seated at left, Dr Moises Broggi lying centre), Torrelodones, Spain, 1937. National Library of Australia Manuscripts Collection, MS6759/5/1.

CE READY FOR
KE
ROW

D WITH IRON DIS-
ABOUR MOVEMENT
NG THE FINISHING
RATIONS FOR TO-
L STRIKE AGAINST
LAWS.

mittee of the General
led at a special meet-
in spite of the Gov-

Miss A. Palmer (holding knitted goods), who recently flew back from Spain, is now going on tour for three weeks for the Spanish Youth Foodship Committee. Here she is seen with the van which will tour Britain.

Workless Leaders Received

LEADERS of the Scottish unemployed workers assembled in Edinburgh after their long march from all parts of Scotland have presented their demands to representatives of the Government, and have been assured that their points will be given careful consideration.

After the 300 men had marched along Princes Street with bands and banners, their deputation was in conference for over two hours with officials of the Ministry of Labour, the Scottish Office, the

TWO BRITISH SHIPS BOMBED

TWO British merchant ships, the Stangrove and the Stanwell, were damaged when the port district of Barcelona was raided by a squadron of five Savoia 81's yesterday morning.

Both ships are owned by J. A. Billmeir and Company, of London.

Department of Health and the Unemployment Assistance Board.

Newscutting from *Daily Worker*, London, 29 November 1938. Working Class Movement Library, Salford, UK.

Aileen Palmer passport photograph, London, 1940. National Library of Australia Manuscripts Collection, MS6759/5/2.

Ambulance Station, Stepney, London, August 1940 (Aileen second from left). National Library of Australia Manuscripts Collection, MS6083/4.

Portrait of Aileen Palmer by Madge Hodges (1938) in background of Vance and Nettie Palmer, Ardmore, Kew, Melbourne, ca1950.

Vance and Nettie Palmer with portrait of Aileen Palmer in background, Ardmore, Kew, Melbourne, ca1950. National Library of Australia Pictures Collection, PIC778/36A.

Helen Palmer, ca1940s. National Library of Australia Pictures Collection, PIC778/273.

Nettie Palmer in 1958. Private collection of John Barnes.

Aileen Palmer, Nettie Palmer and Pushkin the cat, Ardmore, Kew, Melbourne, April 1964. National Library of Australia Pictures Collection, PIC778/21.

Tribute issue of *Meanjin* for Vance and Nettie Palmer, No. 2, 1959.

To Huu, *Poems* (translated by Aileen Palmer), Hanoi, 1959.

Ho Chi Minh, *Prison Diary* (translated by Aileen Palmer), first published Hanoi, 1962.

Aileen Palmer, *World Without Strangers?*, poems and translations by Aileen Palmer, Overland, 1964.

Sketch for the memorial window for the International Brigaders in the Spanish Civil War at the Belfast City Hall. The large stained glass window was unveiled on 24 November 2015. Courtesy of Belfast City Council.

Wording for the brass plaque beside the memorial window features the last verse of a poem by Aileen Palmer. Courtesy of Belfast City Council.

With the agreement of all the political parties, this window was commissioned to reflect the contribution of citizens from Belfast to the fight against fascism in the Spanish Civil War between 1936 and 1939.

About 320 Irish volunteers fought against Franco's forces as members of the XV International Brigade. Of these, 48 were born in Belfast and 12 died in Spain.

For many the Spanish Civil War became an opportunity to stand against the growth of fascism. Men and women from all over the world answered the call to defend democracy and their working class counterparts.

Northern Ireland, already impacted by political and religious divisions, was deeply affected by these events and many local people took part in the Spanish Aid Campaign, including Belfast activists Alderman Harry Midgley, Betty Sinclair, Sam Haslett and Sadie Menzies. They played a significant role at home, raising awareness to support the democratic cause abroad.

Having given all they had to give,
To save from blood and fire and dust
At least a hope that we can trust,
We must remember them – and live.

From "The dead have no regrets" by Aileen Palmer, 1939

Introduction

Portraits

I'm looking at an old photograph of an oil portrait. A young woman's head emerges from a sombre, undefined background. Short-cropped dark hair slicked back from a pale, angular face above a black high-necked sweater – the look is androgynous, bohemian. The artist has painted her subject in half-profile, as if caught in earnest conversation with someone just outside the frame on the right. Her left arm is raised, elbow perhaps resting on an unseen table, cigarette tucked nonchalantly between the fingers of her curled hand, ready for the next puff. The portrait is so immediately striking that you want to know who she is and when it was painted. Where could she be? In a cafe, in Paris perhaps? You feel almost as though you could meet such a young woman walking along a city street today...

I found this portrait when I was in Canberra burrowing through the chaotic papers of Aileen Palmer in the National Library archives. Actually, I had taken a rest from the chaos and was flicking through the photograph albums of the Palmer family in the well-ordered archive of her better-known parents. The portrait is in the background of a faded snapshot of Vance and Nettie Palmer, prominent in the world of Australian literature in the first half of the twentieth century but hardly household names today. They are standing in their living room at Ardmore in the Melbourne suburb of Kew, and look to be in their sixties, which would date the photo to around 1950. The portrait, in a heavy gold frame, hangs on the wall behind them.

When I first noticed the portrait in the background of the snapshot, I wondered if it was of Nettie when she was young. But the pose suggests the interwar period when a cigarette in an elegant woman's hand denoted modernity and independence. Then it dawned on me that it was the portrait of Aileen Palmer I had read about in letters to her parents from London in 1938, but which I could not find among the realia of the Palmer archive. Aileen wrote that Australian artist Madge Hodges (a 'Meldrumite') had asked her to sit for her, explaining: *She didn't think I would be the kind of sitter who would ask her to lengthen my eyelashes, etc. thus more or less inducing her to falsify her work as some sitters do.* Madge Hodges's attitude would have suited Aileen, who cared little for her appearance and even less for the conventional trappings of femininity. Yet it must be said that, while the artist might not have lengthened Aileen's eyelashes, she has certainly trimmed the lines of her sitter's face and lightened her Palmerish profile, inherited from her strong-featured father.

I knew from Nettie Palmer's diary that she had received the portrait when it was brought back to Australia by a family friend in 1940. 'Remarkably good', was her verdict. 'Rather dominant – Napoleonic, conducting the world with a cigarette'. When Vance saw it, he too was impressed. 'Daughters increasing in virtue', noted Nettie cryptically after her husband's response. Ten days later the portrait was framed and ready to hang – and there it is on the wall at Ardmore in a photograph of Nettie and Vance taken at least ten years later.

As I study this little snapshot, I see that the portrait hangs not only behind the couple but between them. Knowing what I do about Aileen, I am struck by the accidental significance of this arrangement. The earnest young woman in the portrait appears to be gazing at her father, who is half-turned towards her while smiling in a slightly aloof manner at the camera. Nettie, head turned away from the portrait and facing the camera, looks a little like a startled rabbit caught in the glare of headlights, but that could just be the flash.

On this particular research trip, I am in Canberra for a month, each morning walking to the library through parks golden with autumn leaves that swish and crackle under my feet, leaving again in the chilly twilight with my head full of the Palmers and, particularly, of Aileen. Each day brings new discoveries and more puzzles and frustrations as the folders of incomplete (and sometimes illegible) bits of correspondence, the unfinished autobiographical fiction pieces that she called her *semi-fictional bits of egocentric writing*, the scraps of poetry, the incomplete diary entries and the envelopes of photographs offer glimpses of the child, the adolescent, the woman who was Aileen Palmer. Tantalising, yet always just out of reach. This is not only because of the fragmented nature of what has been kept; her writing is often oblique, her letters 'abstract' as her mother used to complain, her diaries full of coded initials. Secrecy seems to have been a way of life for this woman.

Aileen, like her parents, was a writer. Like her mother, she was a fine linguist too. She was also a political activist, joining the Communist Party while at Melbourne University in the early 1930s and then volunteering to join the Republican side of the Spanish Civil War in 1936 as interpreter for the British Medical Aid Unit. Her one published volume of poetry is long out of print, but I discovered that several of her poems have recently appeared in an anthology of poetry by International Brigaders in the Spanish War. When I moved beyond paper archives and books into the newer technologies, I found one of her war poems, 'Thaelmann Battalion', being given a stirring reading in Spanish by a bearded young man on a YouTube video.

Intrigued by this woman who was described by one contemporary writer as the Palmers' 'tragic daughter' because she spent many of her later years in and out of mental institutions in Melbourne, I followed a biographer's trail, within Australia and across the world. I visited archives in Canberra, Sydney and Melbourne; I took the tram to Kew and found the address for the family home 'Ardmore', now the site of a block of townhouses. Overseas, I sat for days in the library of Marx House in London, which Aileen frequented in 1935; I stood outside the house the Palmers rented in the village of Montgat near Barcelona in 1936; I travelled to the battle sites of the Spanish Civil War, from Grañén on the plains of Aragon to the mountain-top town of Teruel.

Why, I asked myself, would a young woman of twenty-one volunteer to risk her life in a foreign war? Why did her world then unravel when she returned to Australia in the 1940s? When she suffered her first breakdown at the age of thirty-two, Edith Young, a friend of the Palmers whose London flat Aileen had shared for a while in 1939, wrote to them that she thought there were 'two Aileens': 'the one practical and matter of fact and full of political zeal, the other, imaginative and subtle and unsatisfied emotionally'. She continued that she also thought that there would be a conflict between these two selves that might ultimately cause a breakdown. Reflecting on this idea and in order to imagine my way into her life, I wrote these pen portraits of the two Aileens based on my readings from the archives…

London, 23 August 1936: A vast crowd – 10,000 people, it will later be reported – is milling around the entrance to Victoria Station, jostling to catch a glimpse of the proceedings inside. They had gathered in Hyde Park to accompany the twenty-two volunteers of the British Medical Aid Unit along the route from the London Trade Union Club in New Oxford Street to the channel train, bound for France and eventually to aid the Republican forces in Spain. Well-wishers thrust bouquets of flowers into the arms of the volunteers as they passed along Buckingham Palace Road in a convoy of Daimlers lent by the London Cooperative Funeral Department. Now, on the station platform, a brass band plays as the Labour mayors of six London boroughs in their full regalia mingle with the members of the organising committee and the departing volunteers. Most of those leaving are young men, the bold red cross you can see emblazoned on the white arm and hat bands of their uniforms distinguishing them as medical personnel. A few figures in navy blue stand out among the splash of khaki. These are the female volunteers, wearing the regulation blue coats and caps of the nurses' uniform.

Aileen Palmer, one of the young women in blue leaving for Spain on that Sunday afternoon was not a nurse, but a secretary and interpreter for the unit. Unlike the other volunteers, the twenty-one year old Australian was on her way back to Spain. She had been staying with her parents, Vance and Nettie Palmer, in the little coastal village of Montgat outside Barcelona when the July coup organised by four rebel generals was staged. The Palmers had been there since May on a working sojourn: Nettie writing articles for *The Argus* and learning Spanish, Vance writing a novel, and both of them working on an abridgement of Joseph Furphy's novel *Such is Life* that Vance had been commissioned to undertake. Aileen typed up completed sections of the abridged version, adding her own suggestions and comments along the way.

Her energies at this time were directed mostly towards Barcelona where she had been using her university-learned language skills to translate material for the *Olimpiada Popular*, the People's Olympics organised by the Catalan Communist Party to counter the forthcoming official games in Nazi-controlled Berlin. As the political tensions in Spain escalated, Aileen would discuss the volatile situation with her new friends in a *fonda* in one of the small streets off the Ramblas over plates of octopus or rice with snails. Strikes were paralysing the city, then in July came news of the assassination in Madrid of a prominent right-wing opponent of the elected Popular Front government. *The days passed, heavy with foreboding,* Aileen would write later. *Every day, travelling in by train to Barcelona, you saw reinforcements of Civil Guards pouring into the city.*

When the rebel army generals with their North African militia stormed the city on a sweltering weekend in July, Aileen was staying at the flat of friends so that she could be on hand to translate for the athletes arriving in Barcelona for the games that were due to start on Monday. She was awoken in the early hours of the morning of the 19th by comrades who had been out on the streets all night: *'It's begun. They're fighting in the city now. We've seen the first dead.'*

The rebel soldiers had marched into the city, taking possession of strategic buildings on one of the main boulevards by entering them shouting, *'Viva La Republica!'* At first no one realised they were enemies, but then the workers who began lining the streets tore up paving stones and built barricades, grabbing whatever arms the government handed out. Despite the bloody fighting that ensued, the resistance prevailed and the coup did not succeed that weekend: *By Monday the fighting was over in Barcelona, except for occasional bursts of sniping in the tortuous streets back of the Ramblas. But Barcelona was a changed city.*

Indeed, Spain was a changed country and this was, in fact, the beginning of almost three years of continuous warfare all over the country. Thousands of men and women from around the world poured in to take part in the International Brigades in an attempt to stem the tide of fascism that was threatening to engulf Europe.

Aileen was determined to stay in Barcelona and play whatever part she could, but when her father visited the British Consul he was told the anarchists would take control of the city and the Palmers were urged to take advantage of their British citizenship and leave on the battleship that was sailing for Marseilles the next day. Aileen rushed off to see the chief of the local militia and obtained a document from him assuring that the family would be safe, but Vance remained unconvinced, his main anxiety being that the mail would continue to be disrupted and cut off the income from abroad they were dependent upon. She argued that she should stay while her parents left, but Vance's plea to her to consider how her mother would worry finally persuaded her to give in. This always worked, even though Aileen was aware that her parents operated as a team, one putting pressure on her on behalf of the other.

As the HMS *London* sailed silently out of Barcelona harbour at dawn on 29 July with the Palmers aboard, Aileen made the decision to part with her parents and get out from under what she later called *their august and all-pervasive shadows.* While Nettie and Vance stayed a few days in Paris, Aileen travelled ahead of them to London determined to find her own digs and a job. She met Isabel Brown of the Relief for Victims of Fascism who was forming a committee in answer to an appeal by the Spanish Government for medical assistance. Aileen told her she was *hopping mad* at having to leave Spain and would do anything to help.

For the next three weeks Aileen worked day and night in the two-roomed office at the top of a narrow flight of stairs in the Trade Union Club building in Holborn that was the headquarters of the Spanish Medical Aid Committee (SMAC). Plans were made to secure supplies and equipment and the various volunteers were chosen. Two days before the unit was due to leave she was invited to go for a beer with some of the SMAC members late one night where she was asked if she would consider leaving with the unit as secretary and interpreter. It was put to her that her experience in Barcelona and her ability to speak Spanish as well as fluent French and German would be invaluable in helping the unit get through red tape and foreign regulations. For Aileen, who had not considered joining the unit as she had no medical experience, the invitation was irresistible.

Nettie and Vance, who had reached London by then, were consulted and, while both were apprehensive about their daughter heading off for a war zone, they rallied and supported her. They themselves were writing articles and giving radio broadcasts about the situation in Spain before their return to Australia to take up the cause there. Vance had been feeling guilty about insisting that Aileen leave Barcelona with them; Nettie busied herself attending to practical details like shopping for underclothes and other necessities that her daughter had no time to think about. Aileen's only request was for an adequate supply of Craven A cigarettes.

They did not manage to find her among the crowd at the station to say a final goodbye, but as the train was gathering steam, Nettie caught sight of her daughter's strong Palmer profile under the blue storm cap she wore over her Eton crop. It was an image she would not forget. Aileen was leaning out of the train window shaking hands with the comrades she had been working with over the previous three weeks. Nettie had to admit she looked very happy and told her mother in her next letter home that Aileen deserved to be so, being actually permitted to do something she believed in.

Aileen was to call her time in Spain *my first coming of age.*

Melbourne, Easter 1948: Aileen's head was buzzing. *My mind is so full of the echoes of words that have haunted me...taking out all of the bunkum that some words hold, the poison, the dangerous bunkum that some words hold, that sets me off thinking like this. Thinking too quickly... Remembering things.* Her mind was racing so fast that her fingers on the typewriter could not keep up, even though her trusty portable sometimes seemed like an extension of herself. It had accompanied her in ambulances rattling over the bone-shaking dirt roads of Aragon in 1936. It had sat on tables set up in cupboards or corners of wards or hospital tents that had become her makeshift offices over the two following years, where she wrote letters in Spanish or French or German as the occasion required. It had then travelled in her case from bedsit to bedsit in London during the Blitz where she drove ambulances and tried to ignore the air-raid sirens as she wrote her novel about her time on the battlefields of Spain. Now it was here, back in Melbourne, battered (a bit like herself really) but still functioning – just.

Promised land: that was what Australia had seemed...Songs – the songs they used to sing – foul or comic, brave or nostalgic – haunted her now... Ta-la-la-la-by-by: you want the moon to play with...Everyone of course wanted the moon to play with – something to rouse the lost community spirit, the romantic spirit of peasants and gypsies and children that wore out so soon in the great amorphous cities that spread like a fungus without a heart. Something seemed to have snapped when the gypsy spirit went out of her, and she felt as though she were perpetually perched on a kind of precipice... Gypsies...

Carmela mia, que guapa eres,

La mas bonita de las mujeres...

She had to get out of this dark room where she spent her nights keeping herself awake with cigarettes and benzedrines. There was no time to sleep, so much to write.

She'd wasted the first two years after she returned in 1945, outwardly cheerful, giving radio talks, going to parties, listening to Nettie talk of her very valuable work among the refugees for Australian Spanish Relief. She herself had spoken calmly, collectedly, like an intellectual to the people who wanted to hear her tell of her experiences in Spain, the war in Europe (*comfortable, cushioned people, stuffed men*, she called them privately). But she had felt an inner detachment all through that time, as if sealed off in a cage of glass, in a state she called frozen mind, until recently when the unfreeze had started to set in and the thoughts whirling in her head had left her no choice but to try to get them down as quickly as she could. The bennies had helped and now she couldn't sleep if she wanted to, but at times her hands shook so much they refused to hit the right keys and she had to resort to scribbling on scraps of paper. Nettie had startled her – no, shocked her – one night by coming upstairs and banging on her door in the small hours beseeching her to go to bed, the hysterical edge to her voice driving her daughter crazy. Eventually, Aileen had given in and gone to bed so that she could get some peace. Sent to bed by her mother at thirty-two! *Guilty? Why should she feel guilty now? She had tried all her life to do her best for society, for progress. Then after coming back to the country of her childhood, something inside her had suddenly snapped. 'No hay luna, no hay sol'.*

Vance Palmer sat at his desk on the glassed-in balcony trying to finish the text for the next 'Current Books Worth Reading', the fortnightly national book review he broadcast on the ABC. A sun-worshipping Queenslander, he always sought out the warmest corners and had long since claimed this annexe, which caught the fickle southern sun whenever it chose to appear, as his workspace. The autumn sun warming him here never reached the inner rooms of the rambling old house. Vance was probably distracted from his writing this morning though, not by the warmth but by worrying thoughts about his elder daughter. If only her Spanish novel had been picked up by Gollancz, as had seemed possible at one stage, things might be different now. He'd tried to offer assistance in his letters after she sent drafts of it from London, suggesting how she could better organise the rather messy structure by creating one protagonist instead of the five or so she had started with. The ideas were there; form was what she needed to work on and refine.

In the back garden glossy bushes grew like weeds but hid the neighbour's backyard effectively and provided the illusion of spacious greenery. If he had looked out past the fruit trees towards these bushes, he would have seen Aileen wander across the lawn gesticulating and muttering to herself – or was she singing? – then stretch out on the ground, her head on her arms. Was the grass still damp?

Perhaps he remembered the occasion a few days before when he had mentioned at dinner that their friend Flora Eldershaw had angina, the same condition his sister Mabel had died of in her sixties. It was sad, yes, but Aileen's reaction had been extraordinary. She had gone suddenly white, stopped eating and rushed from the table to her room. She seemed to be in a highly excitable and shockable state altogether, this usually stoic, shy daughter of his. Nettie was beside herself with anxiety, and no doubt the subject of Wob, his younger brother, lay unspoken and heavy between them. It was just as well they had sent for Helen to come and advise them on what to do.

Aileen stretched out on the lawn, cool breeze blowing away the smoky fug from her tired brain, sun massaging her aching shoulder blades. *'On days of doubt, on days of heaviest thoughts about the fate of my people, you alone are my stay and support, oh, brave, strong, true and free Russian language'. Poetry: they could speak poetry, Pushkin and Turgenev, doubt as they might that the world about them would listen to the voice of freedom… Songs of the last depression haunted her mind:*

Once I built a railroad, made it run,
Made it run against time,
Once I built a railroad, now it's done,
Brother, can you spare a dime?

All was quiet in the back gardens of suburban Kew. An exquisite drowsiness washed over her and she closed her eyes. *But now it was the Andalusian wail she heard, the bitter-sweet wail of a people debased by hunger and oppression: cante fondo, out of the depths.*

Go down, Moses: way down in Egypt's land,
Tell, oh, oh, Pharoah! Let my people go!

My people. These are my people, drinking their beer and enjoying a time of full employment, no more rattled than the cockneys were when we came back from Spain and talked about bomb-proof shelters…

The old-fashioned and disorderly kitchen at Ardmore, the family home that Nettie had inherited when her mother died in 1944, allowed only a restricted view of the back garden. Nettie's mind, nonetheless, would have been entirely preoccupied with her daughter's strange behaviour; she didn't need to be able to see her lying on the lawn. Never known for her culinary skills, Nettie was throwing ingredients into a casserole even more distractedly than usual. But instead of preparing a review of a new book in her head or pondering over a lecture she was to give at the university, it was more likely that she was reliving the events of the small party she had attended at the flat of their friends Brian and Dorothy Fitzpatrick the previous night. Aileen had turned up unexpectedly with Flora – in an exhilarated state, red-faced and talking and laughing in a most uncharacteristic way. Although she had seemed her own sweet self since she had come back from England in 1945, typing up manuscripts for Vance and making intelligent suggestions on details, she had also been rather cut off. Nettie worried that it was her fault, that she had pressed her too hard to return and live with them at Ardmore, offering her space to write in and money to help her.

Nettie had watched her daughter carefully at the party because she and Vance suspected she was drinking too much, although they hadn't talked to her about it. While they were unflinching in their literary criticism, neither of them dealt with confrontation well on a personal level. But that night Nettie couldn't blame Aileen's behaviour on alcohol; something else was driving her nervous excess. She had harangued that poor poet mercilessly, accusing him of being a nearly-was poet, a might-have-been poet. Aileen had known him at university years before and Nettie too might have been objectively critical of his work in a review, but this was unforgivable. And when Nettie urged her to stop, she just said airily that there was too much Rimbaud in her head, as if that explained her diatribe. Even when Nettie managed to get her daughter to leave the party with her, Aileen had distressed her by talking loudly in the tram all the way home. They had managed to get her to bed with the help of one of Nettie's mild sedatives, but neither parent had slept. In the morning, Vance wired Helen to come and they started to get in touch with doctors. There had been times over the last few years when Nettie had been almost afraid of her younger daughter's cool efficiency, especially after she joined the WAAAF (Women's Auxiliary Australian Air Force)and looked so formal and untouchable in her uniform, but she knew she could depend on Helen in a crisis. She was due to arrive towards evening, if her aeroplane was on time.

Got to keep telling my mother to leave me alone, telling her not too hard or too casually but saying it somehow enough. Enough for this thing to unravel itself in my mind as I lie on the lawn – the story, perhaps, of my life. The ground was getting hard and the daylight was fading, but Aileen, spread-eagled on the grass, was incapable of moving as her thoughts went on speeding wildly in all directions. *Sick in the guts. It made her feel sick in the guts to read the newspapers they printed in Australia now. Words – bloody words! Yarn-spinning – it had been her main entertainment when she was a child. Yarn-spinning.*

Tom he was a piper's son
He learnt to play when he was young
The only tune that he could play
Was over the hills and far away...

Midsummer Night's Dream. I seen it, I seen the little lamp! Lamps among the ti-trees when they played it among the ti-trees, down at Black Rock. At the Longs' place. Dick Long – went to jail during the anti-conscription campaign. Face like Jesus Christ. Carpenter. Gave them toys...

When that I was a little tiny boy
With a hey-ho! – the wind and the rain
A foolish thing could give me joy
For the sun it rises every day...

Hills of childhood, blue sea and sky of childhood. Bottom the Weaver compose de feux la mer, la mer toujours recommencée...

There was another voice besides that of Paul Valéry in her head now, telling her urgently to get up.

'Go away, I'm busy. Can't you see I'm busy?'

She tried to concentrate on Valéry: O *récompense après une pensée...* But the voice kept on, like an insistent mosquito. Gradually, Aileen became aware that it was her sister's voice, her little sister Hell's voice. She rolled over slowly and looked up to see Helen looming over her, huge against the darkening sky, her face contorted, mouth opening and shutting like a fish gasping for air. Physhies, fishies – these were among those crazy nicknames her sister had for the family. She felt like laughing.

'Aileen, get up. Aileen! Come on, Old Face, can't you hear me? Get up!'

Aileen tried to talk rationally to her sister that day about the phenomenon of delayed shock that she felt she must be suffering from, explaining why her war experiences were only affecting her now, after several years. She might have thought Helen had accepted her very rational explanation; that is, until the young doctor arrived and she was carted off, protesting violently, to hospital.

Nettie was so distressed that she completely forgot she had accepted a dinner invitation for herself and Vance on the Easter Sunday of

1948. On the Monday she sent a note of apology to her friend Jean Campbell, to whom she confided, 'Aileen has had a breakdown & we had to send for Helen from Sydney on her account. We may know a little more about it tomorrow when doctors and appointments settle down a little after Easter: but it will be long. No more just now. We're more anxious than I dare say. Forgive my fumbling admissions. Thanks for your hearty hospitality. Yours, Nettie P.'

PART I

A Promising Life

1

Two Legacies

Aileen was to say that Spain was not her first experience of the bombardment of civilians as she was born in London shortly after the outbreak of World War I. *I grew up feeling ashamed of being a 'pommie', and, when admitting to it at the university, when we were sitting round having our sandwich lunch, said hastily: 'But I was in Brittany before I was born'.* And she was. She was conceived there when Nettie and Vance were on their working 'honeymoon', a matter of weeks before their serene life in the little fishing village of Trégastel was disrupted dramatically with the declaration of war on 4 August 1914.

It was not the Palmers' first visit to Trégastel. Nettie had attended a summer school there three years earlier when she was in the final stages of the International Diploma of Phonetics she had been studying for in Germany and Paris, and Vance had taken time off from his work as a journalist in London to join her for a week. After they finally married, the village that held such happy memories for them was their choice for the kind of working holiday they would seek out many times during their long marriage and productive working partnership. They had simple requirements: sun, sea, quiet, and fresh air.

Janet Gertrude Higgins (Nettie) and Edward Vivian Palmer (Vance) endured a lengthy courtship after they met in the summer of 1909 in the most fitting of locations – the Public Library of Melbourne. Although both were twenty-four years old, their experience of life was very different. Vance, striking with tanned, strong features, blue eyes and sporting a jaunty bow tie, was in Melbourne to follow up some journalistic contacts and had set up his informal office in the library. He had already made two trips overseas and was in fact on a visit home from his base in London to see his family in Brisbane. Nettie, less immediately striking except for her dark eyes and direct gaze, was studying for her final university examinations. The daughter of strict Baptist parents, she had led a sheltered life but was active in politics and the literature club at university. The fact that her accountant father had supported her desire for a tertiary education was progressive for the time, but his sisters had both attended university and his brother, High Court Judge Henry Bournes Higgins, provided financial as well as intellectual support to his niece.

Something had started them talking, and love of writing turned into love at first sight, wrote Aileen of her parents' first meeting. Reams of letters crossed the world and trysts both at home and abroad followed. When they were in Trégastel in 1911, Nettie and Vance decided it was time to tell their families of the engagement they had kept secret for nearly a year.

Nettie would have been happy to declare it to the world when they pledged their love in London in 1910, but the more cautious Vance was not ready, estimating that it would be two or three years before his financial situation as an aspiring journalist would be secure enough for marriage. Later, after Nettie had returned to Australia to prepare her parents for the idea of her marriage and to start teaching, he reminded her of their week together on that rocky coast in the north of France: 'I like to remember the clothes you wore, and the way you walked – the tricky little swing of your body as if your abounding life was making turns all the while with grace. Dear girl, I'll never see a sea-beach until we meet again but your figure will be moving across it, just as it did when I was waiting in the sand and you were coming over from the house. It's great to think that my mate is one whom it's most easy to remember in the wind and the sun: you will understand all that that means to me, dear'.

John and Catherine (Katie) Higgins approved of Vance as a husband for their only daughter once they had established he was a suitable choice. For Nettie, after two years of having the relative freedom to pursue her own interests and make her own decisions, the return home was not easy. Unlike Vance, whose travels to London were for the purposes of establishing his career, Nettie's trip at the completion of her university degree was intended to be a journey 'home' in which she would acquaint herself with relatives and European culture. Once in London, she quickly asserted her independence by freeing herself from her chaperone and travelling to Germany to undertake the phonetics diploma. Back in Melbourne she was immediately reabsorbed into the family fold and expected to take up the duties of a dependent daughter, even though she was now in her mid-twenties.

During this period in Melbourne Nettie tried to persuade her deeply religious Baptist parents that her own and Vance's considered position as non-believers was a legitimate one. She had struggled in her early adult years, praying for faith, but in vain. As she told Vance, her love for him had offered her 'new horizons', adding, 'but I am a bad traveller in spirit worlds: I am like a tiny vessel that can't hold the rivers of joy & faith that flow by'. Their rejection of religion was anathema to her parents who remained intransigent. Nettie's father took it upon himself to write to Vance and urge him to reconsider his faith and to pledge 'total abstinence'. Nettie said she and her mother were 'like two tense strings & I didn't dare snap, because I knew she was strained too'. Aileen was to write, years later, in one of her many 'semi-fictional' attempts to come to terms with her family that *Blake* [Vance] *took religion lightly, but Noni* [Nettie] *had an anxious, tormented time getting free of her parents' religion.* Her mother's problem, according to Aileen, was that *she was essentially almost cruelly honest* and, instead of simply keeping her beliefs to herself, felt she had to argue her case with her parents.

On Christmas Eve 1913 Vance sent a letter to Mrs Higgins thanking her for the money she and Mr Higgins had sent him as a Christmas present: 'I am using it to get a little carpet for my sitting-room that my eyes have been resting on longingly for some time, as it will be filling up my own little glory-box'. More importantly, he asked if they would consider letting Nettie travel to England to marry him. The couple were now both twenty-nine years old. 'I feel that we have waited long enough', Vance argues. 'We are so sure of being happy together, wherever we are, and I have the feeling of being on a sure footing now'. He hopes they will be able to live in Australia eventually, at least he promises they will return for a year in two years' time.

With some reluctance, John and Katie Higgins agreed to Vance's request, but it seems that the burden of her parents' religious strictures still weighed heavily on Nettie's conscience. Eager to join her fiancé, she nevertheless wrote to him suggesting that perhaps they should postpone the wedding if they could not afford to have children straight away. Vance replied, stating the reason he understood to underlie her anxiety and apologising for putting it 'crudely': 'you seem to think that the final act of sex is only tolerable as a conscious means to an end: that otherwise it's a sort of a sin; that it's different in its nature from every other kind of sexual intimacy because it may lead to the conception of a child, and that should always be a thing consciously planned. Mate, I can't put it very coherently but that seemed to me what part of your letter meant'. With a restraint that appears almost noble given that they had already waited five years, he tells her, 'I can say with perfect honesty that your wish alone shall determine all our relations. If you think that owing to circumstances, economical or otherwise, we shouldn't risk having children yet; and that being so we ought honestly to live a sexless life till the time comes when we could have children: then we'll do it. It is possible, though it isn't easy to say so lightly. Our sex-life is only for a few years though and it isn't the only thing that holds us together'. From the outset, the couple regarded themselves as soul mates, joined by a bond that was deeper than physical intimacy.

Perhaps the fear of the ultimate intimacy of sex that overcame Nettie in the months before the wedding had more complex origins than a family legacy of equating sex with procreation. Her ongoing struggle with her emotions at this important point of her life suggests an ambivalence that must have been felt by many of the university-educated New Women of the early twentieth century. Nettie's background would have made it impossible for her to seek love outside marriage. There is no doubt that she was eager to fulfil the role of good wife and mother with her chosen partner, with whom she shared so much intellectually, but she may well have been apprehensive that the independence she sought would remain out of reach when she left one institution where women were expected to be subservient to men and entered another.

At around this time Nettie tells Vance that his letters are never very intimate, a complaint that would become a motif in later years whenever they were separated; Vance, on the other hand, thinks she does not kiss him enough. While this differing understanding of what marks a true expression of love falls along conventional gendered lines, the fact that their relationship was so thoroughly based in all things literary perhaps makes the situation more complicated. Some of Vance's letters do read more like self-conscious literary love letters than spontaneous expressions of his feelings. Nettie perhaps felt that lack. In later years, a persistent criticism of his novels by reviewers and academics would concern their emotional restraint and lack of passion. Another part of the mix, however, was Nettie's particular obsession with words: as a linguist, poet and, later, literary critic. Maybe her lover's efforts at times simply fell short of Nettie's exacting literary standards.

Born into this family of writers, Aileen was to dwell in her later years on the destructive as well as enriching side of this legacy in her autobiographical writings. *We have all been rather too much in love with words, in our own ways*, she wrote in 1961. *It was, in the beginning, a gift imbibed from Nora* [Nettie] *and Blake* [Vance]*, the delight in words, and the capacity to play with words in an exciting way.* Revealingly, it was for Nettie, not Vance, that Aileen reserved her most trenchant criticism. *No basis for tacit understanding had ever grown up between Nora and me. She has always had a passion for verbalising everything. It is almost as though nothing exists for her until it has been put into words.*

The long years that Nettie endured waiting to marry Vance were not only the result of her fiancé's financial insecurities as he established himself as a journalist in London. There was also the matter of his younger brother, William, known as Wob.

In early 1912, just months after she had returned to Australia to start teaching and to prepare her family for her marriage, Nettie received a letter from Vance that heralded a situation that was to threaten their union. In it, he told her of his worry about Wob, from whom he had only received two letters since an illness the year before. And those, he said, had contained only 'bare facts' that seemed to cut him off.

Suddenly, a few months later, Vance left London, just a day after receiving a cable from his family in Brisbane with the news that Wob was ill again. He started a scribbled note to Nettie as he sat on the boat train, finishing it as he waited for his berth on a ship bound for San Francisco, the only route on which he could get a passage at such short notice. 'I've been nearly distracted running round trying to fix things up since I got the cable', he tells her. 'I don't like to think of the journey. Goodbye mate of mine. I'll probably be seeing you soon, though I'll go straight to Brisbane as soon as the boat gets to Sydney'.

On board ship, he poured out his anguish in letters to Nettie. He tells her he received 'such a strange letter' from Wob the very same day the cable arrived in London. He describes his seesawing emotions, how 'fitful gusts of assurance' alternate with 'hours in the pit'. He even dreams of Wob nearly every night: 'I never guessed until now how much he has been mixed up with all I have thought or felt. And we have had such cruelly small fragments of time together in the last seven years. I want him so hard, mate, now. You'll understand'. The man who had been criticised for his lack of emotion in his letters to his fiancée reveals quite a different side of himself in his distress about his brother.

Born in 1887, William Cecil Palmer was two years younger than Vance and the youngest in a large family except for a sister who died in infancy. The boys had a distant relationship with their only other brother, Harry, who was the eldest child. The overwhelming presence of five older sisters probably drew them close together during their peripatetic childhood in Queensland country towns, moving house as their teacher father was transferred from school to school. A mild and bookish man unsuited to teaching, Henry Burnet Palmer was never a success in the education system, but his immense love of literature instilled in his younger sons a passion for reading. Wob's artistic bent led him in the direction of drawing rather than writing and by 1912 he was becoming known as a black-and-white caricaturist. Unlike the rest of their conservative Baptist family, the brothers also shared an interest in left-wing politics.

In his anxiety about Wob, Vance neglected to contact Nettie for more than a week after reaching home in early October, replying apologetically to a worried letter from her that he had meant to wire her from Sydney, but had forgotten. This might sound extraordinary, but the circumstances of his homecoming would have driven everything else out of his mind, even his beloved Nettie. He arrived in Brisbane to find his family distraught and his brother incarcerated, having been admitted to the Wacol Insane Asylum at Goodna on 9 September suffering severe depression after making several attempts to commit suicide.

With an ineffectual father and an absent elder brother, Vance assumed charge of the situation, as his family had hoped he would. He took the train every day 'up the line' to Goodna, located between Brisbane and Ipswich. The brothers spent hours walking in the gardens of the huge red-brick asylum as Vance tried to draw Wob out. Vance found his brother quite coherent, but changed. 'He remembers everything – without interest or emotion', he reports to Nettie despondently. 'And sometimes he tries to "make conversation"! There's not a phrase he has uttered since I've been to see him that isn't quite sane, and yet I know that all the time he's living in another world that he won't let me enter, and that the world we talk about seems quite trivial and unreal to him. He makes me feel so weak and incapable. I've never come into contact with anything like this except in the most superficial way, and it seems that the only thing I can do is to try to make the normal world seems real to him again and to rouse a joy in mere life. I believe if I had him away from there I could do this much more quickly but the doctors won't let him away till all the suicidal ideas are out of his mind'.

This was the beginning of a rather utopian and desperate plan Vance was hatching to take Wob camping in the bush to restore his mind and body and then to take him back to England. Nettie, perhaps fearing that Vance's plan would delay their marriage even further, suggested they might marry when he travelled through Melbourne on his journey back, but he replied that the trip had dissipated his money. He also regretfully rejected her suggestion that they marry and then have her join him in London at the end of 1913.

What they did manage to organise was a week together in Sydney at the beginning of that year, with Nettie bringing her fifteen-year-old brother Esmonde along as her chaperone.

Nettie was both excited and shocked at Vance's appearance when he met her boat from Melbourne. Tanned and lean, he had lost two stone in the three months since he had arrived back in Australia. Although staying, of course, in separate lodgings, the couple spent the week revelling in the summer weather and the pleasures of Sydney Harbour. They took the crowded steamer to Manly for the surf carnival; they wandered through the Botanical Gardens; they watched the sun set at Watsons Bay. The whirlwind tryst and respite from the serious situation with Wob helped them renew their love and their determination to work towards their marriage. When he left, Vance vowed to visit his brother only twice a week and to work on his writing as if he was in England. Nettie wrote to him lovingly, signing one letter with a frivolous 'Your hussy'.

Back in Brisbane, Vance set to work and by the end of March had a long serial of 55,000 words ready to type up and send to his agent in London: 'I feel as if I'd crashed through a long dark tunnel', he writes. 'The whole universe seems to be crawling with words'.

He discussed his plan to take Wob camping with the medical superintendent at the asylum, 'a very clever specialist, though very English and abrupt!' He was fortunate that the superintendent, Dr Ellerton, who took over the hospital in 1908, was a progressive thinker who had initiated vigorous reform and building improvements that supported 'moral therapy', the notion that the mentally ill could be improved if they were living in an uplifting environment. Though a little sceptical about Vance's plan, the superintendent agreed to let him take responsibility for his brother. Admitting to Nettie that it would not be easy, Vance was nevertheless optimistic: 'We're going straight to a place I know in the Blackall Ranges to pitch our tent in the scrub on top of a mountain, where the air's pure and heady as wind...There'll be heaps of exercise from morning till night, working and walking, and there'll be no time to think'. If all went to plan, he intended to leave for England with his brother by the end of June.

A short time later, however, Vance's hopes were dashed when Wob suffered a relapse. Worse, after becoming violent with an attendant, he was moved to a refractory ward among the most seriously delusional patients. Vance was distraught at the conditions his brother was now living under. 'The place', he said, 'was like my notion of an asylum before I'd ever seen one and the associations were harrowing'. He described Wob's state as 'more insanity than melancholia now' and his talk as 'a swift rush of delusions' as he raved about how he had been persecuted and incarcerated because 'he'd written about the Siberian exiles in the *Worker* "till the loneliness broke their hearts and burst their brains asunder"'.

When Vance complained to the superintendent about the horrific conditions, he was told that Wob's incarceration in the refractory ward would do him good rather than harm. At a time when restraint or isolation were the principal forms of 'treatment' available, he was told that seeing patients who were worse than his brother would 'brace up his will, and the main thing in mental cures is to stir up a patient's will'. To make matters worse, Vance was told to visit Wob as little as possible for the next month so as not to stir up old memories in him. No wonder he felt powerless to help. The conditions were so appalling that he even tried to keep the information about the exact ward Wob was now locked up in from his mother and sisters, who had only seen him when he had a room to himself and freedom to walk in the gardens.

If Nettie thought the situation must have reached its nadir, she was mistaken. Vance was so despairing of his brother's condition that, in his next letter, he tentatively broached the subject of breaking off their engagement. He stressed that he did not envisage it as a probability, but that he felt it would be dishonourable of him not to suggest it to her parents. The shame of having a close family member in a lunatic asylum would have weighed heavily on all the Palmers and now that Wob's condition was so grave that Vance could no longer delude himself that he could simply be cured with fresh air and exercise, his thoughts had clearly turned to his responsibility to his future wife's family. While disturbed that Nettie's parents might consider his brother's mental illness to be hereditary, he was also desperate to preserve his own family's good name: 'There is no taint in our blood', he told Nettie. 'I have satisfied myself completely about that, at least as far as is humanly possible. Our people came from such widely different stocks that there was hardly a chance ever of consanguinity. I am not saying this of course to you, mate, but for the satisfaction of a third party if that be necessary'.

How must Nettie have felt when she read those words in Melbourne? And she might as well have been on the other side of the world, unable to sit and discuss the matter with her fiancé, unable in those days even to pick up a telephone. Her reply does not survive, but her outrage and hurt at Vance's suggestion is clear from his subsequent fumbling attempts to explain himself. Her angry words are repeated by him:

'Wob is more important than I am…'

'If I'm only a luxury…'

'I'm not going to read any irony into your phrases, mate', he writes, inflaming the situation further. 'We're too close together to be hurt by misunderstanding of the moment'.

It seems that Nettie was able to convince Vance to take that matter no further. But, on another front, she was puzzled as to why her fiancé would not consider settling down in Australia to work as a freelancer. 'We couldn't live here half as cheaply as in Europe', he told her firmly. 'I've thought it out from pretty well every angle and it seems to me that we'll have to live in Europe for five years or so, and that means I must get back as soon as possible to prevent the few threads I've twisted from unwinding'. Nettie might have been an independent young woman for her time, but where her marriage was concerned, it was Vance who made the big decisions.

Reluctantly relinquishing his plan to save Wob but promising himself to bring him to London when he recovered, Vance organised to return to England in the middle of 1913. He told his brother he was going to Melbourne, which he did, but only for a brief stopover en route to the Northern Hemisphere.

Wob spent the rest of his life in institutions: five decades of it at Goodna. Vance visited him whenever he was in Brisbane. Aileen never met her uncle but wrote about him in several of her pieces of autobiographical fiction, offering versions gleaned from family lore of the story just told. In one, she relates the story of 'Blake' taking his brother camping in the Blackall Ranges as if the utopian plan did actually eventuate. In her version, only after that attempt failed was Wob committed to the asylum.

In Aileen's writing fragments, the connection is made between her own illness and her family's fears because of the precedent of her uncle's mental condition. She refers to the sense of shame, but also guilt, that pervaded the family, encapsulated in the image of Wob's sisters *devotedly* ironing pyjamas for him *so he shouldn't look disreputable and shabby, as did probably most of the inmates of the place where he was to spend the rest of his days.* But *there remained about him something incomprehensible they couldn't forgive, or perhaps forgive in themselves.*

'It runs in the family', they used to say…

2

Ink in her Veins

Nettie finally left for London to be married in April 1914. With a speed that made up for the long years of waiting, the wedding took place at the Lower Sloane Street Baptist Church at 12.30 pm on Saturday 23 May, little more than twenty-four hours after Nettie's arrival on the train from Marseilles, the minimum period on English soil required by law. Vance's preferred venue – the registry office – was out of the question, one of Nettie's parents' conditions being that the couple marry in a Baptist ceremony. The day was hot, suitable for the white silk dress Nettie had brought with her from Australia. An aunt and uncle who lived in England acted as witnesses. Three days later the newlyweds caught the steamer from Southampton to Saint-Malo on the Breton coast.

Nettie organised their rented cottage in Trégastel, quite proud that she 'had it over' the monolingual Vance in that area, especially since her French was 'bonzer' after the weeks in transit from Australia on the French steamboat *Le Sydney.* The stone cottage she found on the sands of an inland bay cost a pound a week and they planned to take it for at least three months. Its white-washed walls, bare boards and unpainted furniture offered the simple style of living they were both to prefer all their lives. Vance even had to collect the daily supply of water from the village pump. Nettie said the villagers thought they were artists. Beyond the kitchen garden and box hedges at the front they looked over the sand and rocks of the bay to the ocean. Spring wildflowers dotted the crops and the crimson summer poppies were just beginning to bloom.

The Palmers' sojourn in Brittany was both a honeymoon and the beginning of a working partnership that was to define their lives together. Within days of their arrival, Vance started spending the mornings writing at the big table near the window in their bed-sitting room. As well as his serious work, such as the sketches published in A. R. Orage's journal *New Age*, in which most ambitious younger writers aspired to be represented, he also wrote what he dubbed 'hack work' or 'potboilers' for money – short stories and serials that were published in English newspapers such as *The Manchester Guardian*. It was a practice he was to continue for many years; fifty-seven potboilers were published under the name of Rann Daly alone.

Nettie observed him at work in those early weeks, reporting to her mother: 'I'm beginning to understand Vance's methods in working: he has to have everything planned beforehand in his mind, so that when once he puts pen to paper he practically never corrects anything...If ever I write even an essay, my rough copies are all upside-down: I do my experimenting on paper, he does his in his head'. The difference between Vance's orderliness and Nettie's scattered spontaneity characterised them in ways that extended well beyond their writing methods, as Aileen was to observe in many of her autobiographical fragments. She aligned herself with her mother.

In the afternoons the two went for long tramps and swam out to rocks in the bay, Vance carrying Nettie back to shore more than once when the tide turned. Summer was upon them by the end of their first month and Nettie told her mother they were both 'vigorously tanning, especially Vance, who cocoa-nut-oils his face, hoping thereby to achieve a beautiful, firm mahogany colour'. The Queenslander's deep tan remained his principal vanity and he worked in the sun in a deckchair whenever possible all his life, whether on the beach, in the bush or in a suburban backyard in Melbourne.

Of the people Nettie had left behind in Australia, her younger brother was the one most sorely missed. Esmonde, eleven years her junior, was in his final year at school when his sister departed. In one of the letters she received from him on the ship he bravely asserted that he didn't miss her as much as he thought he would: 'I do not feel life is altogether unliveable now'. Despite the age difference, brother and sister shared a passion for books, an interest in progressive socialist politics and a love of banter and absurd nicknames. Their close relationship may well have provided a bulwark against the strict conservatism of the Higgins household. Vance had realised he had 'a big world to fill', as he wrote to Nettie before she left home, naming Esmonde as the most important person she was to leave behind. Now, in the early days of their marriage, Vance was showing a side of himself that Nettie had not experienced before and she wrote to her mother: 'He seems much younger than he used to be, & much more full of nonsense & teasing than is quite proper in a solemn married man. I think he'll keep me young. The way Blibb [Esmonde] used to'.

The couple returned to London for a few days towards the end of July, staying in Vance's rooms at 96 Edith Grove, Chelsea. He needed to meet some of his business contacts and also wanted to pack up his flat, storing whatever furniture they were unable to sell. Nettie would have busied herself packing while Vance was out visiting his agent and Fleet Street contacts; she was probably also thinking about the third reason for the trip. Vance was to use his connections to get a collection of the poems Nettie had written over the previous few years published in time for Christmas.

With their various tasks in London accomplished, Nettie and Vance were back in their cottage in Trégastel by the end of July, planning to stay there at least another eight weeks. The declaration of war brought their plans to an abrupt halt.

First they received a telegram with a bag of letters at about 1 pm on 4 August, then later in the afternoon the official sheet was brought back by villagers from the nearby town of Lannion and the news quickly spread: 'War is officially declared: The Germans opened fire yesterday at Nancy and took the customs offices. They have entered the Luxembourg territory'.

The situation escalated with alarming speed, most of the tourists leaving while they could. Within days Nettie was writing home: 'They say England really has joined in, & that her navy is bombarding Kiel, while she is sending troops to Calais, "to maintain the neutrality of Belgium". Germany seems to have spies everywhere. A naturalised (these ten years) German dentist at St Brienc (between here & St Malo) was found putting a bomb under the railway bridge – & was shot'. She hastened to reassure her family anxiously absorbing the shocking news on the other side of the world that she and Vance were not worried for themselves but were a little disturbed that Vance's newspapers were not getting through, perhaps because of censorship. More importantly, the post he relied on for all his business dealings including the receipt of cheques was delayed.

The Palmers were forced to leave Trégastel a little over a month after war was declared. The English mails were blocked and the little fishing village with its picturesque stone houses had been entirely transformed by war. Getting away was not easy. Calais was impossible to sail from as it was swarming with troops and the Saint-Malo to Southampton boat had finished at the end of summer, so they had to take their chances at Dieppe to find a boat that would take them to England.

Nettie and Vance were probably aware of the precious cargo they carried with them on their flight from France for, just before war was declared in August 1914, their first child was conceived. London, when they eventually reached it, seemed 'safe and ordinary' in contrast to France, no doubt to their relief. The couple were soon settled into 11A Hillfield Gardens, an upstairs flat in a row of two-storey houses on a steep slope at Muswell Hill with views over Greater London, situated in an area with open fields and cross-country walks.

Soon after their arrival in London it became clear that Vance's income was in jeopardy even there. Magazines were 'crumpling in all directions' and the pair were faced with living on less than half his normal commissions. On 9 October, less than a month after their return to England, Vance sailed for America to visit the editors of the New York papers in order to try to secure new writing jobs. With ten days sailing time there and back, he spent his few days on land rushing around the scattered New York version of Fleet Street. During his absence, it was arranged that Katharine Susannah Prichard, who was living close by and working for the Melbourne *Herald's* London office, would take over Vance's study and stay at the flat to keep Nettie company.

The two women had known each other at university, though not as intimate friends since Katharine, Nettie's elder by two years, was an evening student. The 'slim and willowy' Katharine Susannah Prichard, as one newspaper described her, was to become one of Australia's most prominent novelists. She later recalled their re-acquaintance in London: 'Nettie had a distinguished scholastic record, was married to Vance Palmer, and was writing poetry. I, a struggling journalist, was slowly making my way into the English press, but could mention a few short stories already published. Vance was in something of the same position. There we were, all three of us, at the bottom of the ladder and gazing longingly at the top'. Nettie, it seems, felt she was on an even lower rung than the other two, who were more widely published and established in their careers, and confided to her mother: 'I hope I know how to behave with Katharine'.

The time together proved to be an outstanding success and Nettie soon wrote: 'She has been a splendid companion & I'm very lucky. Incidentally she has been giving me some professional tips about my writing, so that I may be able to publish some of my stuff now and then'.

Despite the world situation and their financial problems, Nettie was in a mood of steady excitement mingled with trepidation over the next few months. Though thrilled about her pregnancy, she was cautious about telling her family, perhaps waiting to make sure that it was progressing smoothly, perhaps also a little shy about the almost unseemly haste with which she had conceived. It was not until 29 October, after Vance's safe return from his American trip, that Nettie broke the news to her mother in a letter, and then only after two full pages of chat about other things. 'But before I go any further I must tell you the biggest thing that is in our minds now', she ventures carefully. 'I find that I am going to have a child'. She covers her excitement and embarrassment by burbling on that they are both so happy about it and glad that it happened early in their married life as she was not so young that she could afford to have it happen many years later for the first time and that they wanted it soon anyway. Determined to prove herself a good prospective mother, she also asks for hints about baby clothes.

At the same time, Nettie's other life as a newly published poet was providing her with a different kind of elation and her resolutely optimistic letters to her mother over the next few months were an odd juxtaposition of preparation for the baby's arrival, as she diligently embroidered herringbone and chain stitch on little cotton gowns, and modest pride about the publication of *The South Wind.* Her only regret in that direction was that the book had not been published in Australia, but her university friends Christian Jollie Smith and Katie Lush took it upon themselves to distribute copies, while Esmonde was sent fifty copies to distribute too. Anxiety about the progress of the war occasionally darkened the tone of the letters and it appears that Nettie was more disturbed by the whole situation than she admitted. Many years later, Katharine wrote of the time she stayed with Nettie while Vance was away in America, saying that Nettie was 'tremendously distressed' but had tried 'to repress her feelings'. Katharine, drawing on Freudian notions, even suggested that Nettie's repression might have contributed later to 'Aileen's intensely sensitive repressed emotion to people and affairs'.

Nettie was also worried about her sensitive younger brother and, in spite of the danger that might have been involved, she repeatedly suggested to her mother that Esmonde should take a year off between school and university and stay with them in London: 'I quite realise that he's better since that little crack-up in October: that in vacation he's in stunning fine form: but still I see him going on tensely year after year with the same burst of exams in November, and I can't bear to think of it...Esmonde isn't quite like other boys, & thinks harder about his work & lets it take more out of him'. The visit did not eventuate despite Nettie's pleas.

Writing poetry seems to have provided Nettie with some outlet for her feelings during this tumultuous time. Her second volume, published in 1915 under the title *Shadowy Paths*, includes several poems in which she explores the new and almost overwhelming experience of becoming a mother. 'Wonder' and 'Fulfilment' are among them, but it is in 'The Mother' that she reflects on the terrible irony of bringing new life into a world where other mothers' sons are being slaughtered:

In the sorrow and the terror of the nations,
In a world shaken through by lamentations,
    Shall I dare know happiness
    That I stitch a baby's dress?

So: for I shall be a mother with the mothers,
I shall know the mother's anguish like the others,
Present joy must surely start
For the life beneath my heart.

Gods and men, ye know a woman's glad unreason,
How she cannot bend and weep but in her season,
Let my hours with rapture glow
As the seams and stitches grow.

And I cannot hear the word of fire and slaughter;
Do men die? Then live my child, my son, my daughter!
Into realms of pain I bring
You for joy's own offering.

The tiny volume with its mottled grey cover and rough-cut pages is dedicated 'To A. Y. P'.

Curiously, Aileen's name was always pronounced Eileen, and many friends who knew her in Spain and England, but never saw her name written, later addressed their letters to 'Eileen'. Indeed, in the months before the baby was born, Nettie announced to her mother that the names they had chosen would be 'Darrell' for a boy and 'Eileen' for a girl. Just after her birth, Esmonde wrote to his sister: 'Dear scrapface: So her name is Aileen…Is there some subtle difference between Aileen and Eileen? Why this classiness? The poor devil will be always herself & her name mixed – Never mind it is a pretty name'. It seems that Vance was the origin of the confusion, as Nettie explained to her mother: 'I meant to tell you some more about Aileen's name. Beforehand, I made Vance do the thinking about names, as I had the privilege of doing so much else in the way of preparations. He liked Aileen, & I knew you all liked it. Vance took it for granted as spelt with A, so A it was'. They chose Yvonne as her second name: 'a Breton-French name with lots of associations for us, & I like a name with the accent on the end, so as to contrast a little with jog-trot English-accented names like Palmer'. She then details how they are to be pronounced: 'accent on the 'i' in Aileen, the 'n' in Yvonne and the 'a' in Palmer'.

Although she required chloroform and stitches, Nettie's first experience of childbirth was relatively uncomplicated. Aileen later wrote that she was *simply decanted* by Dr Alice Knox at the private hospital, Woodland Villas, where Nettie spent four weeks recuperating and learning basic mothering skills. The new mother was ecstatic about her baby, describing her as having 'black hair but light eyebrows and lashes'. 'Her ears lie absolutely flat against her head', she tells her mother proudly. And with her poet's ability to make the ordinary fresh and vivid, she continues: 'She has a habit of folding her hands crosswise under her chin when she goes to sleep, & of unrolling them like windmills when she's perturbed'.

Vance visited every evening for the hour that was allowed and learned how to settle Aileen in her basket or to lift her out and bring her to her mother: 'I think she likes him to hold her, for he really has a firm grip, – though at first of course he looked as if he were carrying a bomb!' Nettie told her mother that Aileen now weighed over nine pounds, which showed that she was being well fed: 'Sister says I ought to be able to continue as I am, and then Aileen will live happily ever after. Isn't it splendid?'

As well as discovering the wonders of her new baby, Nettie was also overwhelmed by the cuttings from the Australian press about her first literary offspring, *The South Wind*. She said she had never expected the press in Australia to take notice of it. She was especially happy to have been favourably reviewed in *The Bulletin*, even though her poetry was described as 'a slight little feminine song'. To her mother she wrote: 'Altogether it's enough to make one want to continue writing, which one can't say of most criticisms, even when they're favourable...Anyway, my head is swelled: nearly as much as by Aileen? No, not nearly: but still somewhat'. She resolved to put her child before any more 'Immortal Poems' for the immediate future, saying that they could wait, if there was any 'vital spark' in them, until she was older. 'I don't want ink to run in Aileen's veins', she proclaimed, with what could be seen with hindsight as prophetic irony.

By mid-1915 the Palmers were forced by the escalating war situation and the lack of a secure income to relinquish their plans to spend the early years of their marriage in England, and they made the perilous journey back to Australia through submarine-infested waters. Perhaps they also felt the need to take their daughter to safer shores, as they would two decades later when they became caught up in the outbreak of war in Spain and insisted that she leave Barcelona with them. This time Aileen had no say in the matter.

3

Emerald

Aileen's earliest memories were infused with poetry and song: listening to Vance reciting bush ballads or lines from Shakespeare, falling asleep to the gentle sound of Nettie singing German folk songs or reciting Greek poetry. But the first song she remembered learning was taught to her by the bearded poet R. H. Long (Dick), one of the regular visitors who walked the mile from the Emerald railway station to the Palmers' cottage in the bush, calling out 'Coo-ee!' as they approached. Dick Long never needed a bed as he arrived with his neatly rolled swag under his arm, preferring to sleep in the bush. At the height of the political activity surrounding the government referendum to conscript Australian soldiers in 1917, he taught Aileen the anti-conscription song:

Conscription! Conscription!
Every man must go:
I hear Australian voices calling:
NO! NO! NO!

She recalled *I sang with enthusiasm at the age of two years, but the meaning didn't sink into me till years after.*

Within three months of arriving back in Australia with their new baby on 12 October 1915, Nettie and Vance left Melbourne suburbia and headed out of the city to the Dandenong Ranges to live at 'Rose Charman's Cottage'. The simple cottage, surrounded by twenty acres of paddocks and bush at Emerald, had been rented by their friends

Louis and Hilda Esson some years before and was later bought by Katharine Susannah Prichard, who then became the Palmers' benign landlord.

As a child Nettie had been fascinated by 'the remote wavy blue wall' she glimpsed on the horizon as she looked eastward from her parents' modest house in suburban Malvern. Now, at the beginning of 1916, she found that 'the idea of the Dandenongs being a separate world – a green oasis cut off from the great burning spaces of the continent – still persisted. Perhaps it was a legacy of childhood, or maybe the need of a young mother to build up a secure imaginative retreat from the war then raging, a war that seemed oppressively near in London and during the long ship-journey home with dowsed lights'.

The hills provided the solitude of a rural life that Nettie yearned for, while Melbourne was only a train ride away and she was able to keep in close contact with her parents and her brother and friends. Both the Palmers were influenced by the Tolstoyan ideal of a simple and creative life lived in connection with the land. As a young man, Vance had even made an unsuccessful pilgrimage to visit his literary hero when travelling through Russia on his meandering return to Australia from England in 1907. As well as offering seclusion for the creative life, the cottage in Emerald enabled the Palmers to live cheaply in order to fulfil Vance's ambition to be a full-time writer.

Vance and Nettie also started to put into practice their ideas for fostering and supporting Australian literature and Australian writers. Vance became secretary of the Australian Authors' and Writers' Guild and Nettie was active in the formation of the Melbourne Literary Club. In July 1916 she began a regular column in the Melbourne *Argus* called 'Readers and Writers' and that commission heralded the start of a career as a literary critic and columnist that was to burgeon during the 1920s when her influence on Australian literature spread and her work became a crucial part of the family income.

The following year, however, brought near tragedy to the family when Helen was born on 9 May 1917, after which Nettie suffered septicaemia leading to puerperal fever, as a result of medical negligence. For seven weeks of high temperatures, it was felt she had little hope of recovery. And after she did pull through, the recovery was slow. Years later she was to write that 'for many months afterwards I used to feel depression coming over me in great waves…I insisted to myself that now at last I understood life and it was unbroken gloom, it was the black interstellar space, it had no meaning'. What a contrast to the joyful time of Aileen's birth just two years earlier.

Aileen stayed with her grandparents at Ardmore during this period of upheaval and, given the times and the family reticence, probably had little idea why her mother had suddenly disappeared out of her life. No wonder she was jealous when Nettie returned with a new baby. *Probably I was jealous of Gwen* [Helen] *from almost the moment she was born*, she was to state in a 'novel' fragment. *I was a large and corpulent, hefty brute, while she was a tiny tot, very dainty-looking, that I wasn't allowed to bash. When I was two years old, I got the only bashing that I ever got from my father – that I remembered, because it was recollected whenever we went over our childhood memories: I pulled little Gwen along by the ears.*

While life on the domestic front was traumatic for the Palmers in 1917, the world situation also continued to impinge heavily on their lives. The war in Europe was at its most intense and Australian casualties numbered in the tens of thousands. The Hughes government had been returned in May despite the defeat of the first referendum on conscription and on 7 November a new referendum was announced, the same day the Australian newspapers carried initial reports of the Russian Revolution. The Palmers were committed anti-conscriptionists and Nettie could not bear to read the editorials in the newspapers, particularly the conservative daily, *The Argus*, for which she wrote her literary column.

She began a new diary the day Billy Hughes announced the second referendum. The entries are a mixture of domestic life and reflections on the war. The first entry describes the family's daily routine: 'Aileen Yvonne, aged 2½, woke first & came into my bed…V made the fire while I got Baby Helen up (six months) after she had been chucking & waving legs and arms in the air for an hour…Went to the post at midday, Aileen too. A longish walk for her, with two ascents… Came back & found Vance swotting over his novel out in the bush… Scurrying afternoon, with Helen not sleeping & Aileen contrary. Got them both fed & bedded by 6.30. Ran down to the farm for milk while Vance knocked off writing & cut some more wood. Vivid clear cold evening'. By contrast, she continues: 'Italy's got it awfully: worse news every day...Who is to be conscribed? Here in Emerald 110 men have gone. There remain four "eligibles", very semi-eligible. Ten of the 110 had been killed a month ago, & now there are more'.

It was during the following weeks that Aileen learned her first song from Dick Long when the Palmers' anti-conscriptionist friends started traipsing out to Emerald to enlist their help. One Sunday in November, Nettie's close friend from university, law graduate Christian Jollie Smith, came to dinner, after which more friends arrived unexpectedly – among them Guido Baracchi, the Marxist radical who planned to start a biweekly anti-conscriptionist paper of eight issues until the referendum. He wanted Vance to edit it. The little cottage was constantly bustling with people, who spilt onto the verandah where Helen lay in her pram gurgling affably, while her older sister was sometimes so overcome with shyness and excitement that she had to retire inside. On 20 December 1917 the referendum was defeated.

Vance had agreed reluctantly to edit Guido's paper, not because he did not support the anti-conscriptionist position, but because he was working hard to finish a novel, after which he had it in his mind to enlist and leave for Europe. Esmonde had already volunteered as an 'anti' conscriptionist and had left for army training camp. A snapshot taken around this time shows Nettie's smiling younger brother in khaki, sprawled on the grass with a joyful Aileen riding on his back. In early January 1918 Katharine Susannah Prichard made her way to Emerald to try to dissuade Vance from enlisting, showing him letters written by her brother at Flanders about the terrible casualty rates, made so much more poignant by his own death there a month before. She wouldn't stay as she was feeling 'very broken-down' about Alan's death, but neither was Vance to be dissuaded.

One motivation for Vance's decision to enlist was the financial hardship the couple was under as magazines continued to close and Nettie lost her *Argus* column. But his reasons were also more complex. He remained opposed to compulsory service and was well aware of the dehumanising aspects of war. On the other hand, he always aligned himself with 'the world of men' (the title of his first serious book published in 1915) and, after he joined up, he likened the army to a 'guild' or 'a band of brothers', harking back to his pre-war interest in guild socialism in England. *The tradition of masculinity and puritanism in Australian culture* was one Aileen was later to hold accountable for many of its shortcomings and she experienced that tradition in microcosm in her own family.

Nettie supported her husband's decision to enlist but was also devastated. Not only was she recovering from a severe illness, she had two small children to look after. Worse, the financial situation meant that they had to leave Emerald, which she found a 'horrible prospect'. Nevertheless, later that month, after packing up the cottage, the Palmers moved to Killenna, the home of Nettie's Aunt Ina Higgins in Malvern.

Settling in at Killenna proved quite a challenge. Nettie was very fond of her aunt, a staunch suffragist and pacifist who had trained as a horticulturalist and who was active in the Women's Peace Army (WPA). With another stalwart, Cecilia John, she had established a women's farm on land bought by the WPA at Mordialloc in 1915 where they produced vegetables, raised poultry and reared cattle, training young women to run the farm throughout the war. Ina Higgins, like her friend and president of the Women's Political Association Vida Goldstein, was an assiduous Christian Scientist and slept only about five hours a night. From Nettie's diary over this period, it seems that she felt herself to be somewhat inadequate in the face of her energetic spinster aunt, whose pacifism did not allow her to approve of Vance's enlistment in the AIF (Australian Imperial Force) and whose Christian Science beliefs did not make her altogether sympathetic to Nettie's health problems.

While Nettie supported Ina's feminist and pacifist politics, her father's sister also exhibited the streak of puritanism that ran through the family. Aileen was later to dwell often in her writing on the oppressive effect of the family puritanism on her mother's life, which was, in turn, to affect her own. For the moment, however, Aileen was learning to find her way in a new house with stricter rules than those at the bush cottage she knew as home. The things in Auntie Ina's house she was not to play with were called 'special'. Nettie records her asking: 'Is this special or toy? Is this used envelope toy or rubbish?' And later on: 'Mummy, am I special or toy or rubbish?'

In February 1918, Guido Baracchi was arrested and imprisoned for giving incendiary political speeches on the Yarra bank. The poet Dick Long also went to prison. *Long served his jail sentence towards the end of World War One*, wrote Aileen in the 1960s, *when most thinking Australian writers were anti-conscription, if not anti-war. Long was a gentle fellow, opposed to all wars, waged for whatever reason or unreason. He was jailed, Noni* [Nettie] *told us, for 'waving a red flag' in a public place – which meant, for him, pacifism.* A poem Long wrote around that time called 'Peace' puts the case in plain and simple terms that still resonate today, particularly in its final stanzas:

I haven't much faith in
  A Peace that commences
With hacking off limbs
  Or in sniping from trenches.

Yet some say 'tis Peace that
  We're now fighting for;
If THIS brings us Peace,
  What on earth brings us War?

While his friends languished in gaol, Vance tried unsuccessfully to get into Esmonde's artillery unit until finally, on 6 March 1918, he was passed for enlistment. He came home from training camp for a few hours on the afternoon of Aileen's third birthday on 6 April. Then, on Anzac Day, Nettie took her to watch him in a procession from an office window: 'Prawnie very intense, waved without ceasing. Overcome by town in general. "This is a very funny world!"'. Along with learning the anti-conscription song, one of Aileen's first memories was *looking out of a top-storey window (it may have been Collins House) and there was Daddy, in uniform, marching by to the sound of drums.* In a photograph of the family taken in the garden at Killenna, Vance stands straight in his army uniform. Nettie looks up at him anxiously, the months of illness apparent in the angular planes of her usually rounded face. She cradles a cherubic-looking Helen on her hip, while Aileen stands in front of Vance in sturdy boots and gazes fiercely at the camera.

In the fifteen months Vance spent away from his family, he saw only the aftermath of war. Although he had left home on 31 August, he did not disembark in London from the troopship *Barambah,* after the long sea journey from Australia, until 14 November 1918, three days after the Armistice with Germany was signed. He witnessed the war devastation when his battalion was assigned to mopping up operations in France and Belgium, then spent months in London waiting to be demobilised. Esmonde stayed on in England after he was demobilised, becoming a student at Oxford where he immersed himself in Marxism.

Nettie, during this time, looked after her children at Killenna, taught French to private students and gave lectures to diverse groups; she also involved herself with the local political and literary scene, and tried to keep 'that mysterious depression' at bay. She was attempting to grow her hair long, at Vance's request, after having had her head shaved during her illness, but it was still falling out even though she was having her scalp massaged. Feeling like an 'impersonal old blue-stocking', she longed for Vance's return, telling him in April 1919: 'I want to be working in a bush house and cooking ghastly meals for you'. Her periods had not resumed since the birth of Helen and, taking Vance's advice, she plucked up courage in June to visit a gynaecological specialist. He advised her that it was almost certain she would not be able to bear more children.

The specialist's prognosis was unexpected and Nettie was devastated, distraught that she would not be able to give Vance a son and feeling that she was no longer 'a whole woman'. With the slow and uncertain mails, the wait for his reply to her letter telling him of her plight was agonising, but when she finally received it, it was all she could have hoped for and she felt she could begin to forget the news that had 'stabbed me a hundred times a day'. While admitting that he would have liked a son, especially as there would be no more Palmers on the male side of his family, Vance reassured Nettie that he loved her and said: 'Don't be sadder than you can help that we're not going to have any more children. We'll give Aileen & Helen all we have to give'.

After Vance's return in November 1919, the Palmers were able to move back to their old house in Emerald; Katharine Susannah Prichard, who owned it, had moved with her husband Captain Hugo Throssell (whom she had met in London before her return to Australia) to Western Australia. Nettie records Aileen saying: 'This is our real home! I thought Killenna was, but it isn't. There's only one gum-tree at Killenna'. She also demanded that her parents provide her with a 'firm house', a notion she returned to in her later writings about her nomadic family, whom she would fictionalise as 'the Pilgrims', after Chaucer:

Than longen folk to goon on pilgrimages,
(And palmers for to seken straunge strondes)

Life at Emerald settled into a comfortable routine, although Aileen was critical in later life of the way that routine was organised around Vance. In her manuscript 'Pilgrim's Way', Aileen recreates, in the sardonic tone that characterised much of her later work, a scene from her childhood in the Dandenongs. 'Blake' was sitting in his deckchair and the little boy from the farm across the paddock was visiting. The boy and 'Gwen' [Helen] were making too much noise, so 'Noni' admonished them:

'Don't disturb Dad: he's working'.

'He's not working – he's just sitting down', the little boy said.

But Noni had deeply impressed it on me at least (when I was about five or six, and Gwen two years younger, and Blake had come back from 'fighting the savage Germans', as he used to say with a grin) that the work Blake did sitting down was his serious work, or at least it was very arduous. There were two kinds of work, writing potboilers and writing important books.

'Poor Daddy, he's got to write another potboiler', Noni would sometimes tell us.

Potboilers weren't the most arduous kind of work – any fool could write them – but they were a nuisance, an interruption of other things on Blake's mind. It seemed to me silly not to get rid of the potboilers all at once, and then be free for his more important writing.

Once I became twenty-one, I told myself then, and could live by myself, with no one to send me to bed, I'd write all night and turn out enough potboilers to make my fortune, and then be able to write just as I pleased.

Aileen started making up stories at an early age, telling them to Helen as they lay in their beds on the back verandah until her little sister fell asleep, sucking her thumb. Nettie was in no hurry for her children to learn to read and write and they spent their days roaming the tree-ferned gullies, learning to ride their pony, Tommy, running errands to neighbouring farms for eggs and milk, and helping their father gather sticks for the fireplace and the wood stove. Sometimes the whole family went for long walks, one day tramping to the nearby township of Monbulk along the road and then back through the gullies. '10 miles: Helen too, not yet 4!' Nettie recorded proudly.

Thinking people were the background of my childhood, Aileen recalled, and several of her manuscripts feature the stream of *passionately Australian* friends, most involved in the literary scene, who came to visit on the weekends, often staying overnight and yarning around the log fire in the lamplight. *In the 'twenties, most of the people struggling towards putting Australian literature just slightly on the map lived in dire want – if they had to live off their writings, as Blake did.*

Of the *various elders* who visited the Palmers in the Dandenongs, some left more lasting memories than others. Two she remembered with great fondness were the gentle poet Dick Long, who was a carpenter by trade *and gave us kids a lot of ingenious toys, made mostly of wood, carefully planned for the love of it*, and Furnley Maurice, who earned his living by selling books and was probably never paid a penny for his poetry. A contrast to the shaggy Long, he would turn up *in a white collar and his business suit, but bringing, like most people did, sweets for the kiddies.* Playwright and poet Louis Esson (*small, brilliant and waspish*) and his doctor wife, Nettie's schoolfriend Hilda Bull (*tawny-headed and dramatic*), were frequent visitors. Aileen and Helen would listen from their beds on the verandah as Louis's bursts of wit set everyone gathered around the fire laughing – *Noni's laughter mostly louder and more explosive than anyone else's.* With their small son, Hugh, the Essons had taken a cottage less than a mile down the gully from the Palmers, but it was unfortunately burnt to the ground the summer after they moved in, destroying the printing press Hilda had brought back from England to print small editions of Australian poetry and essays. The proofs of a volume of Vance's essays went up in smoke.

Some of the more glamorous visitors Aileen remembered were Edith Young (*a vivid, colourful woman, who spoke dramatically with an Irish accent*) and her younger friend, actress Dulcie Cherry. These *two bright women sat at the feet of Blake, and revered him as a prophet at that period, though neither of them became deeply imbued with Australianism like the others.* They eventually made their separate ways to Europe. Katharine Susannah Prichard was not on the scene much at that time, but Aileen remembered that she was *the most vigorous of all that group, and has had the most lasting influence on my own life, but she lived far away in the West, and exerted a kind of inspiring influence by remote control.*

The child who emerges from Nettie's diary during the early 1920s is highly imaginative, sensitive and rather shy, far from the *corpulent, hefty brute* of Aileen's own memory. She is, however, often contrasted to her sister who was more outgoing and cheerful. Nettie describes one visitor as being 'very sweet to the kiddies & especially attracted by Helen, who is more on the spot than Aileen is'. Aileen suffered from physical problems too that her sister did not share. She was wearing glasses by the time she was about five years old and had to practice with an amblyoscope twice daily to help her stop squinting. And when it became obvious she was left-handed she had that hand systematically slapped by her mother whenever she favoured it, as was the practice then.

Like many imaginative children, Aileen was accompanied everywhere in her early years by her 'little friends'. She later described those imaginary companions as *the people who roamed in my thoughts, and figured largely in the stories I wrote: partly imagined or taken out of the legends Blake used to read to us, by the fire, after tea, before we were put to bed, and Blake put on his pipe, but were also identified with the more glamorous and colourful of the visitors who came to see us at the weekends.* These 'little friends' often feature in Nettie's diaries. On a walk to a neighbouring village Aileen ascribed 'all the bush colour to work of her little friends'. On a trip into town, she was irritable: 'For once town bored Aileen, who vainly pretends to like it more than the bush. She loathes shops: her little friends can't find a home in them'. When the rain pelted down after a hot, dry spell 'Aileen said her little friends were sitting in the tanks & singing'. Before she could write fluently, she painted 'enthusiastic pictures of their adventures…but grieves because their faces don't emerge beautiful'. On her sixth birthday in

April 1921, she 'drew & painted her hero-friend Medista as coming forth from his castle to fight a Horrid Thing that had swords for hands'.

By this time, Nettie was starting to homeschool the children and, gradually, as she became familiar with her letters, Aileen started writing down her stories rather than drawing them. Over the next few years she filled thick notebooks with multi-volumed historical novels, with titles such as 'Lyre and Sword' and 'Nick Hunn', sometimes written under her own name, sometimes under exotic pen-names like Cordelia Charlotte Cecilia Clayfield. A volume of short stories (with a misspelt title that amused Nettie: 'The Spychology of Youth') included one called 'A True Story of my Life'. In it, the narrator, Joan, travels the world for many years with her parents, but becomes bored and misses her friends, Patience and Rosaline. It finishes with an echo of Aileen's complaint about not having a 'firm house': *A good many years have past* [sic] *now, it will be my twentieth birthday soon, but my mother and father are still travelling. But I will remain forever at home.*

Nettie's teaching was, as she admitted, sadly lacking in the area of mathematics, but in literature and linguistics she excelled. And she had a willing pupil. On 12 June 1923 Nettie recorded: 'Aileen started her first novel today, writing it carefully out in a little black notebook. Remarkably bad spelling and remarkably good style'. A few days later she wrote: 'Aileen still passionately interested in her story. Says life hasn't got any interest when she isn't writing'. A few months later, Nettie was recording her daughter's enthusiasm for phonetics: 'Aileen going crazy about phonetics'. A few days later, the earnest student was 'swotting at the Greek alphabet & then beginning a play in phonetics'. Aileen was grateful for the strong grounding she received from her mother in phonetics and attributed her later proficiency in languages to that training, as well as, of course, to hearing her mother recite and sing to her in French or German or Greek.

Nettie also wrote about her daughters in letters to friends like R. H. Long, telling him on one occasion that 'Aileen of course is writing furiously always, with entire delight...She has never tired in her quaint craft yet'. Helen, on the other hand, 'sometimes writes incoherent little stories with lots of illustrations, but letters are her strong point'. Helen also, it seems, preferred playing with friends like Hughie Esson or watching her father play cricket with the Emerald team.

Aileen once commented that, given her upbringing, she *didn't have the least ounce of sense of humour.* And a younger writer whom her mother had mentored said of Nettie: 'She had only one fault, but it bothered me, a complete lack of humour, an excess of intensity'. While Nettie's intensity seemed to outweigh her sense of fun, she did have the facility of being able to relish the funny sayings and happenings of her small children and to express them with wit and compassion in her diary. A more surprising discovery in her diaries is the reference to Vance's theatrical style of humour: 'Vance dressed up as a Velasquez portrait & appeared on the verandah! The children thought he was Shakespeare & fell over with fright. Great jokes afterwards'. But it seems Aileen did not always find her father's jokes amusing.

In 'Pilgrim's Way' she recounts the time he played an elaborate practical joke on his daughters. The children were told that 'Aunt Edith' was coming and they had to put on their best manners: *Gwen* [Helen] *may not have done, as she didn't have quite the sense of responsibility that I had then, but I was terribly polite to Aunt Edith, and let her kiss me, though she looked a bit ugly, in her old grey garb and her whiskers.* After Aileen served her afternoon tea, the old woman went up one of the bush tracks to look for 'Blake': *she chose the one that went past the old well, where the maiden-hair fern grew, an old miners' shaft that we weren't allowed to play around.* When Blake subsequently came in asking for Aunt Edith, they all went along the track to look for her: *There were her discarded garments, shed by the well, and she must have gone down it. I burst into violent tears as, though I didn't like Aunt Edith much, I didn't like stories without happy endings.* Their father then confessed he had been Aunt Edith. *Though drama can have its uses,* wrote Aileen, *I've had enough of it, since I was just about six.*

Just how important it was for stories to have happy endings in Aileen's child world is apparent in a poem Nettie was to write about her in 1938 – one of a series of unpublished poems about her daughters that have survived in Aileen's papers. Called 'Alsia', it recalls, in a lilting rhythm that begs to be read aloud or sung, an imaginary country that Aileen created as a child, which survived war and devastation because she willed it so. It finishes:

Sometimes a sorry country,
        Alsia, Alsia,
But Aileen still kept hold of it,
And every tale she told of it,
Came right at last, all terrors past,
        Because it must be so,
        She loved it, made it so.

The children thrived during their years in the bush at Emerald and the time was also productive for their parents. Vance was often away in Melbourne, involved in rehearsals with the Pioneer Players – a drama group inspired by W. B. Yeats's Abbey Theatre – which he had formed with Louis Esson to produce Australian plays. Their own plays were among those produced at the Temperance Hall in Melbourne in the early 1920s. But the attempt to provide a home-grown theatre eventually failed, partly due to the lack of money to pay for professional actors and to hire a venue more suitable than the cold and draughty hall. They were also competing with the postwar glitter of musical comedies, like *Spangles* starring Gladys Moncrieff at Her Majesty's, and the growing popularity of the cinema. Nettie gave talks and lectures; a landmark in her career was the long essay *Modern Australian Literature 1900–1923*, published in 1924, which won the T. C. Lothian Publishing Company Prize of £25. As well as providing welcome prize money, it opened up new avenues for her literary journalism.

In early 1925, the family was on the move again. Nettie had recorded in 1923 that they were 'beginning to plan for a move to Europe in a year or so', but the move they made in July two years later was to Queensland where they planned to see Vance's mother, who was getting old and frail, and take a cottage for a few months. They left Aileen and Helen at Killenna with Auntie Ina for the last month while they packed up and sold the horses, but it seems that Nettie entertained the possibility of returning to Emerald. As it happened, they were to spend the next four years in the Queensland coastal fishing village of Caloundra.

In 1938, nearly two decades after the Palmers moved to the Dandenongs to provide a secure retreat from war for their family, Nettie's mind was once again focussed on the parlous state of the world when she wrote the series of unpublished poems about her daughters. War was again on the horizon. Aileen was in Spain with the International Brigades while Helen was active in left-wing politics at university. In 'Not Safe', dedicated 'to A and H', Nettie recalls their time at Emerald and hopes that the freedom to learn self-reliance that she and Vance had allowed their daughters will stand them in good stead.

Dears, when we lived in the bush,
In the little house, on the green cleared slope
Between the tangled gully and the high mountainy trees,
I would have held the trees back with one hand,
Oh, I would have encircled the little house with the other arm,
To keep you safe!

What need? The trees were kind,
Full of bird-song against the rising sun,
You camped among them for your play.
The little house was home –
The fire for food, the fire for warmth,
The roof for shelter against the sun, the roof gathering the rain,
Oh, rest, warmth peace –
Yet not safe, not safe.

Not safe?
Sometimes it was the fox startling you both,
In the early night, barking through trees near your verandah,
(And Aileen saying earnestly, clearly,
"Helen, you mustn't think foxes <u>eat</u> little girls – No!")
Or: it was the sight in the darkness of the great trees,
The dead tree, Heart of the Jungle, rising in the midst;
Would he someday fall right on the house & crush it?
Nothing was safe. You knew.

Not safe!
You used to bring in chips for the fire,

Gather dry twigs or bark, carry in a log together,
Oh, wood-and-water joeys, oh good fun!
Oh the fire, that kindly house-friend, patted, coaxed,
Helping us every day.
But then – what was that sound
Behind the thick trees up the hill?
Dry air, dry leaves, dry bark,
And the whole bush was on fire.
The fire warping downhill,
Snapping & whistling in the wind it made,
Now blasting every leaf, now hurling tall trees down…
Ah, we stayed it that time, we burned back;
The wind changed, the air cooled, the fire paused & died,
And down the hill the little house stood unchanged,
And even your swing on the dark wattle-tree.
But fire? Strange friend, we let it in the house again,
With chips & sticks & logs, but it was not safe,
Nothing was safe.

You never lived in fear, but you knew, you knew.
You trotted on the bush-tracks anywhere,
Bare foot, but eyes alert, no snake too quick for you.
In the undergrowth you gathered crimson heath
(Standing at the door, a row of two girls,
Four bunches of stiff heath held aloft as I rode home one grey day,
Voices carolling, intertwining, 'A posy for you, Mummy,
A posy for your birthday!')
In a dry season you carried billies of water from the steeply-hidden creek;
Longing to see a new world, your own,
You climbed the slender crowding wattle-trees,
Not safe; but you had no fear.

Fearless, aware!
This from your childhood you have been,
So you remain; so now you need to be.
It is to hear unflinching the mad cries of the fox in the night,

To be wood-and-water joeys in dangerous places,
To help in fighting a conflagration that threatens the whole world,
To volunteer for look-out duty,
Sure-footed, clear-eyed,
Knowing you cannot be afraid,
Knowing that nothing is safe.

4

Caloundra

Aileen made her first venture into autobiography on her thirteenth birthday, three years after the family's move to Queensland. This simple account of her life covered a mere eight pages of her diary – short by the standards of a girl who filled exercise books with multi-volumed historical 'novels'. In it she recalls her childhood years at Emerald with delight: being taught by her mother, riding the ponies, especially *small, mouse-like, shaggy and brown Dolly,* for whom she held *a devoted affection.* Well-schooled by Nettie, she sketches the landscape in the Dandenongs with a determined effort at poetic description: *Wet, dewy, cool, green, surrounded by high trees that shut out the sun; little gullies with tinkling falls; fronds of tree-ferns dipping in them; gushing cataracts.* Her reaction to the decision to move to Queensland when she was ten is more direct: *We were sent down to Killenna, Malvern, to stay with Aunt Ina, while Mater and Pater sold the horses and packed up. I won't say much about that time. I don't think Aunt Ina was as nice as she might have been, and I'm certain I wasn't. Those times were very troublesome.*

Despite Aileen's misgivings, the move to Caloundra, north of Brisbane, proved to be an inspired one. Vance's eldest sister Emily had married into the Bulcock family, well known in the district, her father-in-law Robert Bulcock being described by Aileen as having been *the Lord of Caloundra once.* The first cottage the Palmers rented in the little fishing village was a small red and white house 'with four rooms and no passages', perched high on Lighthouse Hill and with a superb view of the ocean, the Passage and the Glasshouse Mountains. Transplanted from bush to seaside and from a southern winter to the bright sunshine of Queensland's early spring, the children set about exploring their new environment with delight, swimming in the surf, collecting shells and playing in the rock pools. Aileen described Caloundra as *a beautiful place. The passage – still, crystalline and reflecting everything at dawn and sunset, opalescent by day; the surf here gorgeous, sweeping, bordered with white foam: the rocks, with their pools in which grow seaweed, anamones* [sic] *and wild sea-things of marvellous beauty; the Dickie Beach, with three lagoons; the inland plains, often bedecked with wild-flowers; Bribie Island, to which we travel by boat – it is gorgeous!* Her disposition was not always as sunny as her surroundings, however, and Nettie records her daughter displaying a 'cantankerous *crise de nerfs*' one hottish day and refusing to go for a message. 'Missed yesterday's paper owing to Aileen's nerves' is her next entry. Aileen called her despondent moods *the gloomies* in her diary.

Once settled in the two girls started at the small local school with about twenty other pupils. It was their first experience of school and they took to it enthusiastically. 'They take their lunch & play cricket in lunch-hour', reported Nettie to her mother. 'They are home by half past three. It pleases them both very much. They enjoy the routine, the getting neat in the morning & trotting off with their lunches in their bags. They haven't had enough routine in their lives to make them tired of it'. Aileen, ever eager to practise her descriptive skills, painted a rather unflattering portrait of the teacher, Mrs Taylor, in her diary: *oldish, false teeth, grey hair, shiny complexion, rosebud mouth, coquettish smile.*

She also discovered a new interest – arithmetic – which she had studied little of under her mother's tutelage. Nettie was amused: 'Aileen has developed a sudden passion for sums: division of money. (How do you divide five pounds between four Palmers?)'. She was not so amused at the stilted way the school taught the pupils to write letters, finding Aileen 'too apt a pupil' and apologising to her father for an 'alarmingly dull' letter written to him by his granddaughter, in which she had also tried out arithmetical problems on him. The Palmers' story of noble poverty, relayed chiefly by Nettie to family and friends, impinged on Aileen's mind from an early age and fed her ambition to write lots of potboilers early and become rich so that she could enjoy her serious writing without worry.

Money and poverty were themes she was to return to in her later autobiographical writing. In one fragment, she recalls her puzzlement over being told at the age of four that her family was poor, while staying at Aunt Ina's house in Malvern when Vance was away at the war in 1919: *There wasn't much of that period that I remember clearly, except Nora* [Nettie] *asking me one day: 'Do you think we are rich or poor?' (There were always rich and poor occurring in the stories read to us.) 'Why – rich', I said. Then Nora told me no, we were very poor, but it seemed to me odd, when we lived in a large, two-storeyed house that had been great-grandmother's and a maid and a gardener came to help Aunt Francesca* [Ina].

Later, when Blake came home and we went to live in the Dandenongs, and heard (from Nora, of course) all about how hard he had to work to get us a crust, it became clear enough to me how poor we were; but at Aunt Francesca's, where there was all the ritual of old-fashioned houses, and Uncle James who was a judge [Henry Bournes Higgins] *lived in his immense mansion not very far away, it didn't seem to make much sense that we were poor.* Aileen continued ruefully that, since that time more than forty years before, she *had learnt plenty about riches and poverty, but still had never learnt how to establish favourable terms with money.* But in her early years she wrote profusely about her ambition to be rich, and by the time she was twelve, according to Nettie, she was 'trying hard to keep the family accounts', adding, 'My fault when she doesn't!'

In January 1926, six months after their arrival in Queensland, the family moved to a 'lovely, cool house, with bedrooms like sleep-outs' and a view straight down the Passage, although Nettie missed the wide view from Lighthouse Hill. Living conditions were still basic and frugal. Vance fixed up a bookcase in the sitting room and made a cupboard out of kerosene tins, which he then painted. Nettie cooked on a kerosene stove and ironed with a petrol iron. One luxury they acquired was a gramophone that the whole family listened to in the evenings. It looked as though their planned sojourn of a few months was going to turn into years. Which it did.

During the Caloundra years, Nettie wrote her usual comments on Vance's work in her diary: that he was working hard at serials that he hated or trying to settle into a new novel. Nettie wrote on diverse subjects for a variety of newspapers and magazines: from an article on Henry Handel Richardson for *The Bulletin* (in which she strove to keep her subject's gender unstated as H. H. R. was still thought to be a man) to a piece on blackberries for the *Mirror.* Her efforts were not always accepted and she was outraged on one occasion when *The Sunday Mail* returned an article on Katharine Susannah Prichard 'saying it had published one on the lady two years ago!' Vance suffered rejections too, notably from *The Bulletin*. Just how hand-to-mouth their existence was is evident in such entries as this on 11 March 1926: 'Cheque came from Mirror so we're solvent'.

Nettie's parents provided generous backup, however, and she told her father in one letter that he had given her more five pounds than letters in her life. It seems he also lent them £200 towards the purchase of land in Caloundra. Given the importance Vance attached to his ability to provide financially for his wife and family (as he had avowed in letters to Nettie's father during their courtship), it must have been galling for him to be obliged to accept assistance from her family. His educated but poor rural background meant that he had not received the privileges Nettie had enjoyed as a young woman from an upper-middle class family. As we know, he established his independence early, travelling to London at twenty to forge his writing career. But the war had changed Vance's planned professional trajectory and closed off many avenues for his journalism, while his 'serious' writing made very little money.

Certainly, the well-known critique that Nettie fostered her husband's writing career at the expense of her own creative writing – a critique made by Aileen in her later writings and which has been argued more recently by some feminist scholars – does have validity. But the situation was complex, and it may be that the class factor – which was very much part of their era – has been overlooked in the critical focus on the gender hierarchy that existed between the couple. Nettie's fierce and almost excessive support of Vance's career may have been pursued, at least in part, to compensate for the continuing necessity of her parents' assistance, which she knew would be bruising to her husband's ego. That Nettie continued to develop her poetic skills is evident in the poems that survive in Aileen's papers from the

1930s; that she took the path of journalism and criticism, initially to help the family coffers as well as to help develop a national literature, is hardly surprising. And in her journal writing and her columns – such as the long-running series in the *Illustrated Tasmanian Mail* – her poetically inflected prose is unique and memorable.

Though Vance worked steadily at his writing every day during the sweltering first summer spent in Caloundra, the weather was so hot that he felt it was 'rather like cutting words out of rock'. The children coped in different ways with the heat. Helen went bathing opposite the house with a group of friends every afternoon, while Aileen preferred to bring her friend Alice McIntosh home and they sprawled about reading in silence.

As the weather cooled, the sisters resumed their exploration of the area and, when Nettie was away in Brisbane in June, Aileen wrote happily to *Dear old Adorable* describing their exploits: *I have discovered a new gully at the other end of the marsh (the eastern end) and we have decided to call it Yvonne Gully, if you don't mind...We also gave a name to a tree which overhangs Bullrush pool, on which we often sit and dangle our legs, and throw bits of bark into the water. Though it is not a proper bridge, for it does not go right across, it goes more than half way across, so Helen called it Iris Bridge. When you come back we will name some places in the scrub Janet and Edward to console you and Dad.*

Whether Aileen knew the secret her parents were harbouring around the time she wrote that letter is impossible to know. Given the era, it is likely she and Helen were not told anything; she certainly does not write about it. At the age of forty-one and having been told by her doctor after the birth of Helen that she would not be able to have more children, Nettie was pregnant. Although 'well enough', she confides in her diary that she is simply not able to write and spends her time sewing – not stitching baby gowns as she did in London in 1915, but letting her rapidly growing elder daughter's dresses down and endowing them with pockets. She may have been waiting until she could be sure this pregnancy would run full term before raising her own hopes or giving anything away to the children by sewing baby clothes.

One morning in early September, Nettie collapsed. Displaying her usual stoicism, she did not consider going to hospital. Instead, she spent the next few days in bed, writing to her mother but mentioning nothing of her illness. A few days later, while the children were at school, she suffered a miscarriage and was driven by a neighbour to Beerburrum Hospital. She was 'septic' when admitted. Vance was soon by her side at the hospital and took a room nearby to be with her when it became apparent that, once again, his wife's life was in danger. For several anxious days she was kept on a regime of brandy and other drugs to bring the fever down.

Aileen and Helen were looked after at Caloundra House until Vance's sister Emily was able to come from Brisbane to care for them. What were the children told? Aileen was eleven years old, but it seems neither she nor Helen were given the details of their mother's illness or knew that they might have had a little brother or sister. A letter from Aileen to *Darling old Spooshable* in hospital simply offers the news that the cat has had kittens and that she is going to gather wildflowers with four new girlfriends.

When Nettie was still in hospital but well out of danger, Vance left for Brisbane to begin rehearsals with the Brisbane Repertory Theatre for a production of his play *A Happy Family*. His own 'happy family' joined him there for over a month when Nettie was well enough and they all attended the first performance of the play on 21 October. A few days later, Helen contracted measles and was whisked off to the infectious diseases hospital. Back in Caloundra, Vance and Aileen also succumbed to the measles but recovered at home. Fortunately, Nettie seems to have been spared that affliction, noting in her diary in December that they were all well again though 'rather bankrupt'. Her own and Helen's 'fat' hospital bills had severely stretched their finances, but they would have been even worse had her father not contributed towards her private room in Beerburrum Hospital.

Much of Aileen and Helen's childhood writing survives in their papers labelled 'Juvenilia': Aileen's providing the bulk of the material and displaying skills that are anything but juvenile. Helen often illustrated Aileen's stories and one offering from 1927, '"Potentate

Palace", a story told in letters, illustrated by Helen Iris Palmer' is a handmade book with an illustrated brown-paper cover. Written in black ink with drawings on each page, it has no given author, but the style is Aileen's. It was presented as a gift to Vance on his birthday, book-making being a family tradition

Aileen's thick exercise books include two volumes of 'The History of Alsia' (her imaginary country that Nettie was to recall in her 1938 poem), three volumes of a novel called 'Nick Hunn: a family novel in three books' and a fifty-five page rhyming poem about Guinevere, 'The Borrican Maid'.

An exercise book precociously titled 'Collection of my Literary Works during the year 1926 by Aileen Palmer' contains pieces that reflect her interests during her eleventh year. A story called 'Simplicity' provides an original twist to her growing interest in money. Set around Buderim, it features a rich man, Clayton, and two women. Dorothy Bride, his girlfriend, is a stiff and painted town girl. The other girl, Bertha, tall and dark-haired with full red lips, lives on a farm in the Blackall Ranges. When Clayton and Dorothy's car gets bogged during a country drive, Bertha rides up on horseback to rescue them. Later, Clayton writes to the red-lipped farm girl, saying that he realises now that what he wants is simplicity and slips a five pound note in the envelope. He travels to the farm and asks Bertha to marry him. She refuses, he leaves crushed, and the story finishes: *Bertha stood motionless. 'A hundred pounds! I have got that, during the last month, from admirers; and I bet Miss Bride wouldn't get that much, in three months, from anyone...And it's all because of my simplicity'.*

Aileen was an astute observer and she would have watched and listened carefully when some of the thespians who ran the Brisbane Rep came to visit Caloundra in early 1926 to discuss with Vance the rewriting of parts of *A Happy Family* – the production of which she saw later in Brisbane. One of the actors also left Vance and Nettie a copy of *My Life in Art*, the new autobiography by the famed director of the Moscow Art Theatre, Konstantin Stanislavsky, which they discussed at length with enthusiasm. Putting her new knowledge into practice, Aileen wrote a three-act play, set in the Dandenongs and called 'Cassidy's Farm'. All the characters' names start with 'C'. The heroine Catherine and her siblings are left with their aunt when their parents go to Queensland. Constance Hawkins (who is clearly drawn from Aunt Ina Higgins) is described in detail: *Aunt Constance is a thin, bony woman who would be called tall if she were not so stooped. She has got a crooked nose, grey eyes, hair that seems to have started to go silver but stuck halfway, thin lips, and navy-blue dress, grey shawl, black hat, high-buttoned boots and galoshes.* The play contains good naturalistic dialogue in the Australian vernacular and workable stage directions. Its plot is packed with dreadful incidents: the mother dies of dengue fever in Queensland and the father returns to Melbourne where he is killed when he falls from his horse. Yet, surprisingly, the drama has a happy ending. Perhaps the young Aileen was already feeling the need to separate, at least symbolically, from her parents.

While Helen (known as Sprat) remained 'a sprite and a comedian', Aileen was growing into adolescence. By the time she was twelve Nettie notes discreetly in her diary that the dresses she is making for her are beginning to need to be 'well cut – oh dear!' Puberty did not awaken an interest in boys, however, but rather increased her interest in her own sex. Aileen's historical novels include brave girls who fight duels; in 'Sunset: a story of Rome and Gaul in the 1st century, A.D.', for instance, the heroine declares herself to be in love with another girl. When, on a trip to Brisbane in late 1927, the Palmers went to see a new silent film that featured a cross-dressing, duelling heroine, Aileen's excitement knew no bounds: *'Senorita' thrilling. Bebe Daniels star. Girl dressed as boy. Sword fights. Thrills*, she writes in her diary.

During that year a Caloundra family called the Beasleys began to appear in Aileen and Nettie's diaries. Violet Beasley, the daughter, who was several years older than Aileen, became the object of her adoration. She makes the odd cryptic entry in her diary, sometimes just a row of exclamation marks after Violet's name, but other references are more tantalising: *On the trip to Coolum we had the company of Violet Beaseley, our best Caloundra friend. I'll never forget that climb, or the following night…*Nettie was merely amused at her daughter's crush on the older girl: 'A[ileen] romantically excited about Violet's friendliness & charm'; 'Violet Beazley came in afternoon, & Aileen rode home with her, helping to carry mail. More romance!'

In the Palmer family, diaries were shared family records rather than any kind of private confessional. Vance was a less regular diarist than Nettie, usually filling in the daily entries in her diary when his wife was away. At the start of a year's diary, Nettie might make a comment such as this one: 'Vance ought to inaugurate this diary with some of his more special & luminous notes, but so far it is left to me, his mere rib and crooked part'. Such a statement might seem disingenuous given that, unlike Vance's entries, hers shimmer with sharp observations and poetic turns of phrase that lift the entries far above a prosaic record of daily life, but it seems that her self-deprecation was genuine, even if a little tongue-in-cheek. The habit was to annoy the adult Aileen, who in a letter from England once reprimanded her mother gently: *I wish you wouldn't be so 'umble, as I've often told you – comparing your own letters to bread and those of Vance and Hell to creampuffs and caviare* [sic].

It also seems that Vance may have sometimes borrowed the poet's eye view of Nettie's diary for his own writing. Her entry for 4 September 1925, just after their arrival in Caloundra, reads: 'Spent wonderful afternoon on rocks at low tide: coloured pools, a Chinese dragon of a small octopus, beche de mer, anemones like green brocade'. An article Vance published in the *Daily Mail* on 3 October extends her imagery and turns it, rather laboriously, into journalism. He writes of the octopus in the rock pool: 'Looking at it, one suddenly discovers where the Chinese artists got their idea of a dragon from. Indeed Chinese art must have found a good deal of its inspiration in the marine life of places like this. There are the delicate colourings, the grotesque shapes, the sense of an intense, unreal world of beauty and monstrosity'.

Aileen's diary became part of the shared family record too. When Nettie writes in early 1927 that the children went out on a motor-boat trip, she continues: '(For the day, see Aileen's diary)'. To a young girl reaching adolescence such family sharing might well become oppressive. Towards the end of the year (when Aileen's passion for Violet was at its height) frequent references in her diary allude to the fact that she is writing something that is not to be shared: *Wrote secret*, she confides to her diary, or *Wrote secret in evening*. Who is this disclosure meant for? For others who might read her diary? Nettie responds to Aileen's new behaviour with her usual amused tone, displaying little awareness that her daughter might wish to distance herself a little from the family closeness: 'A[ileen] writing at some long stint just now, "a secret if you don't mind"'.

The decision to send Aileen to board with an old pioneering family called the Petries in 1928 – so that she could attend a larger state school that went beyond fifth class – seems to have been welcomed by her, perhaps not surprisingly. At the end of the 'autobiography' written on her thirteenth birthday in April of that year, she looks forward to it: *I am thirteen, & I wish I wasn't! Is that grammar? I don't care! I'm only in lower Vth, and I ought to be further on. After next holidays I'm going to stay with the Petries at Murrumba, and go to school there. I'm jolly glad. I'm sick to death of this old school. I'll make the best of the hol I have here, because I won't be here much longer.*

Aileen sent cheerful letters home from the Petries, where she had the company of their fifteen-year-old daughter, Poppy Petrie. When she returned home for a week during the August holidays, the family went off for the day to Currimundi, a lake surrounded by wooded cliffs further up the coast. Nettie was glad to see her serious daughter relaxed and wrote to her mother: 'Aileen says Currimundi makes even her feel young! It seemed like it. You should have seen them both playing at being monkeys – hanging by their toes to trees, drawing themselves up by a miracle, chattering & throwing nuts to the ground. It does Aileen good to go quite mad with Helen sometimes'.

The sense of a lost youth was to weigh heavily on the adult Aileen's mind. Several times in later years she recalls that her sister once told her: *'You never were a child'*. Her mother's youthfulness, even naiveté, in contrast to her own lack of it, becomes a theme in her later writing. In a section of 'Pilgrim's Way' called 'Coming of Age' she reconstructs a scene at the village market in Montgat, Spain, when she was twenty-one:

Around the stall would be gathered six bulky women – bulky, as I was then…with long blue cotton skirts going down to their ankles and nearly hiding black stockings and heavy black shoes. I was to them a responsible person as they were, but who was the lady, they wanted to know one day, who came skipping down from our house and down to the beach?

'That's my mother', I said.

They were surprised. They might have been Noni's age – they looked older at least, with their swathes of long black hair, tied in knots at the back...

'Es joven, su mama!' one of them said. ('Your mother's very young'.)

Yes, she was young. 'However long I live', I once said to a friend of hers, 'I'll never live to be as young as Noni'.

Aileen rarely recalls the Caloundra years in her later autobiographical fragments, a silence that indicates they were relatively happy years and didn't need to be worked over, but she did write that she regretted leaving there: *Still, as always happened in our family (Pilgrims all) we had to migrate. No sooner had I got a scholarship to go to the Technical College in Brisbane but my grandfather (John Wycombe* [Higgins]*) died, and we had to migrate south to Chilbrook* [Melbourne], *'to be with mother', that is, his widow, my grandmother.*

In fact, although John Higgins's death cemented the plan, the decision to return to Melbourne had been made earlier, albeit reluctantly, so that the girls could go to secondary school there. Both Nettie and Vance had found their 'retreat' in southern Queensland congenial for living and for writing and they had stayed there far longer than the few months they had originally intended. Neither relished the idea of living in the city again. But return to Melbourne they did, and, after six weeks en route in Sydney, the family reached there in early April 1929. Less than a week after their arrival, Nettie enrolled Aileen and Helen at her old school, Presbyterian Ladies' College.

5

The Getting of Wisdom

As Laura Tweedle Rambotham, the heroine of Henry Handel Richardson's novel *The Getting of Wisdom*, approaches the Presbyterian Ladies' College (PLC) on her first day of school there, she finds the imposing building 'vast in its breadth and height, appalling in its sombre greyness'. Like her heroine, Ethel Richardson was thirteen when she started at PLC as a boarder in 1883. The women of Aileen Palmer's family too had a long association with the gloomy edifice that used to glower over the Fitzroy Gardens in Albert Street, East Melbourne. Aileen's Great-Aunt Ina Higgins was a foundation student there when the school opened in 1875. Her mother followed, starting at PLC as a student in 1900 and returning there in 1912 to teach modern languages during her engagement to Vance. Now, in April 1929, Aileen and Helen are about to complete their secondary schooling within its stone walls.

Aileen was on the cusp of fourteen when she was enrolled at PLC. It was more than four decades since Ettie Richardson had first walked through the school's iron gates, but the shadow of H. H. R. would both haunt and inspire Aileen during her three years at the school. She was already familiar with the expatriate novelist's writing through her mother's critical interest in her work and, by the end of her first year at PLC, both she and her new friend, Brenda Linck, were poring over Nettie's copy of *The Getting of Wisdom*, each determined to write their own school story.

Aileen's first homage to the writer she revered was the rather hagiographical sonnet, 'To a Portrait of a Famous Woman', which was accepted by the school magazine *Patchwork* in mid-1930:

Is this the face of her who is proclaimed
By half the world the greatest of our age?
Whose books will be our noblest heritage,
Long after others have been widely famed;
Careless of whether critics praised or blamed
Nor stayed nor faltered her courageous pen
Through decades of obscurity, and then –
Suddenly the whole world acclaimed.

No one would guess her cramped and thwarted youth:
Her lofty brow betrays no sign or frown,
Her hair is ebon-black, her lips are curled
In half-contemptuous pity for the world;
Her watchful, dark, round-lidded eyes have known
And looked with quiet courage on the truth.

Nettie shared her daughter's amusement at being asked by the editors of *Patchwork* who was meant by the poem before they would accept it. Richardson's name was not well known then as a celebrated Old Collegian as her satirical school story published in 1910 had deeply offended the College authorities. *The Getting of Wisdom* was not held in the school library, nor was her portrait among those that graced the school corridors. Aileen's sonnet is clearly based on a portrait of its subject and the one she would have been familiar with was sent by H. H. R. to Nettie in early 1929 to accompany articles she was writing about her. It would eventually form the frontispiece of Nettie's 1949 biography of the Australian author.

Through her mother's association with Henry Handel Richardson, Aileen received a polite personal response from the author herself after Nettie posted her a copy of the poem and one of Helen's. Privately, H. H. R. was more censorious. 'One of the poems is addressed to me!!' she wrote to her old school friend Mary Kernot. 'They are early following in their parents' footsteps. The verses weren't bad, in fact they were too *good* for my taste. At that age young people shd [should] be wilder'. Like her own heroine, Laura Rambotham, she might have added. In fact, Aileen felt a great affinity with the rebellious Laura, the girl who was convinced of her intellectual superiority but made cruelly aware of her social inadequacies, who became obsessively infatuated with an older student and who had a younger sister who was sweet-natured and more popular than herself. Aileen was to emulate H. H. R.'s sardonic style in the novel she would write a few years later about her own experience at PLC – a manuscript it is doubtful she ever showed her parents.

The Palmers rented a house in Hawthorn, at 13 Chrystobel Crescent, when they arrived back in Melbourne, within walking distance of Ardmore where Nettie's mother now lived alone, managing with the aid of domestic help. Vance and Nettie did not enjoy suburbia after their life in coastal Queensland. Vance sunbathed on the back lawn most mornings but it was a poor substitute for sand and surf. They did enjoy such city pleasures as concerts and the theatre, Nettie taking 'the kiddies' to see the great Russian ballerina, Anna Pavlova. Vance and Helen also took advantage of major sporting events like the test cricket at the MCG. Work soon took precedence, however, Vance writing the last chapters of *The Passage*, his novel set in Caloundra, while Nettie took on a new project, one that she faced with some misgivings.

Nettie had received a double blow the preceding January when she lost her father. Just two weeks earlier her beloved Uncle Henry had died suddenly after suffering a stroke. 'We feel it badly', she wrote in her diary at the time, 'since he was so young: never younger than when he came here for a week last June, nominally 77. He had youthful indignation & sympathies & kindness'. An intellectual radical, Judge Henry Bournes Higgins's lasting legacy was his establishment of the minimum wage in the Harvester Judgement of 1907 when he ruled in favour of 1000 factory workers and set the men's wages by what he determined to be the cost of living. Later, as Sir Justice Higgins, he established the Arbitration Court. After his death, his sister Ina was left with all his papers and it was she who persuaded Nettie to write his biography. Nettie, however, was worried about her ability to write an objective account of her uncle's life and work, as the genre demanded then. The generous regular quarterly income that was attached to the project may have helped her decide to accept the task, for it was a sum that would have easily covered the school fees for Aileen and Helen at PLC.

The sisters experienced intense and conflicting emotions about their new school. 'Helen is purring all the time, Aileen more critical', Nettie reported in her diary at their end of their first week. But a couple of months later, it seems the normally cheerful Helen, whose only experience of formal education had been as a pupil at the little one-teacher primary school in Caloundra, was finding life at PLC overwhelming: 'Helen came home from school in the worst of gloom. She is out of her depth & bewildered & wrathful, poor little dear'. Then, after regaining her usual even temper, the eleven-year-old was hospitalised during the Melbourne winter with a bout of pneumonia. Many years later, a former school friend of Helen's wrote an article about the Palmers in which she remembered Nettie working huddled 'in a tartan rug that had seen many winters', a sight, she said, that was 'pure Abbey Theatre'. The Palmers didn't like the cold, but were 'parsimonious' when it came to heating the house. While the children had been brought up to be hardy, sleeping on the verandah of the cottage in the Dandenongs through their early childhood, their barefoot life in the Queensland sun may have softened them.

Aileen hurled herself into life at her new school with gusto, being promoted from the class she was first placed in within a few weeks. 'She'll enjoy biting into something hard', predicted her mother. In a matter of weeks she was promoted again in everything but geometry and algebra, which were new to her. By early July Nettie was reporting, 'Aileen's whirling along on more dizzy heights, longing to do Latin & German & French well: also bursting into poetry in a private way, papers & papers of it'. For her part, Nettie was working on the biography of her uncle but longing to indulge in some more creative writing of her own. 'Anxious to write a series of spanking poems on Caloundra. Could I? I wonder', she confided to her diary.

The inspiration for Aileen's burst of poetry writing was her French teacher, Miss Hutton, whose name was starting to appear in Nettie's diary in comments written in the amused tone with which she had regarded her daughter's romantic feelings for Violet Beasley in Caloundra the year before. Nettie was no doubt familiar with schoolgirl passions; indeed she had once composed her own Sapphic poems for university friends such as striking, long-haired Christian Jollie Smith, who she wished could have had her portrait painted 'seven times by Botticelli'. You might expect that the seriousness with which she had explored her own turbulent youthful emotions would have made her more understanding of Aileen's, but perhaps her amused tolerance masked underlying twinges of anxiety. She watched her intense daughter closely, noting that she would take herself off frequently on 'fierce' solitary walks, sometimes for hours.

Vance apparently joined in the fun at their daughter's expense: 'Aileen, otherwise Pawpaw, Pawky, or Pork, is haunted by her dreams & thoughts of the lovely Miss Hutton at school. Vance raised Cain by telling her he had just seen an advertisement for Hutton's Pork'. Nettie also noted that Aileen was reading a psychology textbook lent her by the adored Miss Hutton. At the school sports her elder daughter looked on unmoved until Helen introduced Miss Hutton to Nettie and Aileen miraculously appeared behind their seat. A few months later Nettie invited Miss Hutton home to tea, pronouncing her 'quite a charming, solid girl, southern English'. She lent her copy of *The Getting of Wisdom* to the young teacher.

After the ordeal of her end-of-year exams – for which even Vance helped in the preparations, setting her a half-size arithmetic exam to be done in one and a half hours – Aileen plunged into writing her school story inspired by *The Getting of Wisdom*, frequently calling on her sister for advice. According to her mother it was 'very ambitious'. In the new year of 1930 Aileen had to combine her writing with swotting for a supplementary arithmetic exam. Then in February, Nettie commented that her daughter was 'also doing a sudden short three-act play, very feminist & subjective, dealing with the extermination of man a few centuries hence & the survival (for many centuries) of a few charming & deserving women, only too recognisable! She isn't sure if it's a farce or a tragedy: says she meant it to be a comedy!'

Having consciously set out, in the family tradition, to write a potboiler she could perhaps make money out of, Aileen had become bored with her first attempt at a school story. So, when an idea for a play presented itself, she abandoned the school novel with its theatrical little tennis-playing heroine. She might have joked about her new venture to her parents, but her play, 'A Feminist's Heaven', though written in humorous vein, is a serious attempt to explore her unsatisfied longings for love and success. Its sardonic tone predicts some of the science-fiction poetry she was to write during the 1950s and 1960s, such as 'Song from Planet 90' and 'Third from the Sun', where she longs for a world without war. Its utopian theme of a female universe prefigures the lesbian feminist science-fiction genre that was to emerge in the 1970s with the advent of the women's and gay liberation movements.

The central character of 'A Feminist's Heaven' is Varenka Sullivan, of Russian and Irish parentage. In the first act she is *a tall, ruddy girl of twelve, with very black eyes, and soft dark hair,* in love with twenty-two year old Heather Raymond (who, as Nettie was quick to observe, is clearly modelled on Miss Hutton). The time is early in the twenty-first century and the location is *Rossville.* The action moves to the twenty-second century and Melbourne for the second act. Many people have died out, but Varenka, who still looks like a young woman, has made millions from writing thrillers as Imogen Brown, penned to impress Heather, whom she has lost trace of. When Joan, a young newspaper reporter, arrives to interview Varenka, the writer tells her of the dream she once had for a girls' army and the abolition of men: *It was a child's dream, though I've been trying to work it out in this new novel. My army, however brave and numerous, would have been no use against the ghastly science and mechanism of this age. But there is no need for my army now. The human race is dying out of itself. Only we, my friend, will survive!* Joan is discovered to be the daughter of Heather Raymond, who has married several times and who at the end of Act Two marries an Australian communist. Act Three takes place 800 years later in Caloundra, which has become the new capital. The last man dies, Joan falls in love with a girl, and Varenka and Heather live happily ever after. The manuscript of 'A Feminist's Heaven' survives in Aileen's papers in a clean copy handwritten in black ink, obviously a finished product to be shown around. This she did to selected readers.

While Aileen was dreaming of a glorious utopian future, the world was rapidly sinking into recession after the 1929 Wall Street stock-market crash. Soon girls would begin disappearing from the ranks of PLC when their parents became unable to pay the fees as the Depression set in. And freelance work was once again drying up for both Vance and Nettie.

In spite of the dire economic situation, there was much secret excitement in March of 1930 at the Palmer household when the news, as yet confidential, that Vance had won *The Bulletin* prize for his novel *The Passage* reached them. Of course, they told their intimate friends like Katharine Susannah Prichard in Western Australia and the Essons, who were once again near neighbours as they had been in Emerald, having just moved into 4 Chrystobel Crescent. The prize gave Vance the stimulus to organise a trip to London to publicise his novel and renew his contacts in England and the United States. He would also try to place Nettie's now completed biography of Henry Bournes Higgins (which he had cast his structural eye over and relieved of 'some entanglements') with a publisher in London. Travelling third class in a six-berth cabin on a £38 passage, he sailed on the *Ormonde* in stormy weather on 13 May, looking forward to catching up with Katharine Susannah Prichard during the stopover at Fremantle.

Aileen and Helen wrote cheerful letters regularly to their father while he was away. Helen's contain lots of news about football and tennis; she tells Vance that she and her sister both got 'A++ in BIBLE!'; in one letter she proclaims, apropos of nothing, 'I love life'. Aileen's letters are more self-conscious and chiefly about literary matters. She has been reading the mysterious Brent of Bin Bin's latest novel *Ten Creeks Run*, which she proclaims 'bonza', adding: 'I must write to Brent and thank himher [sic] for it. Have you heard that they think she's Miles Franklin?' (Brent gave his address as Seat S9 at the British Museum and rumours flew among literary circles about his identity for years, but the novels were only confirmed to be Franklin's when her papers were released long after her death in 1954, indicating that Aileen had her finger on the literary pulse in 1930.) Inspired by her mother's biography of her uncle, she also tells her father, 'I admired your last two letters, which Mum graciously allowed me to read, and intend to publish them when I write your biography. I've been reading

Katherine Mansfield's letters, so I know something about it'. There is a sense that Aileen is trying to compete (too hard) for the affections of her prize-winning novelist father, whose easy camaraderie with his younger daughter was based, somewhat ironically, on their shared love of sport. 'Dear old Helen', he writes at one point, 'When I come home we'll lie on a rug in the sun, on that patch of buffalo-grass at the back that must be now all smooth and green with constant mowing, and we'll talk for hours, particularly on Sunday mornings. First of all about the Test Match'.

Nettie confirmed Aileen's enthusiasm for Vance's letters: '"Keep all these letters", said Aileen, very sternly: "they're masterpieces". I've never heard her more intense'. Privately, though, Nettie found her husband's letters wanting and her old complaint about his lack of emotion surfaces again. But now his new letters are measured unfavourably against the love letters she once criticised and which she has been rereading: 'God knows I'm glad you love the children & I could never be jealous of them: but do you never remember our intimate life together? What different letters I would be writing you if I had even a hint that you could endure them!' She resumes this intense letter later after a visit from her brother Esmonde, writing a few pages of cheerful chat and pinning a piece of blue velvet to them, noting: 'A frock for Aileen…Her eyes aren't as blue as they were, though'. A good example of Nettie's mercurial nature and volatile temperament, this letter also shows the candour with which she was wont to criticise as well as praise her elder daughter, a habit Aileen took to heart at an early age.

In her next letter Nettie apologises profusely to Vance for her 'need of assurances & reassurances' and Vance responds with concern about the tone of his letters: 'I wish I could write more intimately…Can it be that I haven't shown you how all my life vibrates with thoughts of you?' Both these letters bear witness to the extraordinary value placed on the written word, particularly by Nettie, but also by Vance.

While Aileen was later to find the family obsession with words oppressive, at the age of fifteen her world was filled with their seductive power – reading them, writing them, learning to translate them from and into different languages, especially French and German poetry. Nettie, of course, supported her in her passion, but wrote with some anxiety in her diary of the difference between her two daughters: 'Helen plays endlessly with Hughie [Esson], but Aileen rather sticks about with books – a difficult type, horribly like me'.

Though not sporty like her sister, Aileen was as keen a walker as the rest of her family and Nettie was only too happy to comply with her daughter's request that the two of them take long walks in the evenings, talking exclusively in either French or German, a habit that was to continue for years. At school Aileen had been invited to take part in the Critics' Club, courtesy of her older friend Brenda Linck, joining an inner circle of senior girls who wrote poetry that was published in *Patchwork*, but also verse that was considered too subversive for the magazine – poetry of protest that exposed hypocrisy or philistinism. In her final year at PLC in 1931, after Brenda had gone on to university, Aileen was to be the principal force behind compiling an anthology of verses written between 1928 and 1931 by the group under the irreverent and untranslatable title of 'Je m'en Fiche!', a name Vance and Nettie thought impudent rather than artistic. As well as being represented by six of her poems, she did most of the typing and stencilled the title on the booklet's red cover.

Vance experienced a mixed reception in London. Nettie commented that 'His friends are all prosperous & fat – & not writing at all!' He told Louis Esson that the inner circle of literati was more exclusive than he could have imagined, but he did meet some writers, lunching with Rebecca West and being received by the formidable Henry Handel Richardson at her home in Regents Park Road. Her third volume of *The Fortunes of Richard Mahoney* trilogy had recently been published to international acclaim. Among the accolades *Ultima Thule* received in Richardson's home country was the Australian Literature Society Gold Medal.

Knowing of his daughter's reverence for Richardson, Vance wrote a separate letter to Aileen about his visit: 'I've told Mum about seeing H. H. R. Would you be surprised to know that she drives a car, and is very fond of speeding? And of moving-pictures? – though she only goes to Russian and German ones'. Richardson herself gave her first impressions of Vance in a letter to her friend Mary Kernot: 'He struck me as perhaps being a trifle *vain*. Correct me if I'm wrong; it may have been shyness'. On second acquaintance she liked him better, deducing he might have been scared of her at their first meeting: 'People complain I have that effect on them; though God knows it's quite unintentional. I am really both a simple & *humble* person. (The fault of my *nose*, I say; for which I can't be held responsible.)' She didn't think Vance had achieved much in the way of impressing publishers and critics on his visit to England and personally she found his books constrained and lacking in emotion. Declaring in her reply to H. H. R. that 'his women are of wood', Mary Kernot considered Vance's inhibition might stem from Nettie: 'Perhaps it's rather awful to have a critic at one's elbow, even an adoring one'.

Henry Handel Richardson's friendship with Mary Kernot began at PLC in the 1880s and was resumed by Richardson after the publication of *The Getting of Wisdom* in 1910, resulting in their long-ranging correspondence between London and Melbourne. The character of Cupid in the novel is based on Kernot. Cupid is described as a clever girl, three years older than Laura, who loved reading and who 'had a kind of a dare-devil mind in a hidebound character, and was often very bold in speech'.

The two women's letters appear to have served a variety of purposes, perhaps different for each correspondent. As well as indulging her obvious affection for her old friend, Richardson was able to obtain information about the reception of her books and the state of the literary scene in Australia in a more casual way than, for instance, in her correspondence with Nettie Palmer. Kernot also promoted H. H. R.'s writing in Australia when her readership was mainly European; in fact it was Mary Kernot who had alerted Nettie Palmer to her omission of Richardson's novels in her study of Australian literature published in 1924. For Mary, living quietly with her husband in the seaside suburb of Beaumaris, the relationship would have given her a privileged insight into the literary world and an association with the writers and literary critics who sought her out. Aileen was to write, perhaps perceptively, that Mrs Kernot's relationship with H. H. R. was 'the real romance' of her life. Both women shared sharp powers of observation and sharper tongues, and reading the correspondence that survives is often like revisiting the gossip that was part of the currency of friendship among the schoolgirls at PLC, captured in *The Getting of Wisdom*. Often cruel, it was also often revealing of the writers of the gossip as well as their unfortunate victims.

Richardson showed a keen interest in the Palmers after Nettie had begun to champion her work. Her spy, Mary Kernot, reported on their movements, including the move to Melbourne from Caloundra in 1929. H. H. R. responded to the news with more questions: 'Very glad to hear the Palmers are prospering...Tell me what they, the P.'s, are like to look at. He, with his tiny meticulous handwriting, & she with her ease of expression, & really *natty* journalistic talents. I'll keep your secret'. Mary's immediate response to this request does not survive, but in a subsequent letter she relates a visit by Nettie to her house, telling H. H. R. of Nettie's determination to gather as much material as she could in the way of foreign reviews and even to borrow the German edition of *Maurice Guest*. She describes Nettie as 'active in mind & body & intensely interested in her husband's work'. H. H. R. responds with wicked glee: 'I laughed at your description of your day with Nettie Palmer, her earnestness & energy, & your relief when it was over'. Mary apparently related another of Nettie's visits a few months later, but we only have H. H. R.'s reply: 'Your most entertaining letter of Sept 14th has just come. I do enjoy your pen-pictures of Mrs Palmer's visits. She sounds *most wearing*, & I begin to understand Vance better. Think of living with that always beside you – that paragon of energy & capability. Quite enough to make a man shrink into his shell. The girls too – oh la la! I know the type that prefers to sit & listen to its elders talk'.

Gossip usually promotes the gossiper at the expense of its subject and Richardson's unkind comments about the woman whose indefatigable energy was devoted to championing her work follow a well-worn attitude towards the hierarchies of the literary world. Although the work of critics and journalists was necessary to her survival as a writer, Richardson demeans it as lesser work than the creative work of the novelist, proclaiming herself bored with having to find 'facts'. Of course, critics also had the power to write unfavourable reviews of a novelist's work and Nettie was not always entirely complimentary about H. H. R.'s writing. Richardson mentions Nettie's 'journalistic talents' on several occasions, with mildly condescending comments such as 'The woman's a *born* journalist' and 'She has really a very neat pen'. Of Nettie's biography of Henry Bournes Higgins, however, which Vance had managed to place with the publisher Harrap and which had just come out in London, Richardson was scathing: 'That book left an *arid* impression...I judge from it that N. P. hasn't a touch of the novelist in her, or she wld [would] have made her creatures live more'. With that, Nettie Palmer is firmly put in her place.

When *Ultima Thule* was published to international acclaim in 1929, H. H. R. started sounding out her Australian contacts such as Mary Kernot and Nettie Palmer about how they thought a reprint of *The Getting of Wisdom*, which had been out of print for many years, would be received there. The English reprint came out in May 1931 and Richardson immediately sent Nettie a copy. To Nettie's favourable response, H. H. R. wrote: 'I'm so glad *Laura* has reached you – and pleased you...I hope it will do well in Australia. Most of all, I should appreciate a few words from your pen. You have been one of its kindest and most enlightened friends. A caricature, it was never meant to be. Just a merry and saucy bit of irony. How *can* people take it so seriously?'

Aileen attempted to review *The Getting of Wisdom* for *Patchwork*, but the offer was rebuffed, the principal suggesting she write a review of the trilogy instead. That duly appeared in the August 1931 edition. In one of her jocular reports to H. H. R., Mary Kernot relates being given a copy of the *Patchwork* issue on a visit to the Palmer household on a freezing winter's day, during which she and Nettie and Aileen sat in the only warm spot in the house – Vance's study. With her usual sharp wit, she provides a rather cruel, but probably accurate, pen-portrait of the sixteen-year-old Aileen: 'She was anxious to tell of her attempt to send in a review of Laura. Mr Grey (Principal of College) declined it – said he had never read the book himself, only dipped into it, but a review would displease some old Collegians! but suggested the Trilogy instead – All this Aileen told in nervous bursts. She really is a picture of robust-ness. I always feel nervous about her frocks, they strain. She is coming in these holidays to see me some day. I think all the holidays, playing tennis, hockey, etc would be excellent for her but evidently she is under the weather of her work poor girl!'

Vance certainly comes off best from the gossip between H. H. R. and Mary Kernot about the Palmer family, even if they do demean his writing.

Earlier in 1931 Nettie reported in her diary that Aileen's friend Brenda Linck, who was now at university, had come to dinner and yarned with them during the evening. Brenda tells the Palmers that she has nearly finished a novel on her life as a PLC boarder. Nettie thinks she has 'plenty of grit'. Aileen duly brings her friend's completed manuscript home and her mother remarks that it would 'make "The Getting of Wisdom" seem quite kind & smooth'. Vance reads it carefully and goes through the manuscript with Brenda, Nettie hoping she will take note of his suggestions: 'She has understood them well: a very intelligent, witty girl'.

Unfortunately, no trace of Brenda's manuscript survives, but while Aileen was quietly listening to her father's editorial comments, she may well have been thinking of how to approach her own story of life at PLC.

Aileen was now in sixth form, the highest class at PLC, taking Honours in languages but, according to Nettie, 'most devout in German'. While not happy that her daughter had 'managed to scrape out of gymnastics & singing', Nettie relented when she promised to go for long walks instead. As well as developing her language skills, Aileen's activities with the Critics' Club took up much of her time as she and her friends prepared their subversive poetry anthology. She was also using the listening skills that Mary Kernot joked about to take in the talk about politics that went on around her. She listened when her uncle, who became a communist activist in Sydney on his return from Oxford, came to visit. On one occasion Esmonde teased his quiet niece as he left after holding the floor, tossing over his shoulder as he departed, 'You've been a noisy old windbag, Aileen'. She listened to the talk when the Baracchis came to tea. She even attended at least one of Guido Baracchi's famous parties at Larnoo, their home at Ivanhoe on the banks of the Yarra, where political activists, academics, writers and bohemian art students of the Meldrumite school gathered.

One day towards the end of the year Aileen suddenly cut off her plaits, then called on Vance to tidy up the resulting mess. The next day she bought a second-hand bicycle, which she practised riding assiduously until she crashed it a few weeks later, squashing the bike and breaking her glasses just before her final exams. The bicycle accident happened just days after she was hit on the back of the head by a misdirected stone at the sixth form picnic at Warrandyte. Friend and family doctor Hilda Esson examined her and said no stitches were required but she should be kept in bed. 'Good excuse for doing badly in the exams!' was Aileen's response. She did not, in fact, do badly in the exams and at Speech Night was awarded the German Prize. Helen won two prizes and Nettie noted that she held herself much straighter than Aileen when they went onto the stage to receive their awards.

Nettie and Vance had been making plans for travelling again as a family ever since Vance's return from overseas in 1930. They wondered if they had enough money to all go to Europe at the end of 1932, at one stage suggesting that Aileen could take a job as a governess in the bush for a year after finishing sixth form while Helen continued at PLC. The couple finally decided on several months of camping and writing on Green Island in Queensland during 1932 and invited Aileen to join them while Helen would stay with Nettie's mother at Ardmore to continue her schooling.

It seems that Aileen, however, was investing all her hopes in winning a scholarship to university. In her final exams, she received First-class Honours in German, Second-class in French and European history and Third-class in ancient history. Returning early from a disappointing walking trip with a school group of students and teachers in the February of 1932, Aileen was devastated to discover that she had not been successful in gaining one of the few scholarships awarded. Sobbing inconsolably, she declared she could not bear to go to Green Island with her parents, but wanted to stay in Melbourne. In the face of such a display of emotion, Nettie and Vance determined they would find the money to send her to university even though she was only sixteen and organised for her to stay with Grannie along with Helen while they were in Queensland.

Early in the new year, Aileen had begun typing up the completed manuscript of the novel Vance had been working on since his return from abroad. Unusually structured, the action of the novel, set in Emerald, takes place over the course of a single day, the events of which have their roots in the past. Aileen finished the job in just over a fortnight. She typed an extra copy of the novel (published as *Daybreak*) in February, Nettie noting that her daughter was 'very helpish' after her university plans had been fixed up. She also recorded that Aileen was 'writing something of her own in furious secrecy every evening'. Clearly inspired by the single-day structure of her father's novel, Aileen was beginning to write her own 'getting of wisdom' story, which would eventually cover four thick notebooks of close handwriting and run to over 400 pages.

6

Poor Child!

The single day that frames Aileen's unpublished novel 'Poor Child!' (intriguingly subtitled 'A Posthumous Novel') corresponds to the day after she returned from the school walking trip to Torquay on 7 February 1932. The central character, sixteen-year-old Vivienne Waller, leaves her house early that Sunday morning and wanders the streets around Hawthorn, sits on the banks of the Yarra River opposite the Kew Asylum and crosses the bridge into the poorer suburb of Richmond. She winds her way home at lunchtime and then visits a school friend late in the afternoon before returning to her house at dusk: *Colour was ebbing from the citron-tinted sky. The coolness of evening rose from the ground. In the front gardens of the houses Vivienne passed, hoses were playing. Darkness was descending on the still, implacable city ahead of her. She had been walking all day and had the sense of returning home after long wandering.* During her wandering she relives and reflects on her three years at PLC and charts her journey from shy but egotistical young girl, through a period of depression in her second year when she was in love with a teacher and possessed by thoughts of suicide, to her final year when she determines to relinquish the idea of her creative genius, forget romance, study hard and become a linguist.

In this novel Aileen starts her lifelong practice of renaming people and places in her semi-autobiographical writing. Melbourne becomes, evocatively, Helburne. (It seems her antipathy towards her home city began long before the troubled decades of the 1950s and 1960s when she calls it Chilbrook or Squarebrook in her novel fragments.) Characters based on her family, friends and teachers from PLC appear in 'Poor Child!'. The principal of PLC at the time, Mr William Grey, becomes Herbert (Bertie) Bray, a pompous and verbose man of whom it is said: *'Bullying women is his favourite indoor sport'.* Miss Virtue, the senior mistress, is transformed into Miss Goode who, unlike her counterpart from *The Getting of Wisdom* – the terrifying Mrs Gurley – apparently lives up to her names. Hilda and Louis Esson become Madeleine and Leon Ross and the *glamour* of their *ménage* and their *Bohemian way of living* is contrasted with the Waller (Palmer) household.

Even Henry Handel Richardson appears – as the revered writer Sidney Schumann Davidson – while her friend Mrs Kernot becomes Mrs Russell. It is satisfying to see Aileen unknowingly get her revenge on Mary Kernot when she includes a sonnet about Mrs Russell's friendship with S. S. D. called 'The Shrine'. In it, she describes Mrs Russell's drawing room, which is full of photographs of S. S. D. and has every edition of her work on the bookshelves, even in German which Mrs Russell does not read. The narrator comments after the poem: *This perpetual contact with S. S. D. gave importance to what seemed to Vivienne an otherwise rather trivial existence.*

'Poor Child!' examines Aileen's school years almost forensically. Most of the people and events recorded in Nettie's diary occur in the novel, albeit with different emphasis. The counterpart of the 'charming, solid girl' who was Miss Hutton, for instance, has smooth white skin, full red lips, large eyes and an expression of serenity. There is evidence that Aileen kept her own pocket diaries from which she would have drawn extensively for accurate details of events. Unfortunately they do not survive, but Nettie's meticulous records provide a striking parallel to the novel and indicate just how autobiographical it is.

Unlike Henry Handel Richardson, who wrote *The Getting of Wisdom* twenty years after her school days when she was already an established writer, Aileen penned the novel of her PLC experience immediately after she left school. Yet, while her youth and inexperience show, and the sardonic tone she chooses to adopt often wobbles into the melodrama of her earlier 'novels', her first attempt at serious writing based on her own experience is an extraordinary achievement. Privately a keen student of her father's sense of form,

Aileen succeeds in sustaining the quite complex structural framework of 'Poor Child!'. She eschews the narrative 'I' of autobiography and, although Vivienne Waller shares many of the author's attributes, Aileen's darkly humorous critique of the heroine gives the text a fictional distance.

The subtitle, 'A Posthumous Novel', announces the tone of irony and immediately brings into question how seriously the reader should take Vivienne's various suicide attempts. Like H. H. R.'s Laura Rambotham, Vivienne Waller is no traditional heroine. Described often as obnoxious, conceited, plain or awkward, she is placed in situations where she is usually found wanting next to her peers, as when she is invited to play tennis at a friend's house: *At tennis, of course, Vivienne did not shine...she remembered her woolly dress, incorrect for tennis, her black sandshoes and untidy hair, in contrast to the exquisite clothes of Irene and her friend, who was just back from Paris; the conversation at afternoon-tea – their hostess on Paris, Irene on China, then their hostess's mother: 'And what did you think of Queensland, Vivienne?'*

The central thread of this *Bildungsroman* is the protagonist's obsessive love: first for her French teacher (named Helen Raymond rather than the Heather Raymond of 'A Feminist's Heaven' but also based on Miss Hutton) and then in her senior year for her German teacher, Alexia Garran, who is based on her counterpart at PLC, Miss Jessica Gilchrist. Evelyn Souttar, the object of Laura Rambotham's infatuation in *The Getting of Wisdom* was also based on a real person at PLC – an older student, Constance Cochran – but the novel was written in a different era from Aileen's. H. H. R. herself was to acknowledge this in her autobiography, *Myself When Young*: 'In those days school authorities had not begun to look with jaundiced eyes on girlish intimacies'. Not so when Aileen was writing in the early 1930s. During her years at PLC she became aware of Freudian psychoanalysis and the work of the sexologists on sexual inversion; she also read Radclyffe Hall's *The Well of Loneliness*, a novel with lesbian themes which created a furore resulting in a court case against the novel for obscenity when it was published in London in 1928. 'Poor Child!' consciously rehearses the contemporary debates around homosexuality as it follows Vivienne's growing awareness of her awakening sexuality – a mixture of elation, intense longing and despair.

Clothilde Franck, an older friend and PLC boarder closely modelled on Brenda Linck, serves as the antagonist in these interior debates. Vivienne is ambivalent towards the rather jaded and cynical Clothilde, who psychoanalyses everyone. She is flattered by her friendship and envious of her confidence but jealous of her easy relationship with her teachers, particularly Helen Raymond, who is her senior by only a few years. Clothilde also runs the Poetry Club (modelled on PLC's Critic's Club) which she invites Vivienne to join. The older girl is habitually condescending towards Vivienne in what appears to be a private school tradition. Cupid in *The Getting of Wisdom* usually refers to Laura as 'Infant', while Laura's beloved Evelyn often calls her 'Poor little kiddy'. Similarly, when Vivienne relates the tale of her dreadful holiday early in the novel, Clothilde expostulates with a gasp: '*You* poor *child!*', hence the novel's title.

Early in their acquaintance, Clothilde remarked disapprovingly of a teacher whose attachment to another teacher was well known in the school: '*She's a Lesbian'...*

'What's a Lesbian?' Vivienne had asked.

'Ah, my child, your education is sadly lacking', Clothilde answered.

Vivienne never confides her passions to Clothilde, but listens to the older student's diatribes against what she calls 'hero-worship' among the students, particularly among the boarders. This hero-worship takes the form of being 'mad' on or 'thrilled' on teachers or each other and it is clear that half of Vivienne's French class is 'thrilled' on the amiable Miss Raymond. When she is asked what is wrong with the boarders, Vivienne hazards a guess, *remembering a scene that Clothilde had read her from her novel* and replies, *'Sex-repression'*. According to Clothilde, it was the taboo against sex in the college that led to the girls' passions for their teachers and other students, their instincts leading them to *'unhealthy outlets'. 'Of course, these things aren't confined to boarders', Vivienne interposed. She was angry with Clothilde, for talking as if they themselves, through having dabbled in psychology, were outside and above that sort of thing because they had labelled it. She didn't feel she was beyond it herself. Knowing the names psychologists gave to your desires didn't make them any less: only made you bottle things up inside you, so that they worried you much worse than if they had found an outlet.* But still she kept her feelings to herself, reflecting that Clothilde *had no knowledge of this side of her nature...She would not have considered there was enough of the physical in Vivienne's make-up for her to be classed among those whose homosexual attachments disgusted her.*

At the same time as she listens to (and silently resists) Clothilde, Vivienne reflects on her own history of becoming attached to certain of her parents' glamorous and attractive younger women friends from early childhood: *They wove themselves into her fantasies and became the heroines of her books; but the idea of emulating them did not enter into Vivienne's mind...In the makebelieve dramas which she enacted in the solitude of the bush, it was always the hero's, not the heroine's role that she took.* Aileen must have felt some sense of identification with the masculine female protagonist of *The Well of Loneliness* when she read it and in 'Poor Child!' Vivienne declares she wasn't meant to be a woman. Unlike Radclyffe Hall's Stephen Gordon, however, Aileen's Vivienne Waller comes to the conclusion that she does not want to be a man: *If she had been a man, she would have fallen in love with someone... got married and settled down to a contented and rather commonplace existence.*

Vivienne appears to cultivate a sense of herself as an outsider, with both positive and negative elements. The ironic descriptions of her many shortcomings are balanced by her inherent belief in her intellectual superiority. Perhaps partly born out of Aileen's real differences from her sister, Vivienne's sense of self both reflects and rebels against unflattering comparisons: *She had been a moody and solitary child, prematurely embittered against life, she was not quite sure why. But through all her moments of despair and self-torture, she had guarded the inextinguishable spark of belief in her own genius. Her parents were both intellectual and gifted; surely their children would be likewise... Ideas for innumerable novels thronged her brain; she was confident that she would one day become both famous and rich.* Contrasting herself to her sunny-natured younger sister, Mabel, she *took her own awkwardness as a proof that she had higher gifts than Mabel, that she was singled out by fate from the common herd.*

Vivienne believes her romantic feelings for women to be another positive distinguishing characteristic of her 'difference'; in fact she had thought herself unique until she had come to PLC. The discovery that all sorts of commonplace girls were 'thrilled' on Miss Raymond had almost made her rethink her position. The two women teachers at the school who were an established couple were also a disappointment; they were very ordinary people and even her grandmother liked them! But, convinced that her own desires were of a grander nature and also not the passing phase she had read about in the psychology books Miss Raymond had lent her, Vivienne defiantly continued to be obsessed with her French teacher.

The depression that had descended on Vivienne in her second year at PLC had thrown her fragile construction of self and her private confidence in her superiority into chaos. Her passion for Miss Raymond simply faded away and the loss feeds her thoughts of suicide, but her melodramatic attempts to kill herself are never discovered by anyone. On one occasion she is prevented from stealing the revolver from behind the door in her father's study (a most unlikely scenario) because he is working there; on another, the rope breaks as she tries to hang herself from the apple tree in the backyard because she has forgotten she weighs ten stone. She underlines her stupidity with a quote from T. S. Eliot's poem 'The Hollow Men', published in 1925: *This is the way the world ends / Not with a bang, but a whimper.* But although these scenes border on the ludicrous, Vivienne's constant thoughts of suicide and her repeated assertions that she feels 'dead' and uninterested in life, or even writing, suggest that Aileen went through a period of intense depression, as she would intermittently in later life.

A scene in which Vivienne decides she must give up thoughts of killing herself is both an uncanny precursor of her future and an example of how closely the novel is drawn from Aileen's own experience. On one of their evening walks, Vivienne and her mother Lottie inadvertently find themselves at the gates of the mental asylum. As the huge gateway *loomed up in the dim light…like a pair of cruel jaws*, she reflected that *the thought of going mad had always filled her with a kind of fascinated horror. Wasn't it possible that mad people were possessed of a deeper knowledge than ordinary beings? She had craved, as one craves to know what is beyond the tomb, to know what it is to be mad.*

Vivienne recalls a recent conversation with her mother when she was told the story of her father's brother who had made several attempts at suicide before descending into a *settled melancholy* that had seen him institutionalised in a Queensland mental hospital, where he remained. Her father had been in Europe, rushed back home, took his brother camping – all to no avail. It is the 1912 story of Vance's brother that is related here, complete with the fiction that Vance had actually taken Wob camping in the Blackall Ranges. Aileen maintained that story on several occasions during her writing life, so it appears that Nettie might have embellished the original.

The effect of the story on Vivienne is profound. *Listening to her mother, Vivienne realised acutely what her parents had suffered together. Her mother's absorption in him would not let her father suffer anything alone. Her father's sympathies were not so easily aroused, he did not form so many and deep friendships, you were less aware of him as a being ever giving his utmost to life and those around him: but there was a quiet strength about him that could be relied on in a crisis – Vivienne remembered his tireless devotion when anyone was ill. How he must have spent himself for his brother!* Vivienne takes herself to task for contemplating giving her parents further pain and vows to relinquish her *egoism and folly* and accept whatever life offers: *Vivienne had resolved that evening to act – do anything to prove to herself that she had a will, as capable of moving from the vicious circle in which she had been rotating.*

She resolved to buy Clothilde's pushbike and learn to ride it. We know from Nettie's diary that in early October 1931, Aileen had tried to buy Brenda's bicycle only to find she had already sold it, 'so they dashed into town together to buy another second-hand bike for Aileen'. She also cut off her plaits, perhaps symbolically renouncing childish things, though not her androgynous identity as she now sported a boyish Eton crop.

At the end of February 1932 Aileen entered Melbourne University as an Arts student, majoring in French and German language and literature. She began March with a symbolic burning of volumes of her childhood writing, including nine exercise books of the historical epic 'Lyre and Sword' by 'April Nightingale'. 'What a sibyl she is!' commented Nettie indulgently in her diary. Excited and always disorganised, Aileen rushed off to university each day, one day distraught at not being able to find her pen so Nettie lent her hers, which her daughter managed to lose too.

At Easter, the new student took the train to Mount Dandenong with the crowd from the Labour Club, of which she was now a member, for their annual conference. Among the speakers were Nettie's brother Esmonde and Guido Baracchi, both of them, as Nettie recorded, 'Aileen's uncles at Emerald once'. (Given her background, how could Aileen have avoided being drawn into her two sometimes conflicting passions – literature and politics?) On the 29th of the month she returned home from the conference, 'very *ungeschlafen* [unslept] & fierce, with a cold'. Two days later, Aileen and Helen moved to Ardmore to stay with their grandmother before seeing their parents off on the SS *Dimboola* on 2 April, bound for Queensland and their sojourn on Green Island.

Since beginning 'Poor Child!' in early February, Aileen had somehow found time between her exciting new ventures to continue writing her novel. She had filled one thick exercise book and was well into the second when she wrote 'Stuck. March 1932' at the bottom of page 205. Her writer's block occurred as she was beginning to write of the effect on Vivienne of her dissipating feelings for Helen Raymond during her second year at PLC. Her French teacher had become engaged and would soon leave the school. She was no longer teaching Vivienne and on the rare occasions they met on the tram, the schoolgirl found little to say to her. The page on which Aileen had got 'stuck' ends with the words: *Others before Helen had come and gone, without leaving a trace. Of some of her predecessors, Vivienne still had memories, bitter or sweet; of others she had forgotten even the names: but there had been no disillusion afterwards, no self-torture.*

When Aileen resumed 'Poor Child!' on page 206, she was attempting the difficult task of writing about her alter-ego's depression, caused by the realisation that her infatuation for Helen Raymond had been driven by egotism rather than genuine love. Vivienne's belief in herself had also dissipated with the loss of her muse: *For with Helen's going went all her soaring hopes: her fatalistic theories showed their reverse sides. Doomed to disappointment, doomed to failure...With the desire to shine in Helen's eyes went all urge towards intellectual activity. The Poetry Club – what did it matter? She kept it going in second term, contributing poems she had written earlier in the year, and assisted by various enthusiastic class-mates, but all her own enthusiasm had vanished.*

During the long vacation at the end of that second year at school, Vivienne revisited the thoughts that had possessed her over those dreadful months: *Phrases went round and round in her mind: 'Fool, idiot, madman, why don't you kill yourself?' and Tolstoy's observation, that she had once heard one of her parents' quote: 'This is my son, who has all the faults of a genius, without being one'.*

The guilt that seemed to be a constant part of Aileen's feelings towards her parents, particularly towards her mother, manifests itself in this early work in the following sequence where Vivienne resolves to make Lottie Waller's life easier: *Her mother had written poems when she was younger, then her life had been taken up with household cares and when she had gone back to writing it had only been potboiling journalism that didn't absorb all of you: if only she could relieve her mother of all her burdens, she might be able to go back to poetry. What a pity she had abandoned it to have children!* In keeping with the ironic spirit of the book, Vivienne's *dream of self-abnegation* fades as she tries to imagine herself as an efficient housekeeper and she resolves instead to *make her last bid for brilliance* in her final year at school and become *a successful linguist.*

It appears that bound up in Vivienne's desire to 'shine' in her French teacher's eyes was the desire for acceptance by her mother. If she was not to be a creative genius, she could at least aspire to become a linguist like her mother. Aileen also wanted to shine in her mother's eyes. The irony of Nettie Palmer's decision to set aside writing poetry after her daughter was born in 1915 because she did not want 'ink to run in her veins' acquires a particular poignancy in this context. It was the ensuing upheaval of war that made Nettie take up journalism to help the family finances; the war also made her question the importance of writing poetry in such a world. Without that war, the responsibility Aileen felt for simply being born might have been allayed. Unconsciously, and rather chillingly, Aileen uses Nettie's metaphor in 'Poor Child!' when she describes Vivienne's inability to show her feelings: *But to her teachers Vivienne was a slippered scribe devoid of emotions, whose blood was red ink and whose skin was parchment!*

During her final year in the Honours sixth form, Vivienne Waller becomes caught in the thrall of passion once more as she falls under the spell of her German teacher, Alexia Garran. As with her infatuation with Helen Raymond, her obsession causes her both elation and misery and she more than once resorts to thoughts of suicide again. But this relationship is different and it suggests that Aileen is describing her own development into adulthood. For one thing, Aileen appears to have kept this passion a secret. There are no teasing jokes at her expense about Jessica Gilchrist in Nettie's diary as there were when her infatuation with Miss Hutton was an open book. The only reference to the German teacher is this one in April 1931: 'Aileen to meeting of German Club with Miss Gilchrist'.

Not surprisingly, an invitation to Vivienne by Alexia Garran to accompany her to the German Club at the university forms a major scene in 'Poor Child!'. Vivienne delays telling her mother of the invitation until the last minute, afraid that she will want to come too: *Alexia might be invited out to tea, as Helen* [Raymond] *had been, and there would be all sorts of other developments; but something in her – was it snobbishness, Vivienne wondered? – baulked at the idea of Miss Garran's sitting in their dingy little kitchen-dining-room and eating her mother's spaghetti and jam-tart; and – yes, she didn't want Miss Garran to know her as part of a family – the fool of the family; and, above all, the great thrill about Monday evening would be having Miss Garran all to herself.* Of course, the evening proves to be something of a disaster. Just before it, Vivienne catches a cold: *the spirit of bathos that guided her destiny always contrived for her a cold in the head at the critical moments of her life.* When she finally meets her beloved teacher, she is struck dumb as they sit in the *Brunswick cable-tram lit by dingy yellow electric-light*, Miss Garran exquisitely dressed in a pale green and brown matching outfit, Vivienne in her mother's black coat.

This relationship is different on another level too. Whereas Helen Raymond was depicted as approachable and friendly *and wore a kind, angelic expression*, Miss Garran is altogether more challenging and Vivienne had at first disliked and feared her. Although the schoolgirl had thought her black hair, pale skin and Grecian profile beautiful, she felt *there was something cruel about the curve of Miss Garran's lips and the steely glint of her eyes.* And where a goodbye kiss on the cheek from Miss Raymond sent fourteen-year-old Vivienne into ecstasy for days, the sixteen-year-old girl's feelings for Alexia Garran are expressed more obliquely and with a subtle eroticism through their shared exchanges of German Romantic poetry. In one scene, Vivienne wangles a German class with Miss Garran alone and teacher and pupil work together on a Heine ballad: *Miss Garran reads it through in German. Though the language is very simple, Vivienne soon loses the thread of the story; but the mere sound of the words has an effect on her like that of exquisite music. And Miss Garran's voice: when she speaks English, her accents are precise, inclined to be affected; but reading German, especially German poetry, there is something melodious, something soft and caressing about it.* Vivienne then haltingly provides her translation of the ballad: *When Vivienne raised her eyes from the page, she met those of Alexia looking full into her own... She looked quickly away. And yet she was divinely happy.*

Aileen wrote much of 'Poor Child!' during her first year as a student at Melbourne University. She signed off the last page of the fourth thick, black-covered exercise book: 'February 28th, 1933. Aileen Yvonne Palmer, aged seventeen'. Another exercise book identical to those that contain 'Poor Child!' also survives in her papers. This contains a curious journal. She kept it for just over three months between 30 June and October 1932, during the time she was also working on her novel.

It seems she started the diary because she had recently been received into the ranks of a small and select group of female Arts students who referred to themselves as the Mob. Older than Aileen, her new friends set about initiating her into Mob philosophy of spontaneity, free love and a worship of trees. Aileen's nickname became 'Twig', indicating her status in the hierarchy of the group. These unconventional young women were studying in an era of university education far removed from that of today. Now the emphasis is increasingly on vocational training; then an Arts degree offered a broad, liberal arts education – less a training for a specific profession than an education for life. The young women's studies focussed on literature and European languages. So, while the secret society of the Mob provided its members with a safe space in which to explore their passionate friendships, the erotic currency of these friendships was integrally bound up with the heightened language of poetry and music. In a typical entry, Aileen writes: *D and I walked on ahead. She told me she had made up a new song that morning! I asked if I could walk home with her that afternoon and hear it. It had to be heard that day.*

Aileen begins her journal as a private diary, but it soon becomes part of the esoteric exchanges that take place between Mob members. In return for lending it selectively to other members she is offered the privilege of reading their diaries. Sometimes there are annotations in Aileen's diary by the person being described in it, thus the entries become a kind of conversation. The young women also write *billets-doux* to each other. Poems and songs are copied into the diaries, almost as gifts for those reading them. Aileen offers Christina Rossetti's 'A Birthday' ('My heart is like a singing bird') as well as poems of Heinrich Heine in German. She copies the traditional 'Coventry Carol', which is one of the 'Mob songs', into her diary in Middle English. 'Lullay, lullay, lytel child' is usually sung by Dorothy Adams, the leader of the group, who was actually a tutor in the English department when Aileen was accepted into the Mob in 1932. The young women discuss their favourite authors, who include the Brontës and Shakespeare. One of the group, known only by her initial 'K', is writing a thesis on New Zealand writer Katherine Mansfield, who had recently died of tuberculosis. Aileen tries to 'convert' Dorothy to the novels of Henry Handel Richardson, but the worldly-wise tutor finds her *too restrained, even in 'The Getting of Wisdom'*. Aileen vows to lend her *Maurice Guest*!

The diary is replete with code words, such as 'collecting', which appears to refer to a special connection forged between two of the young women, although these are not exclusive relationships. New members are 'collected' by one of the group. Aileen writes of her initial collection: *The day I was collected has never been diarised, & probably never will be.* She is 'collected' by several different Mob members through the course of the journal and, as she becomes more confident, she also initiates the process. The group meet outside university as well as during their days at the 'shop' (as the university was known by its students) and Aileen's description of one gathering is typical: *Nellie and I hugged in the hall and went upstairs with our arms around each other; and drank honey and ambrosia sip for sip from a cup in the bathroom. I sat on the floor between Isobel and Jo…Nellie and Dorothy were being m- on the other side of Jo. Then Jo began to stroke my hair and gripped my shoulder with her sensitive, supple fingers. I was as happy as I have ever been; – and happier, because this love will last and could have no jealousy and bitterness in it.*

The code initial 'm-' is one that is used frequently but never spelt out. From its context it could be short for something like 'maudlin', elevating its meaning from 'sentimental' to 'sensual'. At one point, Aileen allows a younger friend, Shirley Campbell, who is still at PLC, to read her diary when she stays overnight with her: *Shirley assured me that I hadn't sunk in her estimation after reading my diary, but I am not sure. I will never be quite certain whether it was partly perversity or wholly horror of maudlinity that prevented our love from expressing itself in physical emotion.* Later they talk as they lie in their separate beds: *She said she wasn't used to being maudlin; I said neither was I before I joined the Mob. I had hated the kids at school who were, because in people of their inferior mentality it was just sloppy. With the Mob it was the real thing – not a game with the emotions.*

The gentle sexual experimentation reported in the diary is verified in a fictionalised memoir written by Jill Golden, the daughter of another Mob member ('K' of Aileen's diary). 'K', whose real name was Kathleen Cooke, left diaries and letters that are contemporaneous with Aileen's diary and, although their names are fictionalised in the memoir, the women from the Mob are easily recognisable. Aileen becomes 'Pearl' and extracts from her diary are quoted, although with the substitution of the fictionalised names.

Sometimes I have felt that working on Aileen Palmer's autobiographical writing, in which actual people and places are given fictional names (and not always the same ones), is a little like entering a hall of mirrors where nothing is quite what it seems. Jill Golden's fictionalised memoir based on the real letters and diaries of the group of young women at the University of Melbourne helps to illuminate the arcane and mysterious world of Aileen's diary at the same time as it adds another cryptic layer. But Aileen's diary *itself* further confuses the boundaries between fact and fiction by including some of the fictional characters from 'Poor Child!' in it.

'Edna', who appears only briefly, is clearly based on Miss Hutton, but the person outside the Mob who appears extensively in the diary is 'Alexia Garran'. Why doesn't Aileen call 'Alexia Garran' by her real name of Jessica Gilchrist? There is one mention in the diary of 'Gillie' (the PLC students' nickname for Miss Gilchrist) who is directing a play that Aileen's friend Shirley is appearing in, but when Aileen attends a rehearsal she writes that *Alexia took very little notice of me.* The conflation of the real and fictional person remains puzzling, but a possible explanation lies in the last few pages of the diary.

These final pages are exuberant in tone. Aileen is at home feeling *horribly full of beans* at the end of a German Club outing to the Dandenong Ranges. She spent most of the day in Alexia Garran's company, walking and talking with her as an equal. For the first time, the teacher is not on a pedestal. Aileen finishes her account of the day with: *I've invited her to Selby* [a Mob meeting place in the Dandenongs] *at some vague time (forgive me, Mob!) & promised her a copy of my novel if it's ever published. I don't quite know how collected I can call her, but I know I'm happy – a steady, assured happiness that is none the less intense.* This passage suggests that 'Alexia' might be inducted into the Mob through Aileen's initiation. It also contains the curious promise to provide her ex-teacher with a copy of 'Poor Child!', indicating that Aileen has developed beyond her schoolgirl alter ego. The diary finishes on page 81 with a joyful *Attagurrrrl!*

Perhaps the positive account of 'Alexia's' *collection* on the German Club outing was written as an attempt to balance the account of the devastating school camping trip in 'Poor Child!'. In the novel, the trip is the catalyst for the protagonist's day of wandering and reflection that forms the story's framework. On that occasion, 'Alexia Garran' had failed to attend the trip in spite of her promise. The parallels between the novel and Aileen's life are clear. That Aileen was in a fever of anticipation of the excursion to Torquay is clearly marked in Nettie's diary, though not the reason for her excitement, that is, that Jessica Gilchrist was going. On 1 February 1932 Nettie writes: 'Aileen set off with full pack up: no cardigan or blazer'. Five days later, she reports that her daughter has returned early, unexpectedly. In 'Poor Child!', Vivienne leaves the group early because of her misery at Alexia's failure to arrive and catches the bus back to 'Helburne'. As well as her failure to win a scholarship, it was that awful holiday on which she had pinned all her hopes for reaching some sort of understanding with Alexia that provoked the tearful scene with her parents in which she refused to go to Queensland with them.

In her diary, Aileen refers to her *frenzied intuition* that led to her refusal to go to Green Island, but adds: *My salvation came through my staying here, but from an unexpected quarter.* It was her association with the Mob that had saved her, not pursuing a relationship with her German teacher. As the erotic currency of the Mob's passionate friendships was intimately bound up with words – billets-doux, poetry, story and song – it is possible to suggest that the passion for 'Alexia' is brought to its narrative consummation in Aileen's diary. Perhaps it was necessary to keep 'Alexia' alive in her diary so that it could end with the reversal of Vivienne's unhappy walking-trip experience, giving the story the sort of 'happy ending' Aileen had craved as a child.

Aileen's coming-of-age novel is her first sustained piece of largely autobiographical writing, and it prefigures the fragmented, semi-autobiographical 'novels' that she wrote during the 1950s and 1960s. In 'Poor Child!', her adolescent alter ego is concerned with establishing an identity for herself that is separate from her parents – one in which she can resolve the ambivalence towards them that governs her existence. Her 1932 diary contains a passage in which she responds to a letter from her mother on Green Island canvassing plans for the family to visit Europe the following year. With the new confidence she has acquired as part of the Mob, Aileen feels she will be able to concur with her parents' wishes without losing her sense of self: *Will I hurl myself again against fate? No, I won't be so filled with frustrated longing & self-pitying tears; I won't have the feeling that the words my parents utter torture my exposed nerves; there will not be the clash between my admiration for them and the expansion of my stunted individuality; there will not be the feeling that I have never lived.*

7

Young Communist

Aileen and Helen are posed in front of bushes in the driveway at Ardmore. It is 1932 and the snapshot shows the two sisters at radically different stages of their lives. Aileen, the university student, looks ten rather than two years older than Helen. In fact she looks almost matronly, her sturdy figure garbed in coat, hat and gloves, clutch purse under her arm, glasses on her nose and an aloof, humourless smile tightening her lips. Her hat may well be the brown felt one that Nettie sent to her after the Palmers reached Cairns, saying she wouldn't be wearing it in Queensland. Helen, a gawky schoolgirl in jumper, bulky skirt, white stockings and shoes with straps, stands to attention smiling on cue. They both look distinctly uncomfortable. It takes no stretch of the imagination to guess that their grandmother is behind the camera, perhaps having told the girls they should have their photo taken while they are neatly dressed for church so that she can send it to their mother.

Nettie was anything but neatly dressed on Green Island, which she described as being 'like a flat hat immensely over-trimmed with green plumage'. She and Vance had set up camp on the coral island towards the end of April, starting each day bathing naked in the warm sea and then settling down to work. Vance, having donned a pair of shorts, would sit on his deckchair in the sun, typewriter perched on his bare knees, pipe dangling from the corner of his mouth. Nettie, in a crumpled cotton dress, preferred a shady spot for her deckchair, where she wrote in her notebook, bare feet nestling into the sand. In the evening she cooked over the campfire, often fish Vance had caught in the late afternoon. They would then sit outside their tent under a black sky dotted with stars, reading by the light of the petrol lantern Vance had rigged up, talking about books and writers, discussing their plans for the future or just reminiscing.

It may sound like an idyllic way to escape the Depression, but the Palmers were well aware of what was happening across the world. Inevitably, talk of the Depression's devastating effects crept into their conversations and it was a subject Nettie wrote about too: 'But where was there any chance of escape? The wheels are slowing down all over the world, hopes being trodden underfoot, vitality ebbing. Even in this lotus-eater's paradise – well, look at the tents of the unemployed on the Cairns racecourse'. Even though their circumstances were very different from the thousands of unemployed who were forced to live in tents, the Palmers were also, in effect, homeless. They had given up their rented house in Hawthorn, making one of their periodic retreats from the city to restore their creative energies – and to save money.

Aileen was homeless too. It had been her decision to stay in Melbourne and not to accompany her parents to Queensland, but no matter which choice she had made, the result would have been the same. She once again had no 'firm house' to live in. She had been transported from the freedom of life at Emerald to Auntie Ina's when she was three after Vance enlisted, then left again with her aunt at ten years old while her parents organised the move to Caloundra, and she was now obliged to live with her little sister in another elderly relative's house. This time it was her grandmother's rules she had to follow, one of which was attending church. At least at seventeen she could deal with the situation by spending as little time at Ardmore as possible.

If Nettie *was* sent the constrained photograph of her daughters dressed up for church, she was unlikely to have been as impressed by it as her mother would have liked. But Katie Higgins was worried, particularly about Aileen. As Helen reported to her mother in a younger-sister telltale way, 'Granny is getting a teeny bit anxious about Aileen moving about in an atmosphere of Communism & Labour Clubs'. Nettie, however, was already well aware of her elder daughter's political interests. Aileen had, after all, returned 'very *ungeschlafen* & fierce' from the Easter Labour Club conference just before her parents had left Melbourne. So it might not have been too much of a surprise when, early in their Queensland sojourn, Nettie and Vance's old friend Guido Baracchi sent them a copy of the first issue of the Melbourne University Labour Club magazine, *Proletariat*, and congratulated them on the fact that Aileen had become a member of the Communist Party of Australia (CPA). The CPA's new recruit had just turned seventeen.

Aileen had plenty of precedents close to her. Her great mentor Katharine Susannah Prichard had been a foundation member of the Party in 1920, as had her mother's friend Christian Jollie Smith (a lawyer), and her own 'Emerald uncle' Guido Baracchi. Her real Uncle Esmonde had joined the CPA on his return from Oxford, where he had been active in communist circles, even visiting Moscow. He and Ralph Gibson, another young Australian intellectual who had an English master's degree, had led the study circles at the Easter conference Aileen attended. The review of the conference in the first issue of *Proletariat* stated: 'For the first time this Easter the Labour Club went into the claims of Communism and clarified the points of difference between Communist and Parliamentary Socialist'. It asserted that the two brilliant young students of sociology, Higgins and Gibson, had both been previously aligned with social-democratic policies but had adopted Marxist–Leninist theories and policies through 'the force of intellectual conviction'.

Aileen's ASIO (Australian Security Intelligence Organisation) file states that she was a member of a family 'all noted as Communists or at least strong supporters of the Party'. This, like many ASIO assertions, is not entirely accurate; Nettie and Vance, while remaining broadly left-wing in their allegiances, did not ever become Party members or even strong Party supporters. In fact, Esmonde's embrace of communism caused something of a rift between sister and brother for years, and Nettie's friendship with Christian also suffered. How she and Vance responded to their adolescent daughter joining the Party is not something that survives in diaries or letters, though Nettie did write what seems to be a deliberately non-committal response to Helen on receipt of the *Proletariat* issue and Guido's news: 'It's a very competent magazine indeed & the Party seems to be sound at present. Aileen's languages will help her to study the Communist movement abroad'. Ever the fussy mother, Nettie also tells her more practical younger daughter to make sure her sister wears a singlet (shortening the straps if they are beginning to sag) and a cardigan under her coat. Obviously, even a young communist can catch a chill.

Today, post–Cold War and with the knowledge of the extremes of Stalinism, it is perhaps difficult to imagine the idealism of those Australian men and women who flocked to the CPA in the early 1930s, driven by the massive unemployment of the Depression and the creep of fascism, derisive of what they called 'bourgeois democracy' and frightened of another global war. From the mid-1920s the Australian Government had introduced harsh laws aimed at the militant unions, and Joseph Lyons of the United Australia Party had campaigned on a platform of stamping out communism when he was elected Prime Minister in January 1932. Fascist paramilitary organisations flourished during this period of social unrest and the New Guard in Sydney lent its support to Lyons during his electoral campaign, handing out tickets for his policy speech at Sydney Town Hall, which was delivered under the banner 'SMASH THE RED WRECKER.' Such was the tense atmosphere in Australia when Aileen joined the CPA.

The Labour Club at Melbourne University had been formed in 1925 and contained a nucleus of communists. Guido Baracchi had re-enrolled as a student in 1931, at the age of forty-four, and was in his element giving lectures at the Labour Club and hosting club functions at his home at Ivanhoe, which Aileen had started to attend while still at school. Considered highly radical, the Labour Club was constantly in conflict with the more conservative campus elements, including the university magazine *Farrago*, the editors of which Aileen declared to be fascists. Simmering enmities came to the boil in the month she joined the Party, culminating in the dunking in the university lake of one of the more flamboyant members of the Labour Club, Sam White, by a gang of right-wingers led by Edward Dunlop (later 'Weary' of war-hero fame). The hardline CPA leadership under J. B. Miles was not too impressed by the campus intellectuals and Miles criticised the first issue of *Proletariat* for 'the unspoken liberalism of its editors' and the inclusion of articles by non-communists.

Helen reported to her parents in Queensland that there had been several university rows 'centring around Mr. Samuel White'. Aileen also wrote to her parents (in a different tone from her sister) updating them on her political activities, telling them on 1 May that she had just come home from the May Day afternoon on the Yarra bank, that 'Flunk' (Helen) was helping her write up some notices for the Labour Club that she'd been commissioned to do, and that she was going to Guido's for an all-day conference the following Saturday.

Nettie, meanwhile, was playing peacemaker. She told her anxious mother that she was being terribly kind to her 'two sprouting daughters with their appetite & interests' and tried to reassure her about Aileen's activities. 'Aileen's all right, I think', she wrote. 'She was always self-contained as Helen was not. It's a prime need with Aileen to be able to call her soul her own in all sorts of matters, small & large: and this year she's experiencing more sides of life than ever before, growing very fast'. To Aileen she wrote carefully: 'Dearie mine…Granny seems rather worried about you. The way she put it is that she hopes you tell me all you're doing as she can't pretend to know: not so crudely as that. I want to assure her that you're all right & that I know all about you and/or even when I don't know all about you I know you're all right. That is so, dear. I can trust you to make your own mistakes – lots of them – or to tell me, if you can, & if it's not letting someone else down'.

Far from confiding in her mother, Aileen continued to write cheerful, newsy letters that gave nothing away of her private feelings. In August she sent her mother a pair of stockings for her birthday, apologising for her lack of inspiration*: but what the dickens can you send people living on an island? A string of beads to wear round your middle?* And when the third issue of *Proletariat* came out in September, she informed them there was an article in it on proletarian songs *quoting Mr. Louis Esson & Mr. Vance Palmer.* To her diary, however, Aileen confessed her discomfort about her treatment of her grandmother, asking herself *Am I a selfish little beast?* But she added, with a touching honesty: *I feel much more callous than I would with the parents – not a doubt that my life is more important than hers.*

In July, Helen reported that Aileen had 'gone off to some Labour Conference down at Sandringham'. 'She's never home', she added, 'except for bed & breakfast!' The Sandringham conference was at the bayside home of the bearded poet Dick Long, who had taught Aileen the anti-conscription song at Emerald when she was two years old. In the 1932 diary she started after her 'collection' into the Mob, she noted that she found him *the same, but more subdued.* She also noted that she left the conference after the second session.

Aileen's life had changed with the advent of the Mob around the middle of the year. Although some of the Mob members were also involved in the Labour Club and her diary is dotted through with references to making and pasting up posters, she seems to have become less absorbed in politics and more consumed by the exhilaration of being with her new friends and discovering a new emotional dimension to her life. Her desire to devote herself to the Mob meant she had little energy for anything else, including Labour Club and her studies. When told she had been put on a sub-committee to do research on armaments, she wrote in her diary: *Blast! I feel utterly lazy where Labor* [sic] *Club's concerned.* Her political zeal was to return with a vengeance, however, in her ensuing university years.

Aileen continued her close association with the Mob throughout university, but the all-encompassing intensity of her first year among them diminished over time. The Mob's alluring leader, Dorothy Adams, seems to disappear from view; perhaps she left the university and the group lost its coherence. For two years Aileen spent part of her long summer vacation with Mob members at the property of Nellie Stewart's family in Shepparton. After Nettie and Vance returned from Green Island towards the end of 1932, Nettie found Christmas to be strange without her elder daughter at home with the family. While Helen and Vance spent their days at the cricket (including coming home 'bubbling' over 'that marvellous boy' Bradman), Nettie seemed depressed at being back in the city after her eight months on the island. She was spending her days with her mother and reorganising her plans for her Green Island book, and commented in her diary, 'Horribly difficult, in this world of indifference & cowardice'. The book never eventuated, but there is a section on their island experience in her published journal, *Fourteen Years.*

By May of the following year, Nettie took the advice of a doctor who treated her for a lingering bout of pneumonia 'to find a warm, sheltered place in the Dandenongs' and she and Vance moved from their rented flat in South Yarra to a 'spindly cottage', sans electricity, perched on the slopes of Kalorama in the northern part of the range.

For the rest of their university and school years, Aileen and Helen remained based at Ardmore, but spent much of their free time at Kalorama. They would travel up by train, usually separately and often accompanied by friends. Aileen took some of the Mob members or her old school friend Shirley Campbell. The young people often walked the five miles from Croydon station to Kalorama and then tramped the hills on day picnics, Aileen sporting her favourite garb – jodhpurs. She was also immersed in living up to her ideals as a communist who rejected bourgeois capitalism, refusing to buy new clothes and combing the hills for blackberries and apples. 'She has a passion for whatever can be got without price', noted her mother. Around the house, she eschewed domestic chores in favour of outdoor tasks such as helping Vance stack enough wood to last the winter. Nettie often recorded that Aileen seemed well and happy during this period of her life. One relaxed image from the time is of her daughter cleaning her shoes in time to the Emperor Concerto playing on the gramophone.

Early in 1934, her third year at university, it seems that Aileen was working 'furiously' on a new novel, about Melbourne, the first chapter of which introduced a number of different characters 'as if glimpsed in a crowd'. Nettie must have been allowed to read it as she commented at one stage that it was 'very difficult & with too many characters, but full of virtue'. It seems to have been a less autobiographical project than 'Poor Child!', which she had finished in March 1933. Given the earlier novel's sometimes critical portrayal of the protagonist's parents and the highly autobiographical account of Vivienne's emotional journey and lesbian infatuations, it seems unlikely that her parents ever read it. Nettie never mentioned it (although her 1933 diary does not survive) and, while Aileen wrote of her childhood historical novels in later years, she never referred to 'Poor Child!'. It is as if that quite extraordinary piece of extended writing never existed. Yet the first notebook of the manuscript of 'Poor Child!' and her 1932 diary are found together in the papers that she put together for preservation. (The three later notebooks of the novel are found in a different set of papers containing Aileen and Helen's 'Juvenilia' donated later to the National Library by friends.) Interesting questions arise that cannot be answered. Reticent about her sexuality in later life, did Aileen leave these notebooks as clues for later readers of her archive or was their inclusion accidental?

No more is mentioned about the new Melbourne novel after February and no trace of it exists; it may well have been shelved when Aileen's final university year started in earnest. For one thing, she had to make a decision on her thesis topic for French Honours. Her activities in the Labour Club also took up much of her time and she was joint editor of *Proletariat* for the August issue. As well as acquiring an article on Soviet students by Katharine Susannah Prichard for it, she herself wrote a long article titled 'Fascism and Culture'. In this didactic piece, she denounces the *phrase mongers* of fascism who seem to offer a change from the *blatant commercialism of the age*. After denouncing the work of Western writers like Pound, Lawrence, Huxley and Eliot for, variously, their mysticism, Catholicism, or anti-communism, she turns to the Nazi terror under Hitler's regime, the *crowning act of barbarism* of which was the burning of books in May 1933. She concludes: it *is clear, from the experiences of the Soviet Union, that only the abolition of this system by the revolutionary working class* can raise the level of culture and allow *the creative forces lying idle under capitalism* opportunity for expression.

During the four-week university vacation in August, Aileen decided to write on Proust for her thesis. She also brought a new friend to Kalorama to stay for several days. Margaret Kemp was also involved in political activities – being secretary of a committee against censorship – and she was older than Aileen. According to Nettie, when Margaret was at Kalorama, Aileen 'oozed happiness'. During her stay, the young woman spent the evenings in long family talks around the open fire and Nettie gave her verdict on her in her diary: 'Margaret shy & shrewdish in her questionings: a little too willing to admit her own deficiencies & limitations & to abide by them. Humorous enough to sit on Aileen for having been a convinced feminist by the age of five: "I didn't think like that until I was nineteen!"' After she went back to town, Margaret left a present of four breakfast cups and saucers at Ardmore for Nettie, who remarked, wryly, that she must have 'spied the great nakedness' of the cottage in Kalorama.

Nettie doubted if Aileen was getting much 'orthodox work' done in her final year as her energies were devoted to the Communist Party in the anti-war movement. She was probably right. Her daughter's political activities were ramped up even more when the Czech-national, Paris-based Jewish writer and communist Egon Erwin Kisch made his controversial visit to Australia in November as an invitee of the Movement against War and Fascism to speak at an anti-war congress. Government officials attempted to prohibit the activist from entering the country and refused to let him disembark when the RMS *Strathaird* reached Fremantle.

Like many Australian writers and intellectuals, Aileen was already active in protests against the Lyons government's increasingly strict stance on censorship. The works banned were usually those that promoted left-wing or communist views even if the official reason was indecency. So she was ready to give her all for Kisch's cause when the situation arose. As it became clear that Egon Kisch was to be prevented once again from disembarking from the *Strathaird* when it sailed into Port Melbourne, she threw herself into helping to organise protest meetings, spending days on the ship as it lay in port. On the 13 November Nettie decided to go with Aileen to the ship, which was due to leave for Sydney that day. She took with her a copy of Vance's new novel *The Swayne Family* as a gift and, after a short talk with the confined activist, pronounced him to be 'clearly a literary man'.

Nettie left the ship after visiting Kisch, but her daughter remained on board. A few hours later, Aileen was on hand to see him jump five metres from the deck to the wharf, breaking his leg in the fall.

Even after this desperate act, the injured man was not permitted to stay in Melbourne, but was taken on the ship to Sydney where he was allowed to disembark for hospital because Justice H. V. Evatt decreed the prohibition to be illegal. It was then that the government forced Kisch to take the now infamous dictation test which, under the Immigration Act, was able to exclude 'aliens' who could not pass such a test in modern European languages. Kisch posed something of a problem as he was multilingual, but it was a reasonable assumption on the part of the authorities that Scottish Gaelic was not among the languages he spoke. New Attorney-General Robert Menzies was a key player in organising the ruse to ban the communist dissident.

When Kisch failed the test, he was once again deemed to be a prohibited immigrant. Appeals were organised, with Christian Jollie Smith heading his legal team. While they were being heard, Kisch spoke at some of the many protest rallies organised on his behalf.

Katharine Susannah Prichard, Louis and Hilda Esson, the artist Max Meldrum and Aileen's father were among those intellectuals active in the protests. At a huge rally in the West Melbourne stadium on the 18 November, Vance was one of the speakers addressing a crowd of 4,000. During the rally another prohibited invitee to the anti-war congress – New Zealander Gerald Griffin, who had failed a dictation test in Dutch – was escorted onto the stage by a bodyguard of communists. The crowd stood in hushed silence as the lights were extinguished while he spoke. A second large protest rally in Melbourne in December, at which Kisch and Griffin spoke again, drew nearly twice the number of people, and a later rally in the Sydney Domain drew close to twenty thousand.

For Aileen, the time was hectic. Not only was she on the organising team for the Kisch protests and attending anti-censorship meetings, she also had to face her final university exams in early December. And to top it all off, during the week before Christmas she took a sales job at Mullens the booksellers, probably organised for her by her parents.

There was no rest for Aileen after Christmas either. January saw her totally immersed in her thesis on Proust, which had to be submitted by the end of the month. At first she stayed in Carlton with friends, an idea her mother privately thought was not a good one. Nettie was proved right when Aileen arrived with luggage and books at the house in Kalorama a few days later, deciding she might work better there. 'What a family!' declared Nettie.

From then on, the thesis became a Palmer family affair. Nettie read it as Aileen wrote, declaring it to be a 'terrific assemblage of Proust & his illuminators'. The fireplace filled with screwed-up sheets of green paper. Helen started typing long sections of the thesis, while Aileen prepared and corrected the sheets further on. By the 25 January, she was writing the conclusion. Vance bound two copies on the 27th, declaring that the carbon copy was more readable as the typewriter ribbon was old and pale. Aileen started rereading and correcting in the afternoon, mainly putting in by hand the French accents that were not available on the typewriter. Helen took over, then Nettie, and the process was finished by midnight – sixty-nine folio sheets. The next day Aileen packed up the manuscript and took the morning bus to town. 'A peculiar calm descended on the house', recorded Nettie.

On the evening of the day Aileen submitted her thesis at the university she attended the inaugural meeting of the International Writers' League (Australian branch) where she was elected secretary. The Kisch protests were the inspiration for its formation. The following night she headed off to a big party at the Essons' house in Hawthorn to farewell Katharine Susannah Prichard who was leaving for Perth the next day. Nettie, who was also there, noted that it was 'an extraordinary party' with a dazzling array of people and 'a great deal of obliterating wine'. She also observed how 'devoted' Katharine was to Aileen.

Aileen finished the hectic month of January by refusing to go on a camping holiday with her family as she was too busy with committees and gathering names for an anti-censorship petition. Her decision was not popular with her parents and sister, perhaps understandably, after the effort they had all put in to help her get her thesis submitted on time.

Towards the end of the previous year Nettie and Vance had started forming plans to take the long-postponed trip to Europe with their daughters. They were aiming to leave in 1935, as Aileen would have finished university and Helen could take a year off before starting her university studies. Nettie gained a grudging agreement from her mother about the family leaving her while they went overseas. Grannie said 'the girls would be very fortunate to travel so young, most people having to make their own way at the end of a career, at 50 or so'. They then managed, with some difficulty as bookings were heavy for February/March, to obtain passage on the French ship, MM *Eridan*, sailing on 21 March 1935.

While the other three spent February organising for the trip – Vance zealously burning things, Helen and Nettie sewing clothes, all of them packing up their belongings at Kalorama and taking cases of books to Ardmore – Aileen stayed with friends in Fitzroy and continued her activities with the Writers' League, the Kisch protests and the anti-censorship movement. On a rare visit to Kalorama she was annoyed to find that the old clothes she had planned to give to the Communist Party had already been distributed elsewhere. She was also joint editor for the forthcoming April–June issue of *Proletariat* (in which she had an article: 'Some Censored Australian Literature') and that had to be organised before she left.

Aileen's parents were not pleased with her lack of involvement in their preparations for the trip and, after a discussion with her husband, Nettie wrote her a letter on the 7 February 'sketching some protests'. She felt her daughter was 'a little too casual & devoid of realism in her plans'. Vance also wrote to Aileen, pointedly saying he was too busy 'making pounds' before they left to speak at the inaugural meeting of the Writers' League. What Aileen replied to the accusations about her lack of 'realism' is not on record, but she was passionately absorbed in her political activities. As she was not going on the overseas trip with her parents through any wish of her own, she may well have felt frustrated by their admonitions and Vance's reluctance to involve himself in the League. A few years later she did apologise to her mother and father in a letter from England for her single-mindedness during that time in 1934–5: *You remember when I cursed Dad years ago for not speaking on the Yarra Bank with Katharine at the time of the Kisch campaign, and going for a walk with you instead, which he could do on every other day of the year? It was partly because I felt that Katharine and other people were putting all their guts into the struggle, and that you two didn't think it was important.*

The publication of Aileen's university results in the newspaper on 22 February helped redeem her in her parents' eyes, although only after some confusion. She had forgotten her number and assumed in her panic that she was the one with the Second-class Honours. As it turned out, through Helen's more practical interpretation of the coded list in the paper, Aileen had been awarded First-class Honours in French – 'it seems', Nettie said, 'by reason of her astonishingly original thesis: "Proust et la Personnalité Dissociative"'. Unfortunately, no trace of the thesis survives.

A few days later, while Aileen was busy preparing for the planned torchlight procession through the streets of Melbourne to commemorate the Reichstag fire in 1933, after which Kisch had been briefly imprisoned by the Nazis, it was announced that the appeal against him had been dropped. The condition was that he was to leave Australia in order to avoid prison. He left in March in a blaze of publicity, taking part in the Reichstag commemoration procession and speaking at other functions. At a dinner held for him on 2 March, Aileen, as secretary of the Writers' League, sat next to the 'Great Man' who made a speech in English that, according to Nettie, 'was witty and alive'. Kisch later wrote a book (also witty and alive) about his Australian experience called *Australian Landfall*, published in 1937. In 1935 Aileen had been promised the job of translating it into English from German, but by the time it was ready for publication she was on the warfront in Spain.

The final 'maddish, whirling weeks' before the Palmers departed for Europe flew by. Ardmore was a scene of 'chaos', but Aileen was 'still deep in plans & papers'. Nettie managed to get her into Broothorn studios where she and the girls had their photographs taken, Aileen's showing a 'good Palmerish profile' that satisfied her mother who said she was not easy to photograph. (Nettie had always made Aileen take her glasses off for photos when she was a child.) An evening party was held for the family at the Essons, then a farewell lunch at Ardmore where Nettie's mother was in good spirits. At the lunch, Auntie Ina told Nettie she hoped she wouldn't let the girls learn to smoke as it was bad for their future character and motherhood. Little did she know, and Nettie was not about to tell her, that Aileen had already taken up the habit at university.

The Palmers left by train for Sydney on 16 March. During the few days in Sydney before the *Eridan* sailed, they dashed about meeting friends, often separately. Aileen scoured Sydney for friends from university, ending up one evening at Pakie's Club in King's Cross, a well-known haunt of writers and artists. She and Nettie met up with Christian Jollie Smith for lunch the day before they left and they discussed the Kisch affair. Also on that day, the Communist Party of Great Britain wrote a letter to Aileen granting her the transfer from the CPA for which she had applied and welcoming the new 'comrade'.

The ship sailed on the 21st for Marseilles, from where the Palmers were to travel to Paris and then London. According to Nettie, Aileen enjoyed 'an orgy' of languages on board, talking with passengers from many nations: French, of course, as it was a French ship, but also German, Russian and Italian. Although she did not know it then, Aileen's knowledge of languages was to provide her entry into a decade of active participation in the fight against fascism.

Years later, in an autobiographical fragment, Aileen wrote about being taken abroad in 1935: *I hadn't come to Europe to pick up impressions, nor from any urge on my own part at the time, when there was plenty going on in Australia. But I remember Noni* [Nettie] *saying to someone, 'We want the children to see something of Europe before it's blown up'. Which seems a frivolous way of putting it now, since I've seen a bit of what blowing-up can be like…*

8

Europe in Turmoil

Aileen's Bachelor of Arts degree was awarded in her absence on 6 April 1935 – her twentieth birthday – as she was on board the *Eridan* putting her First-class Honours French into practice and readying herself for a one-week immersion in French culture. When the Palmers reached Paris they followed their usual tendency of hiving off in different directions during the day and meeting up in the evening to share their experiences. Nettie reacquainted herself with the city she had last seen as a student in 1911, ducking into the bookshops on the *rue de l'Odéon* where she befriended the well-known book proprietors, American Sylvia Beach of *Shakespeare and Company* at No. 12 and her counterpart across the road at No. 7, the 'markedly French' Adrienne Monnier of *La Maison des Amis des Livres*. Vance and Helen may well have gone off exploring together; they often did. Aileen spent days in the Louvre.

As soon as the family reached London at the end of April, Aileen immediately threw herself into political activity again, taking part in a May Day march from Hyde Park to Shoreditch while her parents went flat-hunting. If Australia had provided Aileen with ample opportunities for anti-fascist activism, conditions in Europe were palpably more volatile. Tension was mounting as fascism spread like an insidious poison across its internal borders: the Paris riots of February 1934 had almost plunged France into civil war; Italy was under the firm control of Mussolini and his Brownshirts; Hitler's power had escalated exponentially since his election as German Chancellor in 1933. In London the atmosphere was turning ugly as the paramilitary

Blackshirts of the British Union of Fascists led by Sir Oswald Mosley (*the spectre of Hitler in Britain*, according to Aileen) provoked violent confrontations with Communist and Jewish groups.

Nettie and Vance were looking for a furnished flat for the family, but eventually, after finding the flats they saw 'horrible and dear', settled for an unfurnished maisonette at 27 Calthorpe Street in Bloomsbury, within walking distance of many of the city's attractions: theatres, art galleries, concert halls and the British Museum. To Aileen's delight, Marx House on Clerkenwell Green was a brisk walk round the corner and along Farringdon Road and it would soon become one of her favourite haunts. Its library had opened in 1933 with 5,000 volumes on socialism and the house had become a gathering place for those with Aileen's political interests. It also offered courses on such subjects as the history of the working class movement, Marxist philosophy and public speaking.

First, though, all four pairs of Palmer hands were needed to make the unfurnished flat habitable. After scrounging second-hand furniture, they painted tables, chairs, cupboards and even the floors, hung curtains, unpacked their luggage and settled in. While Aileen might have complained about not having a 'firm house' to live in when she was a child, her family's frequent moves made them all adept at creating an instant home with relatively scant resources, a facility that would stand her in good stead over the next turbulent decade.

Nettie declared that she felt more at home in Calthorpe Street than she ever had at Muswell Hill where she and Vance had lived when Aileen was born. Proximity to the places that fed her soul was likely to have been the main reason. While Nettie was off visiting the Wallace Collection and the British Museum, Aileen and Helen felt that every hour was important for protesting: *We had no time for pondering over old art works in galleries and museums, as the sense of a war was pressing upon us, and we had to be busy, though we were both too young and inexperienced to be very intelligently 'busy'.*

On 10 May, just over a week after the family's arrival in London, Aileen attended a protest meeting on the anniversary of the Nazi book burning of 1933. The book burning had taken place just two years before; students in the squares of university towns across Germany had made huge bonfires of books deemed subversive by the authorities. The writers of the thousands of books destroyed in this orchestrated symbolic act of cultural control were a rollcall of European, British and American thinkers: novelists, poets, philosophers and theorists. They included writers who had special significance in Aileen's life. Heinrich Heine, the poet she had studied with her beloved German teacher at school, was one; Egon Kisch, for whom she had campaigned tirelessly in Australia, another. The works of Marcel Proust, on whose novels she had written her Honours thesis, were sent up in flames, as were those of Karl Marx, whose writings she now followed as a convert to communism. During this period, Aileen Palmer's political zeal was deeply personal, as all she had been taught to value began crumbling around her in a world experiencing dramatic upheaval.

In 1929, the experience of moving from the little fishing village of Caloundra to a city that was beginning to feel the effects of economic depression had made the adolescent Aileen acutely aware of the social ramifications of class and education. Attending a privileged private girls' school in Melbourne had heightened that awareness. Her years at university during the period when fascism was on the rise and paramilitary groups such as the New Guard were making their presence felt in Sydney further kindled her activism. Above all, the attempts by the Right to curb intellectual freedom, including censorship of left-wing writing in Australia and extending to such acts of atrocity as the Nazi book burning in Germany, fired her revolutionary spirit. Vance and Nettie had taught her to believe that the world could be transformed through literature. They had instilled in her the importance of creative work over wealth and the acquisition of material possessions. So, when Nettie became worried about Aileen's increasing involvement in politics in 1935, she might have reflected that her intense and intelligent elder daughter had perhaps learned her parents' lessons too well.

One of the speakers at that London meeting on the book-burning anniversary was a brilliant Cambridge student with brooding Byronic looks who was already a published poet. John Cornford, almost the same age as Aileen, had joined the Communist Party at sixteen and later went on to become a leader in student politics. Though a powerful and riveting public speaker, he was, apparently, quite unable to make small talk, a trait which made him, according to the recollections of a fellow student, 'a laughable contrast with the type of professional *charmeurs* whom the Cambridge Union produces'. The year before Aileen encountered him in London, he had published an article in *Cambridge Left* in which he attacked the work of young poets like W. H. Auden and Stephen Spender, denouncing their writing for its separation of art and life, calling it 'the poetry of revolution as a literary fashion, not as historic reality'. 'No wonder Spender is the pet of bourgeois-liberal critics', he wrote. 'If this is the revolution, then there is no need to fear such an idealist romantic affair! But this is not the revolution. This is only the intelligentsia playing at revolution'. He then compared Spender's elegant pathos with the stirring lines of the French communist poet Louis Aragon: 'I am a witness to the crushing of a world out of date / I am a witness drunkenly to the stamping out of the bourgeois'.

While we do not know the exact content of Cornford's speech at that meeting in 1935, his beliefs were to profoundly affect Aileen's thinking about the place of art as a revolutionary tool, bringing together her two main passions: writing and political activism. She was to meet the charismatic John Cornford again the following year in circumstances she could not have begun to imagine that night in May just after her arrival in London.

Towards the end of June, while Aileen and Helen attended a peace conference in London, Nettie set off once more for Paris as an official delegate to the International Congress of Writers for the Defence of Culture, organised by leading French intellectuals to rally the European intelligentsia to fight the rise of fascism. Many of the speakers were writers who had been targeted in Hitler's book-burning purge: André Gide, André Malraux, Louis Aragon, Heinrich Mann, Bertolt Brecht, Anna Seghers and numerous others. Some of the German–Jewish writers at the conference had fled their homeland and were living in exile in Paris. In her diary Nettie posed the question of what life was like for those refugee-writers: 'How can they sing the songs of Zion in a strange land?' Harking back to an address by Australian poet Bernard O'Dowd on 'Poetry Militant' that had influenced her at university in 1909 (just as John Cornford's similar pronouncements were influencing Aileen in 1935), she guessed that 'what they write will surely be a poetry militant – not triumphant'.

The mood as well as the poetry in Paris was militant and tempers were running high. Just a week before the congress, surrealist André Breton had assaulted one of the organisers in the street. Russian communist Ilya Ehrenburg hated the surrealists, arguing that they were non-political and merely exhibitionists, even pederasts and fetishists, and wanted them banned from the congress. Surrealist René Crevel tried to negotiate over the next few days and when his attempts failed, returned to his apartment, switched on the gas and killed himself.

The five-day congress opened on 21 June at the *Palais de la Mutualité* in the Latin Quarter during a torrid summer heatwave. The audience of nearly 2,500, which packed the hall, sweltered in the close conditions as chairman André Gide delivered the opening address, stressing that culture is 'our common heritage, is common to all of us, and is international'. The Australian delegation was made up of writers who were based in Europe at the time: Nettie Palmer, the young novelist Christina Stead, and John Fisher an Australian journalist who was the son of former Australian Prime Minister Andrew Fisher. In their address they described the campaign against the increasing censorship in Australia and urged the congress to send protests to the conservative Lyons government.

Aileen later wrote an account of the Paris congress for the Melbourne University Labour Club magazine *Proletariat*, published in what was actually its last issue at the end of the year. Though written in the present tense as though she herself was in the audience at the congress, her article must have been based on her mother's recollections. It echoes the didactic style of her earlier contributions to the magazine as she emphasises the need for 'common action' in the face of 'the imminence of the fascist menace and also that of war'.

The Paris Congress was one of the most important intellectual events of the mid-1930s. International solidarity was its purpose and for many European intellectuals communism appeared the only force able to combat the rising tide of the 'fascist menace'. Speeches emphasising a fervent belief that communism was the solution to the world's considerable problems resounded throughout the hot summer days of the congress. In an address on the individual writer and society, Gide (whose long, angular face Nettie likened to a stone Easter Island figure) quoted André Malraux's line: 'Communism restores to the writer his fertility'.

Most of those present at that Paris Congress in 1935, however, would have been unaware of the purges being carried out in the Soviet Union under Stalin's regime and the imprisonment and execution of intellectual dissidents there. In her article for *Proletariat* Aileen laments the absence of Maxim Gorki, who was to have led the large Soviet delegation, stating that he had 'become ill just the day before intending to leave Russia' and noting that his message of greeting to the congress was read out at one of the sessions. In fact, Gorki was virtually a prisoner in Moscow at that time and would be dead within a year, his murder likely to have been carried out on Stalin's orders.

At the end of Aileen's article, the editors noted: 'Aileen Palmer is a former editor of *Proletariat*. She is at present hiking through England, and intends shortly to visit the U.S.S.R'. No mention of this projected visit to Russia is to be found in her papers or in Nettie's diary and the visit was not made. I wonder if Aileen's unwavering belief in the Soviet Union might have been shaken had she encountered firsthand the hunger and poverty there. Perhaps not. Both Guido Baracchi and Katharine Susannah Prichard had remained committed to communism after making visits to Russia in 1933. Although they could not have remained unaware of the appalling conditions under which people were living, they still felt the building of the new socialist civilisation, though flawed, was the best alternative to capitalism with its unemployment and threat of war. They were impressed when shown the golden fields of grain on a Ukrainian collective farm used as a showpiece for the agrarian collectivisation process; they were told by their guides to ignore the displaced and starving people they had seen as being the consequence of resistance to modernity. Guido and Katharine each returned to Australia full of praise for the regime, hiding their ambivalence, perhaps even from themselves. Katharine's resolve to continue to embrace communism, which she had devoted her life to, was made all the more urgent by the tragic discovery on her homecoming of her husband's suicide during her absence. If she had faltered in her beliefs, her efforts would have been in vain.

In July, Aileen took time out from her activities in London and set off on a walking trip through the Lake District with Helen. The two young women climbed the steep mountain paths with heavy packs on their backs, collapsing to lie in grassy meadows in the summer sun. It was rare for the sisters to spend extended time in each other's company now that the difference in their ages seemed so much more marked; their trip recalls the days when they roamed the bush around Emerald together or explored the beaches and rock pools at Caloundra. But the differences between them resurfaced as they wound their way back by train, stopping off at Stratford to take in a Royal Shakespeare Company production. Aileen's basic garment was still her jodhpurs and she wore them, Helen reported back to her mother, even to the theatre, which Helen felt might have been just permissible in the standing room area where their tickets were, but not in the 'posher bar' to which they had access and where the audience was in evening dress.

Politics was never far from Aileen's mind and she left Stratford for a farmhouse camp in Derbyshire where a youth peace conference was taking place, while Helen travelled to Grafton Regis where their old Caloundra friend (and Aileen's first serious crush) Violet Beasley was staying with her conservative church-minister father. Aileen was to join them on her way back to London and Nettie hoped that her tomboy daughter would borrow one of Helen's frocks to wear to church. When the sisters arrived home at the end of July, Nettie, always concerned about Aileen's weight, noted with approval that she was 'brown and lither' and had lost a stone.

The sisters spent more time together at the end of August when Aileen joined the rest of her family at a friend's house in Sussex where they had spent the month. She and Helen went off exploring the area on bicycles every afternoon, Nettie noting that Aileen wanted 'to cover ground in every direction at once' while Helen pointed 'sternly at the map'. Beyond the marked difference in development between the university graduate and the schoolgirl, the difference in their personalities remained constant – one was impetuous and scattered, the other practical and steady. In later years, Aileen would comment that people always thought Helen was the elder sister because she was so much more sensible.

Early in their London stay the Palmers had made the acquaintance of Dr Helene Scheu-Riesz, an Austrian playwright and writer of children's novels, a campaigner for women's rights and a socialist activist. A columnist for *Die Neue Freie Presse* in Vienna and a publisher in Austria and America, Scheu-Riesz was once described by an American poet who encountered her on a lecture tour as 'a pocket-sized dynamo. The air snaps and crackles about her constantly: whatever topic she speaks upon becomes an exciting issue'. Nettie and Vance were concerned about Aileen's future career and were delighted when the vital Frau Scheu-Riesz was 'full of suggestions' for her. Aileen could perhaps become a literary agent in England like the many female agents in America, but first, it was decided, she should get secretarial training. And if she did, she could come to Vienna as Frau Scheu-Riesz's secretary in November, develop her language skills further and be introduced to her host's extensive circle of prominent colleagues. Already an accomplished typist, Aileen enrolled in a course in shorthand and started working on some of the Viennese author's work. Over the next few months she translated a poem Scheu-Riesz had written on the American feminist Jane Addams, made a synopsis of a German serial for a film producer, and translated one of her novels.

As the year wore on, Aileen also immersed herself more and more in politics, attending mass meetings, selling copies of the communist newspaper *Daily Worker* on street corners and beating a path between the flat in Calthorpe Street and Marx House. Nettie noted that she was 'restless like a cat, who presages a move' and that she was 'longing to see the last of us'. The day after the general elections on 14 November (won by Conservative Stanley Baldwin but with a reduced majority) Aileen boarded the train for Vienna where she would stay in a room at the top of Frau Scheu-Riesz's house, situated almost at the edge of the Wienerwald and a half-hour tram ride from the centre of the city.

In a radio broadcast on the BBC at the end of 1944 Aileen recalled her impressions of Vienna in 1935, describing it as *a charming city, combining the compact intimacy of a little country town with the alertness of a cosmopolitan centre. Vienna was once the hub of an empire; its people are a mixture of nationalities; it's a sort of crossroads, and every language in Europe is spoken there. Yet everyone seems to know everyone else in the cafés along the Ringstrasse. Those roomy, leisurely cafés, where you go to read the daily paper and meet your friends, make social intercourse very easy and pleasant.* But she went on to say that *there was a cloud over Vienna* in 1935, that its *gaiety* was *subdued.* The people already had a foretaste of what life would be like under a totalitarian regime with a servile press and a secret police force that threw people into prison without trial. *The dominant element in the atmosphere of Vienna*, she said, *was apprehension, and acute awareness of the country's peril, hemmed in as it was between two avaricious powers.*

Aileen settled in to life in Vienna, translating for Frau Scheu-Riesz and teaching English to private students. She found the Austrians friendlier than the English, but, given her somewhat spartan upbringing and her political ideals, the grandiosity of the buildings and the Viennese love of opulence, from fine fabrics to rich food, were not entirely to her taste. No letters to her parents survive, but in one to her grandmother she describes what she calls the 'ceremonious' quality of the Christmas celebrations with the extravagant decorations and present-giving. She also laughs gently at the Viennese habit of going out, even when it was not excessively cold, wearing 'heavy furs on their winter-mantels as if they were preparing to go out into blizzards all the time'. She does not describe the grand palaces on the Ringstrasse to her grandmother but writes of 'the magnificent workers' flats that were built by the Socialist municipalities...built out of a housing tax and rented very low'.

A scene in the unpublished novel Aileen wrote after her return to London from Spain in 1938 also offers insights into life in Vienna in 1935 and into the Scheu-Riesz household in particular. And it is not all complimentary. She writes of *the Viennese habit of flattery just to give pleasure, the elaborate courtesy, the excessive compliments that seemed overdone to foreigners.* The character of Irma Stein, the *Frau Doktor* who holds court in her house on the Wimpelgasse, is clearly modelled on Aileen's host. Irma is described as an *actor* and *stage-manager* of the *performance* she puts on for the many distinguished visitors to her house – *the centre of the whole thing, a small vivacious widow with sudden enthusiasms and an unshakeable belief in her own capacity for managing other people.*

The central character in the scene is Kay, a young Australian woman who is staying at the house to study music and learn German. Totally non-political, she is causing a stir by encouraging a suitor with Nazi affiliations. Also staying in the house is another young woman, Joan (the name Aileen used for her fictional alter ego in most of her adult writings). Before she arrived in Vienna, Irma Stein had told Kay that Joan was an intellectual and very serious – not Kay's type at all: *And one glance at Joan, with her short hair combed straight back, her drab-looking coat and skirt and clumsy shoes, convinced Kay she was right.* To Kay, Joan seemed to exist in a world apart from *the excited clamour of the Wimpelgasse*, content to *slog away* at the work she was doing for Irma Stein, *though it was obvious she didn't take Irma seriously for a moment. Their scepticism about Irma's omnipotence was the only point of contact Kay had with Joan.* When Irma makes it clear that Kay's young man is not welcome at her house because of his political connections, Kay turns to Joan for sympathy and is rebuffed. She immediately puts it down to Joan's lack of interest in men: *She had never known any other girl so completely devoid of interest in the opposite sex.*

Gradually, Joan makes Kay aware of the political situation in Austria, one day pointing out of the window to a policeman who is standing on the street opposite the house: *'There he is again, the same evil-looking brute. It probably hasn't struck you yet, of course – or you just think it's funny – all these policemen here, standing about with their guns. But that's Austria now. They're scared, these people, scared: they try to forget it, with their little intrigues and claims to omnipotence. They sing and chatter away like birds in a cage.*

The 'omnipotent' Helene Scheu-Riesz was of Jewish heritage but, like many Jews, had converted to Protestantism because of the anti-Semitism that was rife in Vienna. She was to become 'scared' enough to leave Austria for America in 1937, thus avoiding the *Anchluss* of March 1938, the so-called union between Germany and Austria when Hitler's forces took control of the country and Jewish families had their property confiscated and their lives destroyed. In the United States, Scheu-Riesz continued to cut a colourful figure, taking writing workshops in the early 1940s on Ocracoke Island in North Carolina, where she was remembered for her thick German accent and Austrian dress – laced bodice, blouse, gathered skirt and headscarf – as well as for her teaching. She returned to Vienna in 1954 where she died in 1970.

In early February 1936 Aileen wrote to her parents that she would like to leave Frau Scheu-Riesz's house to get a room on her own, asking if they could provide a pound a week for her keep. Was she finding life under her hostess's roof too restrictive? Did she have a lover, perhaps? She had made friends with several women her own age while she was in Vienna, one of whom, Frieda Leib, visited when she returned to London; another was a young Indian woman she plied with books by Tolstoy to 'feed her with European literature'. Always reticent, understandably, about any romantic attachments, she did write to Helen from London in later years asking her sister if she had found her Vienna diary among documents she had sent and, if so, to hide it from their parents as it contained private material.

Nettie was not impressed with Aileen's request to move from Frau Scheu-Riesz's house into her own room. 'Horribly unsatisfying and disappointing' was her comment to her diary – perhaps partly because of the money, but mostly, I suspect, because she was anxious for her daughter to come back to London. Helen had sailed for Australia on the *Strathever* in January to start university and Nettie was feeling the loss of both of her daughters, in fact she confided to her diary that she was 'quite at sea'. The English winter was bleak and miserable and she and Vance suffered colds and fevers. She seems depressed and flat.

Life had not been easy for Vance and Nettie on this trip to London. Just weeks after they arrived, Nettie commented to her diary: 'V rather shivery under the hail of returned mss [manuscripts]. If my shower is smaller, it's because I've sent almost nothing out yet'. The acclaim Vance had enjoyed on previous trips had faded: his mentor A. R. Orage had died, the literary scene had changed and the experimentation of modernist novelists like Virginia Woolf had made Vance's adherence to the radical-democratic tradition seem outdated. Aileen was to write many years later in one of her semi-fictional pieces that it had not occurred to her at the time that her father *had been depressed, coming back to London in 1935, to find the reputation and status he had once had, gone with the wind.* Nettie did make some inroads into radio broadcasting at the BBC and Vance had serials published in English newspapers. They both continued to send articles home to Australia, but money was always tight and the cheques slow in coming through.

Nettie had made two overnight trips to Henry Handel Richardson's home in Dorset – in July and December – and subsequently wrote favourably of the author in her published journal, *Fourteen Years*: 'Her alert talk is what stays in the mind, its vigorous questions, its firm outlines'. A few months after the second visit she published an article on Richardson in *The Sydney Mail.* In letters to Mary Kernot, Richardson was less generous in her account of her first actual meeting with Nettie, no more generous in fact than she had been when Nettie was promoting her work in Australia in the 1920s. After saying that Nettie was 'a very pleasant person', she proceeded to denigrate her as talkative and rambling. 'How wrapped up she is in Vance & the girls, too!' she added. Nettie must have confided her worries about their work situation and Richardson comments, rather smugly: 'The poor things are having a hard time to make ends meet...In many ways I feel *very* sorry for her; & wish I cd [could] do something. But sitting religiously aloof as I do, I've no power at all'. Nettie's second visit in December only served to cement H. H. R.'s unfavourable view of her. Telling Mary she was going to London the next month, she writes: 'I shall make a point of seeing Vance and contrasting the two of them: he as silent as I am, & she one long dreary flow'.

Aileen remained at Frau Scheu-Riesz's house until her departure from Vienna a few weeks after her letter to her parents, in time to celebrate her twenty-first birthday with them. Allowed to choose where they would go, she opted for *The Fall of St Petersburg* at Shoreditch Town Hall, with her friend Frieda Leib in tow. She brought back some more translation work of Helene Scheu-Riesz's to London and was hard at work on a manuscript of her own (which does not survive), but no mention was made of any more substantial career moves. Nettie wrote to William Ifould of the Mitchell Library in Sydney to see if there might be any prospects there for her daughter, but it seems Aileen had other things on her mind, Nettie noting acerbically that 'A[ileen] would like to live in Bloomsbury a long time'.

After so many months in a large city, Vance and Nettie were hankering for somewhere quiet and warm where they could work cheaply for a few months, and Spain fitted all their requirements. Australian writer Brian Penton dropped in to the flat, looking 'brown and springy' and urged them to go to Malaga where he had just completed his second novel, but the Palmers decided to try to find a quiet place on the northeast coast not too far from Barcelona. They also had a project to fund their journey; Vance's luck had changed when he was offered a job by Jonathan Cape in late April – abridging Joseph Furphy's sprawling 1903 novel *Such is Life*.

Borrowing Henry Handel Richardson's copy of the Furphy novel, the three Palmers set off for Spain on 11 May 1936, Nettie planning a series of articles on Spain for *The Argus*, Vance planning to work on the abridgement and continue a novel (then titled 'Homage to Sanderson'), and Aileen planning to contact the Communist Party of Catalonia and offer her services. The Popular Front socialist government had been elected to power the previous February and, although the situation was fragile, hope was in the air.

After the Channel crossing and a trip to Notre Dame in Paris, they headed for the station and the Spanish train, Nettie noting, 'Piled in, ready for anything'. They were going to need to be.

PART II

A Decade of War

9

Barcelona – No Pasarán!

In the beginning was Barcelona before the war burst, when the furtive rich sat in the shady cafes, looking out. Then I was also a tourist, an outsider, sitting in cafes and watching the river that never stopped flowing and passed me by: the Ramblas, whirling thoroughfare grown from an ancient river, like all the sunken roads that wind from the Catalan hills to the sea.

When you stand on the beach of the village of Montgat facing south and let your eyes follow the curve of the bay around to the distant point where land meets sea you can just make out the Barcelona skyline through the sun's glare and the city's pollution haze. Turning away from the beach you face (across the railway line and the busy main road) the irregular row of houses leaning against the hill that make up the *Calle Monsolis* (or *Carrer del Marquesa de Monsolis* to give it its Catalan name). Towering incongruously behind and to the left of these houses is the mansion of the Marquesa de Monsolis that gives the little street its name. At the end of the *calle* on the right is the *Fonda Marina*, now an upmarket restaurant, in 1936 a local cafe that sold meals and daily provisions and was the hub of the village. Known as Roca's after its owner, it was to this establishment that Aileen was directed by the tourist office in the Ramblas, just down from the Hotel del Centro where she and her parents stayed when they first reached Barcelona. Dispatched to do the negotiations because she spoke some Spanish, she was to find the principal language spoken in this part of Spain – Catalan – quite a challenge.

On 14 May 1936 the Palmers moved into the conjoined house at No. 11 *Calle Monsolis*, for which Vance had had to pay *a dragon of a senora* a year's rent in advance. Unlike the stuffy, enclosed terraces of London, this simple, airy house had mosaic tiled floors and straw mats. Behind it, a cool white courtyard was dug into a hill that was kept at bay by a high concrete wall overhung with white trumpet dahlias. In front of the houses between the narrow *calle* and the beach road lay long, narrow gardens used by the locals for growing vegetables. The beach road is a multi-lane highway today but it was busy even then with motor-lorries piled high with baskets of food, horse-drawn carts, and cars with noisy engines augmented by the continual tooting of horns. At least in 1936 the railway line was up on the cliff, not between the road and the beachfront as it is now.

For the first week the newcomers experienced slate-grey skies and spring storms, and then the sunny days they were waiting for broke through. Slipping across for an early morning dip, Vance and Nettie found the picnic parties from Barcelona, fourteen kilometres away, already setting up their striped tents on the beach. Their spirits lifted; they forgot the English winter as the sun seeped into their bones and they settled down to work.

Although it was Vance who had been commissioned to abridge Joseph Furphy's *Such is Life*, it seems that all three Palmers were involved, and principally Nettie. She worked on the project during the day, finding it hard to 'boil it down enough'. After a few days, she had cut 36,000 words but had to get it down by 50,000. Vance spent the days working on the novel that would eventually become *Legend for Sanderson*, looking over Nettie's efforts on the Furphy novel at night. Aileen then started furiously typing up the revised manuscript, for which she was being given a cut of Vance's fee. By 25 May, Nettie records: 'All of us considering & arguing about SIL. Afraid to throw good things out, yet guarding against longueurs. Problems in every chapter. Aileen's suggestions very acute & clear'.

Aileen pored over the Catalan newspapers every day, able to make out the subject matter if not to make an exact translation. She spent days in Barcelona in between typing, making contacts among the politically active young people and looking for work, sometimes bringing home new friends like the Finnish-born Lisa Gedeke, who like Aileen, spoke several languages. By the time she finished typing up the revised manuscript of *Such is Life* (which her mother said was 'excellent work, thoughtfully done all through. No ordinary typist could have attempted to make sense of it') she had started working for the *Olimpiada Popular* organised by the Popular Front government, which planned to boycott the Berlin Olympics.

This counterblast to Hitler's Olympics was to be held from 19 to 26 July in Barcelona. Athletes from twenty-two countries registered, most sponsored by trade unions, communist and socialist parties, and workers' clubs, and included German and Italian contingents made up of exiles. Spending her days at the Olympiad's office Aileen did anything that was required, mostly typing and translating material. Towards the end of June she sent off an article entitled 'Counter Olympiad' to the *New Statesman* but it was not published, perhaps because of the ensuing events that caused the Olympiad to be cancelled.

But it was grown too swift, too turbulent, that river of young men and women that never stopped flowing between the double row of trees, colour-splashed by the flower-stalls and the scarlet placards on the newspaper-kiosks. The furtive men who sat in the shady cafes feared the rejuvenation of the river. In the meantime, they sat drinking coffee and anis – fat, fish faces, looking out through glass…

Then one day I came to Barcelona and there was no anis to drink. The shady retreats were all shut up. You didn't realise at first what it was that had changed the whole aspect of the city. Then you noticed the red placards everywhere: Vaga dels Ramis Gastronomics! Visca la Vaga!

Strike! And strike at the spot that produced the most immediate reaction on the city's parasites…a city of burning sunlight, and nothing to drink…

By June the atmosphere in the city had become volatile as the strikes intensified and everyone was on edge. Late one night Aileen and Nettie went to hear Dolores Ibárruri (*La Pasionaria*), the communist activist who coined what was to become the catchcry of the Republicans: *'No Pasarán!'* ('They shall not pass!') They ended up walking the fourteen kilometres home after the trains had stopped running. Aileen also met with her new comrades Arthur, Herman and Frieda daily in a little *fonda* off the Ramblas to listen to the arguments, often between Arthur and a Catalan student, who used to discourse on the doctrines of the Catalan Trotskyist party, the P.O.U.M.

In July came news of the retaliatory assassination in Madrid of Calvo Sotelo, a prominent right-wing opponent of the elected Popular Front government.

Then the storm. First it was just a cloud that thickened on the far horizon of Madrid. Monday: 'Calvo Sotelo is dead', Frieda announced, as she joined the usual group at the fonda in the early afternoon.

'Viva!' the student said. 'There's a fascist out of the way!'

Frieda turned on him.

'No, you fool, don't you see what this means? It's what the fascists have been driving for all along. Their whole policy of provocation has been directed to this end. Now they have a slogan, a rallying-cry: "The Reds have killed Sotelo!"'

On Saturday 18 July Aileen set off for Barcelona, intending to stay at her friends' flat while she acted as interpreter for Olympic delegates at the alternative Games. These were scheduled to begin the next day at Montjuic Stadium, high on the hill that dominates the city (later to be the site of the 1992 Barcelona Olympics). She promised to get tickets for her parents for the opening ceremony and the following week's events, telling Vance she would try to get him in as a journalist, not as a parent, so that he could meet other journalists in the press box. Nettie had ironed and packed some clothes for her daughter for the week in town; she had also taken over translating one of Helene Scheu-Riesz's novels as the Austrian writer was demanding its completion and Aileen's mind was entirely elsewhere.

Aileen was awakened in the early hours of Sunday morning by friends, who had been on the streets all night, bursting into Frieda and Herman's flat where she was staying and announcing that the fighting had begun and that they had seen the first dead. She had visited the station of Radio Barcelona the evening before where Herman was to speak about the People's Olympiad and was aware that government communiqués were pouring in about fighting here and there. She had tried to pick up the thread of the crescendo of voices around her in her hazy Catalan, but had assumed they were safe in Barcelona. Others were more alert, but they were still unprepared for the infiltration of strategic buildings by the rebel soldiers during the night who shouted 'Viva la Republica' to cause confusion.

No one realised they were enemies at first and no one resisted. But, when the situation was grasped, the Government of Catalunya passed out what arms it had to the workers who lined the streets, and, even without arms, the workers rose, tore up paving-stones, built barricades, and fought...

Below us in the city the guns boomed on, but by afternoon Barcelona's fate was decided. We were as happy as if the fate of all Spain had been decided that day. Fighting continued elsewhere, but it was remote, unreal.

In the afternoon we walked down into the city as far as the Plaza de la Universidad. People were strolling about the streets as though it were just any Sunday afternoon – sitting in cafes exchanging the latest news, or just ordinary gossip.

Now and then a lorryload of Civil Guards would pass, and the people would greet them with the clenched fist salute, cheers and applause...

Over the next few nights, the city where traffic usually roared through the night was still and quiet and people outside after dark were warned to return home by the newly formed Citizen Guard patrolling the streets in working clothes and with old-fashioned rifles.

But with daylight the voice of the city burst forth again in greater volume than ever before. There was a continuous circulation of traffic on the Ramblas: commandeered cars and lorries, roughly daubed with the letters that stood for the parties and trade unions who had banded together in defence of the city – CNT, PSUC, Estat Catala, POUM – armed guards sprawled along the running-boards, or seated on the bonnets – horns tooting continuously the one-two-three signal of the CNT, radios pouring over the streets their floods of oratory ('La Republica La Republica'), and the songs that had become the continuous refrain of those days, 'Himno de Riego' and 'Els Segadors', the medieval dirge that an embittered and oppressed people, the Catalans, have taken for their national anthem – the loveliest and most poignant anthem I have ever heard.

Nettie's first knowledge of the insurrection in Barcelona on the sweltering morning of Sunday 19 July came when she overheard the village milkman telling her neighbour that there was '*revolucion*' in the city. Running down to the beach where her husband was bathing, she could hear the cannons and the rattle of machine guns. Vance had heard them too but supposed the firing was a salutation to the Olympiad. When told what was happening, his immediate concern, and Nettie's, was for the safety of Aileen.

With the trains not running and the telephone cut off, they set out for Barcelona on foot but were stopped at the first barricade. Though finding the situation hard to grasp, over the next couple of anxious days they heard that the worst of the fighting was over but that Barcelona was full of suspected fascists. They heard that General Goded (who was captured in the uprising) had led the revolt and that it had been organised to coincide with others in the garrison towns all over Spanish Morocco and Spain – Ceuta, Seville, Saragossa and Madrid. Their own house was searched by local militia for firearms one morning, Nettie recording that the men ransacked cupboards downstairs and upstairs, 'earnestly peering into my harmless diaries and notes on Spanish literature'. On the Tuesday morning she and Vance managed to get a ride into Barcelona in a lorry packed with armed unionists heading for Saragossa.

They found a city in ferment, with many buildings and churches gutted by fire, shops and banks closed, the streets still lined by barricades made of road blocks and sandbags. Where to start looking for their daughter? They walked up the steep hill to the Montjuic stadium where the People's Olympiad should have been in full swing. Missing Aileen at the office there, the pair headed back down to the Hotel Olimpic in the Plaça d'Espanya where the French athletes were being farewelled. Missing her there too and failing to find her at the Hotel Coulon off the Ramblas, Vance and Nettie reserved a room at the Hotel del Centro where they had stayed on their arrival from England just a couple of months earlier. As they were recovering their energy and working out their next move over lunch at the hotel, Aileen suddenly appeared – 'gay and grubby in the blue cotton frock and white shoes she set out in last Saturday'. (So much for Nettie's ironing and packing.) Excited and exuberant, Aileen was busy helping interpret for athletes marooned in the city and sending telegrams home to say they were safe. She had not forgotten her parents, but the telegram she had sent them arrived after they returned to Montgat.

Aileen believed the actual attack on the Spanish people by the rebels had given them a mandate to retaliate and establish their legitimacy. She was not alone in feeling that. Many idealistic young people were exhilarated by the routing of the rebel generals and eager to take part in the retaliation. George Orwell, for one, had come to Barcelona with the idea of writing newspaper articles but joined the militia almost immediately: 'When one came straight from England the aspect of Barcelona was something startling and overwhelming. It was the first time that I had ever been in a town where the working class was in the saddle'. Aileen's exuberance, though not diminished, was put into perspective by her German friend Herman who warned her that those behind the revolt were more than *just a pack of ambitious generals. He was right, of course – though in that first week when the rebel militarists were stamped out from power in Catalunya, there were not many in Barcelona who saw the war in perspective. We knew there were 'fascist nests' in different parts of Spain; that the rebels held Seville, Burgos and Saragossa; but there was something more – some grounds for real alarm behind those newspaper-headlines, shouting with what seemed unnecessary emphasis: NO PASARÁN!*

Vance and Nettie walked back to Montgat the next day after farewelling Aileen who was joining the procession of Olympians marching to the funerals of anti-fascist fighters. Vance set about writing articles on the Spanish situation for the overseas press. He thought Aileen would probably want to stay on in Barcelona and couldn't blame her as he wished to stay himself. A few days later, however, he returned to the village from Barcelona at about four o'clock after trying unsuccessfully to cash international traveller's cheques. He was warned by the British Consul that the anarchists, who were more influential in Barcelona than anywhere else in Spain, were taking over the city and that the Palmers should leave on the warship that was taking British citizens back the next day. Just as unreliable mail delivery, affecting their livelihood, had forced Vance and Nettie to leave Brittany for London at the onset of war in 1914, so the fear of losing connections to the outside world led them to leave Barcelona in 1936. Nettie had lain in the sea on that very hot day gazing up at the row of houses with the mansion of the Marquesa behind them (now offered to the authorities as a hospital), reflecting on the unexpected situation the family found themselves in. So when Vance told her they must prepare to leave at once she did not remonstrate with him. 'At once!' she wrote in her diary, ruefully repeating Vance's ultimatum: 'So that was why Monsolis and the whole of Mongat had seemed to lie in my hands all day like a scroll, perhaps rolling up very fast'.

Aileen, on the other hand, was furious when she returned home and was told she would have to accompany her parents to London. She went at once to see the head of the local militia, who typed out a document certifying that the Palmers would remain safe if they stayed in Spain. But to no avail. She reluctantly gave in and the next morning, on 29 July, she left by taxi with her mother and father for the HMS *London*. She went ashore for the day to say goodbye to her friends, returning to the ship that evening (much to Nettie's relief) and telling her parents that the city seemed almost 'normal' and that the shops were open. She managed to give Nettie a further scare when she disappeared for an hour to have a drink with a friendly British officer in his cabin where he showed her a red tie with a hammer-and-sickle he had picked up in Barcelona. On her return, Aileen found that her mother was more distraught than she had been when Aileen went missing for days. *Maybe she thought I might have jumped off the ship*, she wrote later with grim satisfaction.

An article written by Vance came out in the London communist paper *Daily Worker* on 1 August while the Palmers were en route to England. In it, he unequivocally supported the actions of those who had risen up against the rebels in Barcelona: 'The Left Front was a living reality, its courage and decision had swept into its ranks middle-class elements that might have wavered or even gone over to the enemy. An unarmed and unprepared people attacked by men sworn to defend them above everything else; organised, paid, equipped with the latest weapons, given the peculiar freedom of Army power. Even the ordinary bourgeoisie felt this was unforgivable treachery'.

Aileen's resolve to get out from under the shadow of her parents meant, as we know, that she was back in Barcelona just over a month later as part of the first British Medical Unit to travel to Spain. After their heady farewell at Victoria Station they had experienced an equally enthusiastic welcome during their stopover in Paris. Back in her familiar haunts, she nevertheless found Barcelona to be an altered city: *its colours dimmed, a ragged look about the streets. People walked about with a strained look on their faces, like those who have gone without sleep for many nights under the stress of a strong emotion, and who are now making the descent to ordinary life, to find their reserves of energy have left them. That 'morning after' feeling we all know, after a night of intense excitement when we have not slept and, in other parts of Spain, the rebels were advancing, the government forces, deprived of arms, giving ground.*

Vance had booked his passage back to Australia from Montgat before the July crisis. Planning to leave in October, he had intended to return home earlier than Nettie and Aileen, the plan being that they would stay on in the village (the rent was paid for a year, after all), attend the next writers' congress in Madrid in February 1936 and then probably return to Australia. The rebels' attempted coup had completely disrupted those plans and Nettie, eager now to return to Helen and her elderly mother, managed to secure a berth on the *Moldavia* on 4 September while Vance stayed in London, winding up his business with his literary contacts there and waiting for his booked passage on the *Orama*.

Aileen wrote an optimistic letter to her father from the Lloret Hotel on the Ramblas in early September, saying that she had met up with the people she knew before and that Barcelona was *not at all sinister when you're inside it again* although it was *bloody hot.* Her unit was waiting for its lorry convoy of five vehicles to arrive and then they would be moving to either the Saragossa or the Madrid front. To her sister in Melbourne *(Dear Louse)*, she wrote an ebullient letter a few days later saying she was about to leave *for some point on the Saragossa front.* Enclosing one of the red rags sold plentifully on the Barcelona streets, she finished: *If by any chance I get bumped off I'd prefer these to any other circs. to get bumped off in.*

Vance of course relayed Aileen's 'cheerful' news to Nettie on board ship, reporting that their daughter had met up with her friends and quoting her belief that the city didn't seem 'sinister'. He didn't pass on the news that she was expecting to leave for one of the war fronts, but later told Nettie he had popped into the Spanish Medical Association office and was told that Aileen would be acting as a liaison officer in Barcelona indefinitely. Towards the end of the month he confessed to Nettie that he was 'itching' to get back to Barcelona to see their daughter as he had always felt guilty about their hurried departure from Spain, as though they were running away from something. But his plans came to nothing when he had a letter from Aileen around that time written from 'a hospital inland'.

Vance left for Australia in October without meeting up with his daughter, little realising how many years it would be before he saw her again.

When Aileen returned to Barcelona on leave after three months at the English Hospital at Grañén on the Aragon plains she found it once again an altered city.

Barcelona had got used to the war by then, and life had settled down to a normal, easy-going pace. Freshly painted, the city dazzled your eyes, when you returned to it from the infinite grey-brown desert of the Aragon plains.

In Barcelona there were shops, cafes, cinemas – unheard of things – but not so much of the martial music as before.

During her three days' leave in Barcelona in December 1936, Aileen was photographed with a small group of Australians, standing in the central Plaça de Catalunya, from where the Ramblas leads down to the port. Behind the group to their right an ornate fountain replete with rollicking cherubim plays in front of the sign to the underground entrance of 'Metro Norte'. People loll in the midday sun, reading or chatting around the base of the gushing fountain; two squat, elderly women in headscarves sit with their arms folded on their ample laps beside the steps leading out of the plaza, dwarfed by the statue of a woman in flowing robes rising from the bushes behind them; to the right of the group a Catalan man in a long coat and peaked cap stops mid-stride on his journey across the square to stare at the camera: it seems to be a frozen moment of a normal day in the life of a busy city. Except that filling the space at the back of the photograph is the Hotel Colon, which has been taken over as the headquarters of the combined Socialist and Communist Party. Draped across its elegant facade is a banner reading PARTIT SOCIALISTA UNIFICAT DE CATALUNA (PSUC) and it also displays portraits of Lenin and Stalin and stylised posters of men with upraised clenched fists. Aileen commented on the photograph she sent her parents: *Notice how even the statues return the 'Popular Front' salute.* And it is true that the white figure of a youth rising from the greenery appears to perfectly mirror the raised arm of the comrade on the U.G.T. poster on the Colon.

The two men in the group photograph are John Fisher (the journalist who had been one of the Australian delegates with Nettie at the Paris Congress in 1935) and volunteer Jack 'Blue' Barry, who is just about to leave for the front where he will be killed in a few weeks' time. Four Australian nurses with them pose awkwardly for the camera. Recently arrived in Barcelona, they had stopped wearing hats after they were taken for part of the detested bourgeoisie, but they still sport neat court shoes and gloves. Diminutive Mary Lowson, at forty-one, is the eldest of the nurses. She had been the first to respond to the call for volunteers put out by the Australians for Spanish Relief Committee, headed by Nettie Palmer. A committed communist and the most political of the four nurses, Mary was joined by a fellow nurse from Lidcombe State Hospital in Sydney, May MacFarlane. Una Wilson, who was a theatre sister originally from New Zealand, stands out among the group with her blonde hair and stylish clothes. The fourth nurse, Agnes Hodgson, had joined the group at the last minute when another nurse withdrew. She had experience nursing overseas but, unlike the rest of the group, had no political affiliations. Agnes recorded her impressions of Barcelona on her arrival at the beginning of December in her diary: 'Unshaven men carrying guns and wearing dirty white and black rope-soled sandals. Black of eye, dark-skinned and bearded. Everything scrutinized – we realized we were in a country at war...Atmosphere of suspicion everywhere, among the foreigners, at least'.

The seventh member of the group portrait is, of course, Aileen Palmer. Looking altogether less conventional than the neatly attired nurses, she stands with her feet in their flat lace-up shoes firmly planted on the paving stones of the Barcelona square, hands in the pockets of her leather trench coat, short-cropped hair. She directs a slightly amused gaze at the camera. This is a young woman who, unlike her companions, is quite at home in her surroundings. Unlike her companions, she has already experienced three months on the Aragon front.

For a long while I didn't see Barcelona again. There were International Brigades being formed in Albacete, and our medical group was moved up to serve the Madrid front, where there was more to do.

But life always brings you back to Barcelona. It is like a fatal motif in your life that you never escape. It is washing about us now with its waves of staccato sound – the familiar tunes of the street-organ, the scream of the knife-grinder's machine (only now that reminds us of air-raid sirens), the crackle of staccato voices that is the rising river of voices in the street.

And on Sunday they'll bury Hans Beimler in Barcelona. They will march down the Ramblas carrying white flowers, and they'll play (I wonder if they'll play it when I'm dead) that anguished and most haunting of requiems, 'Els Segadors'.

10

Digging Shit

The village of Grañén straggles over a rocky plateau on the Aragon plains, 220 kilometres inland from Barcelona. At the highest point stands the village church, its decaying belltower fringed with huge storks' nests, their long-necked inhabitants peering over ragged bundles of sticks at the buildings below. Pigeons scatter as the church bells toll the hour then return to their niches in the crumbling walls. There is a sense of desolation about the place. When Aileen arrived there in early September 1936, she described the village even then as being *rather lousy and stick in the mud*, but at least found something in Grañén that reminded her of home: *I went for a long walk all morning over these plains that are very Australian in colour and atmosphere – half-tones of grey and brown, with craggy mountains jutting out; houses that might be rocks showing a cluster of villages here and there – houses that might be rocks, and rocks that might be houses. Beyond the ranges to the north, glimpses of the Pyrenees newly capped with snow.*

It was Peter Spencer aka Viscount Churchill, cousin of Winston and a Spanish Medical Aid Committee member, who chose Grañén as the site for the first English Hospital. Spencer found the village on a Michelin map as he and Kenneth Sinclair-Loutit, the administrator of the new medical unit, drove from Barcelona towards the Aragon front in search of a suitable location for the hospital. Grañén was about eighteen kilometres behind the fighting front that ran between the towns of Huesca and Saragossa, both held by the insurgents. It was on the railhead to Lérida and Barcelona and situated at a road junction. These were all good strategic reasons for Spencer's choice, but they were not good political ones. Ignorant of Spanish politics he had unwittingly chosen a village that was an anarchist stronghold. Its flamboyant, black-moustached, pistol-toting mayor, known as 'Pancho Villa' after the famous Mexican revolutionary, had abolished money, and goods and services were bartered through the village committee. He had not been consulted about the hospital and regarded it as representing interference from the central government.

Aileen was well aware of the different allegiances of the parties that gathered under the banner of the Popular Front government, but many of the newcomers from England were deeply confused by what Sinclair-Loutit described as 'the acronymic labyrinth of Spanish politics'. While the various parties of the Left were united against the rebel army generals, who represented the right-wing Falange and the religious Carlists, there was nevertheless intense acrimony between them. In Catalonia and Aragon, historically the anarcho-syndicalist centres of Spain, the internal politics were at their most fractured. Those in the anarchist movement were fighting for internal social revolution and opposed the centralisation of the government. The most powerful was the CNT trade union (whose one-two-three signal Aileen had noted being tooted on horns continuously in the days after the July coup), while the FAI political party and the POUM (the dissident semi-Trotskyist party) also opposed centralisation. The UGT, the socialist-communist trade union, was rapidly growing as was the PSUC (the combined communist and socialist party). These latter organisations saw the wider implications of the conflict as a fight against fascism and the PSUC was the party that the British Medical Aid Unit was most closely aligned with.

Like most of the foreign volunteers who headed to Spain to fight for the Republican government, Aileen supported the centralisation movement and believed that the conflict was not simply a *civil* war but one that presaged a world war if Franco's Nationalist forces were not stopped. All her life she regarded the 'Spanish *Civil* War' to be a misnomer. On the Aragon front in September 1936, it was the local militias of the various anarchist parties and trade unions that were most active, although poorly armed and disorganised. English communist poet John Cornford described what he found when he joined the POUM militia on the Huesca front: 'There are some workers with experience of street-fighting, some who have been trained in political fighting organisations; but the number who have evaded military service is incredibly high – it is an army of anti-militarists. Of the different parties the P.S.U.C. are far the best organised...P.O.U.M. is disgracefully organised'. He wrote a moving poem about the experience of waiting on 'the last mile to Huesca'; Aileen would later use the line as the title of her novel about Spain.

In what must have been a bizarre encounter, Spencer, English member of the House of Lords, and Sinclair-Loutit, Cambridge-educated medical student, confronted the obstructive mayor and somehow, in inadequate Spanish, negotiated with the Grañén village committee for the use of an abandoned farmhouse in which to establish the English Hospital. The farmhouse's owner – a doctor of fascist sympathies – had fled the village after it was taken over by the anarchists. When the rest of the medical team arrived from Barcelona in the unit's lorries a few days later, hot and tired after joggling over the dusty, pitted roads, everyone set to work on the task of transforming the filthy, rat-infested building and courtyard deep in muck into something that resembled a hospital.

We long and painstakingly created our own order out of chaos, furnishing and mending a great rambling semi-collapsed barn of a place, and cleaning the yard by a species of Walrus and Carpenter work, known as 'digging shit', reported Aileen to her parents. Welsh theatre sister Thora Silverthorne recalled: 'We were a sort of pioneer unit. For the first week or so we scrubbed and cleaned. The great thing was that we were all young and enthusiastic people...We set up an operating theatre, which was my little province, because I'd done a lot of theatre work, and a couple of dark little wards'. As well as being young and enthusiastic, the volunteers were in a novel situation and Aileen entered into the spirit of things: *Last night a mob of us slept out on an unroofed veranda generally used for sunbathing and just about half an hour after we had dropped asleep one of these sudden Spanish storms was upon us, and we were dripping wet before we had picked up ourselves, our bedclothes and stretchers and rushed inside. Even inside there were various holes in the roof and places by open windows where pools of water had formed. However we are still at the stage when you can get lots of fun out of such incidents.*

Just a week or so after the unit's arrival, Tom Wintringham, a journalist from *Daily Worker* (and a close friend of Aileen's Uncle Esmonde at Oxford in 1920) reported back to London from Grañén with less enthusiasm: 'The position of the medical service on this front is tragic: wounded bleed slowly to death while being carried on springless lorries over hill roads for hours. There is not enough organisation to run a cafe'.

John Cornford, whom Aileen had heard speak in London the year before, was one soldier from the Aragon front who was to spend time at the medical unit's hospital, not wounded but suffering from exhaustion and food poisoning. He wrote of his experience in his poem 'A Letter from Aragon', which has the repeated line 'This is a quiet sector of a quiet front'. But even on this quiet front, the Cambridge activist learned much about the realities of war:

In the clean hospital bed my eyes were so heavy
Sleep easily blotted out one ugly picture,
A wounded militiaman moaning on a stretcher,
Now out of danger, but still crying for water,
Strong against death, but unprepared for such pain.

Cornford returned to England after his short hospital stay and formed the company that later became the nucleus of the British section of the International Brigades. Less than two months later, on 28 December 1936, one day after his twenty-first birthday, he was killed in action on the Cordova front in the rebel stronghold of southern Spain. Although Aileen hardly knew him, Cornford was an enduring inspiration, and she mourned his death for the rest of her life. She wrote several poems that reference his work and titled an article she wrote on Spain and Vietnam for the Sydney magazine *The Realist* in 1966 'Heart of the Heartless World' after one of his poems. Quoting the first few lines:

Heart of the heartless world,
        dear heart, the thought of you
is the pain in my side,
        the shadow that chills my view…

she describes it as *one of the most moving and memorable poems of our time.*

It is clear from Aileen's and Thora Silverthorne's letters home that the members of the unit did not expect to be in Spain for long. As the weeks wore on and turned into months, their initial enthusiasm turned to frustration. *Our work is, of course, very spasmodic,* Aileen explained to her parents. *For instance, two nights running, after days of idleness occupied, rather fruitlessly, with our own internal affairs, you have cases requiring laparotomies – operations on the guts – brought in after midnight, and the chief surgeon, theatre nurses, anaesthetist (who is also the administrator) and maybe one or two others such as myself who hang around to make tea and help clean up working till after three or four. Then another day when no wounds arrive, and people quarrel for lack of occupation, and because they dislike the shape of each other's ears.*

Time hung heavy and tempers became strained during the *terrible becalmed weeks* when there was little to do but play ping-pong and argue. And the stress was due to more than the perpetual seesawing between frustrating idleness and the horrors of ministering to the wounded and dying. A basic diet of beans cooked in olive oil was alien to English stomachs and many suffered diarrhoea and at first were able to eat little more than the bread. (Aileen was not among them, being proud of her cast-iron digestion. Perhaps Nettie's cooking had prepared her for anything.) A basic flysheet with the punning title *The Grañén Griper* was set up to ease the boredom, but it did little to alleviate the animosities that broke out among the disparate group. 'Pancho Villa', the mayor, continued to create havoc for the medical unit, trying at different times to cut off the staples of food and fuel, while the local peasants swarmed through the hospital and enjoyed, according to Aileen, *spreading atrocity stories about the English doctors.* Some members of the unit left or were recalled to England and new staff arrived, but the situation did not settle. The tension increased as it became apparent that the Aragon front was at a stalemate, at least partly through the lack of arms and disorganisation of the militias but also because the centre of the action had moved to Madrid about 250 kilometres away.

As well as personality clashes, class and political tensions surfaced among the members of the unit. Some of the working-class drivers and mechanics resented the Cambridge-trained doctors, while the non-communists resented the communists, feeling that they were running the unit. There was also a degree of competition between the young medical officers and particularly between Archie Cochrane and Kenneth Sinclair-Loutit. 'Idleness bred a fantastic web of petty jealousies and spiteful intrigues', Cochrane was to recall years later. But he, a non-communist, was certainly not immune from making criticisms himself, believing that there were a number of 'secret Party Members' who felt it was their duty to control the unit, possibly a barbed reference to Kenneth Sinclair-Loutit.

Aileen was secretary to Sinclair-Loutit, the administrator of the unit, who was the focus of much of the resentment on account of his youth, his class and his political affiliations. Long-faced and with a slightly supercilious air, the twenty-four year old Cambridge graduate had not yet finished his medical training at St Bartholomew's Hospital in London. Unlike the staunch communist and trade unionist Thora Silverthorne, with whom he soon began an open relationship and later married, Kenneth had only joined the Party just before leaving London with the unit. This made some of the committed communists suspicious of him for different reasons from the non-Party members. Yet Aileen remained loyal to Sinclair-Loutit throughout this difficult period and he and Thora became her closest friends in the unit. Years later, Thora was to remember Aileen as 'our secretary, our interpreter, our dogsbody. Everybody exploited her. She was absolutely wonderful, she really was. She held things together'. Kenneth remembered Aileen as 'a terrific quiet indefatigable worker, the key to the Secretariat. Total self-abnegation...She was a sincere and educated Marxist of the most unpreachy sort. She did not know how good she was...she kept my courage up when from sheer physical pressure I was ready to drop'.

The aura of intrigue about the unit that the non-communist Dr Archie Cochrane noted was indeed partly due to the regular secret meetings held by Party members. The reason for the secrecy goes back to the formation of the Spanish Medical Aid Committee, which was set up as a voluntary organisation at the beginning of the military rebellion in Spain. The *Socorro Rojo Internacional* (International Red Cross) based in Madrid had initially made a request to Isabel Brown of the Relief Committee to the Victims of Fascism, and in response the committee had been created, made up of members of the Socialist Medical Association and left-wing politicians. An uneasy relationship developed over the ensuing few weeks between the communists and the more moderate members of the committee. On 22 August, the day before the unit left for Spain, Viscount Churchill, who was to be SMAC's representative in Spain, and five of the original seven Party members (including Aileen) met as a secret 'fraction' with Isabel Brown. She urged the communists to conceal their Party membership both to avoid publicity for the unit and because of the inter-party conflict and the influence of the Anarchist movement in Spain. Tom Wintringham from the communist newspaper *Daily Worker* joined the unit in Paris on the way to Barcelona, and over the next few months new Communist Party members joined the unit and others left or were sent back to England.

A document authored by Kenneth Sinclair-Loutit and Aileen Palmer titled 'Survey of a year's work with the British Medical Unit in Spain' survives in the Russian State Archives of Social and Political History and it makes fascinating reading as it reveals the Party intrigues and backstabbing that occurred over that period. Relations between the factions at the unit's administrative bases in Barcelona and Grañén were tense and acrimonious and various leading members of the CPGB (Communist Party of Great Britain), including writers Sylvia Townsend Warner and Valentine Ackland, were dispatched to Spain to report back to headquarters. Individuals were sent back to England for various reasons including drunkenness, troublemaking and inefficiency. Some left of their own accord because they were 'hostile' to the unit's administration. Some were returned because of sexual misdemeanours, in a 'clean up' that one of the so-called hostile doctors, Dr Ruth Prothero, reported elsewhere 'smacked of Stalinism'.

The 'Survey' mentions only two people in regard to sexual misdemeanours and it is not surprising, given the Communist Party's somewhat misogynistic attitude towards women, that both were nurses. One newly arrived nurse was returned because her 'sexual promiscuity seemed to shock the Spaniards', but the other, Nurse Doris Bird, who had come to Spain with the original unit, was sent back for conducting 'a passionate Lesbian love-affair' with Vita Felber, an Austrian exile who had been working in Barcelona and who had joined the unit as an interpreter. It was also noted in the survey that

Felber was under suspicion of espionage because of her previous connections, but after being investigated in Barcelona she returned to the unit.

This latter case drew comments beyond the survey by both of its authors. Years later, when Kenneth Sinclair-Loutit was interviewed about the unit's members, he returned several times to comment, almost lasciviously and certainly condescendingly, about the Bird–Felber affair. Among these comments, he joked that 'Radclyffe Hall was not yet in paperback' and that 'the Popular Front did not have a gay chapter' so the affair 'had to end'. He described the nurse known as 'Dickybird' as a 'dumpy little figure in khaki britches' who spent her days 'being one of the boys' with the unit's drivers and her 'delicious evenings with giggly cuddly Vita'. Aileen does not mention Doris Bird but devotes quite a bit of space in her diary to Vita Felber, who she detested and called on one occasion *a lying little bitch.* Apparently Vita also had affairs with some of the men of the unit and ended up marrying one of the transport drivers Denis Prout, referred to by Aileen as *poor Hamlet.* Aileen related the tale of the *Viennese creature* and her marriage in a letter to her parents, but did not mention her lesbian affair with Nurse Bird.

It is tempting to speculate why Aileen was silent about Doris Bird but so vocal about her dislike of Vita Felber. Did Vita usurp her position as interpreter perhaps? Aileen was, after all, fluent in German and held the official position of interpreter for the unit. Or was she disapproving of the woman because of her affairs with both women and men? Perhaps the sense of specialness her own awakening predilection for women had given her at school and university was being shaken in the raw and often brutal world she was plunged into at Grañén. Perhaps, realising that Nurse Bird was regarded by her colleagues with some derision, she had started to reflect on the moralistic attitudes of the Communist Party in general, particularly towards homosexuality. The situation in Catholic Spain was even more acute where communist women as well as men regarded the rare cases of lesbianism with rejection and disgust.

It seems Aileen kept her feelings about her sexuality to herself, simply appearing non-feminine to her comrades. She was never interested in clothes or how she looked, but perhaps she accentuated these qualities as a strategy to make herself unattractive to men. In a letter to Thora in late 1937 after she and Kenneth had returned to England, Aileen writes jokingly from a temporary posting: *I am the only woman in this place, supposed to supply the feminine touch (!!!).* Years later, she also accentuated her lack of femininity when relating an incident from her time in Spain. While stationed in Teruel in late 1937 she was sent to ask for medical equipment for the hospital: *The 'comandante', in Assault Guard uniform, looked at me curiously, and kept asking me, 'Eres hombre o mujer?' (Are you a man or a woman?) Spanish men weren't used to women without any lipstick, long hair, and the rest of it, and I was wearing whatever I could grab. I never dressed up, all the time I was in Spain.* For his part, Sinclair-Loutit seems to have assumed Aileen was merely shy or immature. When interviewed in 1984, he commented on her neglect of her appearance and simply noted: 'no boyfriends (there was clearly a block there)'. Since he was so interested in Nurse Bird's lesbianism, he would surely have mentioned it if he had suspected Aileen of being interested in women.

The situation at Grañén continued to deteriorate as confidence in Kenneth Sinclair-Loutit waned and accusations flew, often by disgruntled members of the Party. Perhaps because of her loyalty to Sinclair-Loutit, even Aileen's worth was discussed at one meeting where she was accused of being inefficient and it was recommended she should be sent back to London as soon as another interpreter could be found. It was suggested that Australian Margot Miller, who was present at the meeting, should take over her secretarial work. The flamboyant Miller had been wounded soon after the unit's arrival in Grañén and had been hailed as a hero and interviewed by the press during her convalescence in London. Aileen and Sinclair-Loutit's survey, however, offered no praise but simply mentioned her 'taking unnecessary risks at the front', so it seems she was no friend of the Sinclair-Loutit camp. Interestingly, Aileen never referred in her letters home to the fact that there was another Australian in the unit during the three months at Grañén.

At the end of November, Kenneth Sinclair-Loutit was temporarily recalled to England. His own explanation when recalling events in 1984 was that he went to argue the case for the unit to become part of the newly formed International Brigades (which it did at the beginning of 1937). But his departure was also prompted by a document, sent to SMAC and signed by seventeen members of the unit, which complained of his cliquish style and his lack of leadership. Aileen wrote a long, impassioned letter to Comrade Robson of the CPGB supporting Sinclair-Loutit and claiming that he *as titular head* had been forced to bear the brunt of much of the infighting that had occurred between Party members: *The members composing this unit have been a queer lot for the most part – I suppose a venture like this is bound to appeal chiefly to people who are a bit off their rocker in one way or another. And some of the most unreliable have unfortunately been the party members.* She writes that she hopes Sinclair-Loutit is not made a *scapegoat* as she has seen *what hard work he has put into the thing* and that *he's a bloody good comrade.* Her summary of the conditions they were working under is apt: *To have carried out our work successfully in the peculiar conditions in which we are living we would all have to have been superhuman; unfortunately, we have all been too human, in one way or another – everyone has yielded to the acute personal likes and dislikes which inevitably arise. You know what a long sea voyage is like. Well, our slack periods are something like that – always the same people, that you can't get away from – alternating with periods of intensive all day and night work when the rushes of wounded come.* Aileen was aware of the recommendation that she too should leave the unit but says defiantly that *as this effort has been my engrossing interest for three months, I will not be leaving unless it is definitely decided that I can be no use here.*

The report of the October meeting where it had been suggested Aileen should be sent back contains a curious sentence that implies that she spied on her colleagues, albeit rather inefficiently: 'She is known in the unit as Pad-Pad and Eagle-Eye, which shows how unsuccessful she was in her "spying"'. Given the atmosphere of suspicion that existed between unit members, perhaps those at the meeting thought she was 'spying' for her friends. Maybe she was, but another explanation is also possible. Aileen was still committed to becoming a writer and in reply to a letter from her parents almost as soon as she arrived at Grañén she assured her father of this. Vance had suggested that what she was experiencing would make marvellous material for a novel but did not think she would realise that until later. *Actually*, she tells him, *everything I experience begins to take novel-shape in my mind, even when I am in the middle of it; though naturally the final shape of the novel I'll write about this is not at all clear to me.* She said she would try to write descriptions of the work there, although it would be difficult to do so in a life *utterly devoid of privacy*.

Echoes of her distress about the lack of privacy appear in a gossipy story told to the Australian nurse Agnes Hodgson, who was in the group photograph taken in the Plaça de Catalunya in December. Hodgson was sent to Grañén in January 1937 after Aileen and others from the unit had left to join the International Brigades. In her diary Hodgson writes of being told about the Australian who 'was always snooping round and making notes' and who 'tried to commit suicide because of someone who read her diary'. In a scene reminiscent of one in 'Poor Child!' where the protagonist Vivienne threatens to jump out of a school window, Aileen is said to have jumped from a window onto the floor below when no one paid attention to her demand to know who had read the diary. She was unhurt and was subsequently offered brandy. Writing from the lofty perspective of a thirty year old, Hodgson concludes: 'These young things should not be allowed out, this one was too sensitive and not sensible yet'. But Aileen had grown up with her family's expectation that diaries were public property and she had struggled as a teenager to establish a writing space that was for her eyes only. By the time she was in Spain, she had apparently impressed on her parents her need for privacy and Vance warned Nettie before he left England not to tell *anyone* in Australia exactly what she is doing because of Aileen's aversion to information about her: 'it's enough to say that she's with the Medical Unit'.

In that three months on the Aragon front, Aileen underwent a tumultuous initiation, not only into war, but also into adulthood. She worked hard and established fierce loyalties and aversions. As well as being secretary to Sinclair-Loutit, she was an interpreter in several languages. Sometimes she accompanied ambulances to other villages along the front following the call to stand by for wounded, as there were French, Italian and German volunteers fighting as well as

English and Spanish. Sometimes she translated between doctors and patients in the hospital. Occasionally she relieved nurses on night duty. Occasionally she also had the grim task of packing up and sending home the *efectos de los muertes*, the pathetic bundles of belongings of those who had died. She embraced some of the distractions that accompany living on the edge – smoking heavily and drinking with her comrades, sometimes to ease tension and blot out the close-up witnessing of pain and death; sometimes to cope with the boredom of the times when they waited for the next lorry-load of wounded. She picked up a fine array of swear words that she used freely with her comrades, but which she curbed in her letters home. She also learnt to be circumspect about her sexuality.

She might have still been prone to adolescent outbursts like the one related by Agnes Hodgson in her diary, but she had also developed a new confidence, displayed in her letter to Comrade Robson on behalf of Kenneth Sinclair-Loutit. She might also have become disillusioned with certain members of the Communist Party who were part of the unit during those months, and she certainly remembered the period at Grañén with some horror. But although the sensitive and sheltered young woman was made to 'come of age' quite brutally, she never wavered in her commitment to communism itself. Sinclair-Loutit reflected when talking about the time decades later that there were 'shades of commitment' among the Party members he had dealings with, but the two he named first as being 'total in their engagement' were John Cornford and Aileen Palmer. He also summed her up accurately as 'a Marxist, but not a party fanatic. Preaching did not interest her, action did'.

11

On the Move

Life in Spain changed radically for Aileen in January 1937 after the British Medical Aid Unit was absorbed into the International Brigades and its members dispersed. Instead of being based at an established, if rudimentary, hospital like the one they had set up at Grañén on the Aragon front, the medical teams became mobile units within the various brigades. They set up hospitals along the constantly shifting frontlines in former hotels, disused mansions and summer villas of the rich, from the foothills of the Guadarrama range to small towns on the outskirts of Madrid, from snowy mountains in winter to the heat, dust and flies of the plains as summer progressed.

By the beginning of that year the military rebellion had escalated into full-scale war. The Popular Front government of France under Léon Blum, from which the Spanish Republicans had expected support and arms, had formed a non-intervention policy with England under pressure from Stanley Baldwin in August 1936. Eventually twenty-seven countries including Germany, Britain, France, Portugal, Italy and the Soviet Union signed the non-intervention agreement. France closed its borders and volunteers from England were no longer able to travel to Spain openly but had to undertake a treacherous journey through the Pyrenees on foot. However, Italy and Germany flagrantly broke the policy of non-intervention and were supplying General Franco and the Spanish Nationalists with aircraft and weapons: Mussolini directly, Hitler via Portugal.

The International Brigades supporting the Republican government were established under the auspices of the Soviet Union and started taking shape in October 1936 at the brigade headquarters at Albacete, southwest of Valencia. Volunteers found their mission was no longer voluntary as they came under the command of hardline French Stalinist André Marty, appointed by the Comintern, who became infamous for ordering the imprisonment and execution of dissidents or defectors from within the brigades. Ernest Hemingway was to create a devastating portrait of him in his novel *For Whom the Bell Tolls*: a heavy old man with 'watery grey eyes' whose 'face looked as though it were modelled from the waste material you find under the claws of a very old lion'.

It was to Albacete that some of the British Medical Aid Unit, including Aileen, travelled in early January, after handing over the hospital at Grañén to the Spanish under the leadership of surgeon Dr Aguilo, whom Aileen respected and said they would miss. Some of those she would not miss were members of the unit who stayed at the hospital – *internal differences*, she said, *solved by an arrangement of sheep in one place and goats in the other, or vice versa.* As Aileen and her comrades travelled south with a French convoy, they found the Spanish people openly enthusiastic for the Republic: *When we crossed the border after dark, the driver got out and brought us a couple of sprays from an orange tree – 'Maintenant nous sommes en Valence – on est plus chez soi'. Along the road whole populations of villages stood giving the red front salute to the French convoy for the International Brigade, and in one place where we stopped a whole crowd of children from a school stood to sing the International.*

On reaching Albacete, their mood changed. A drab town situated on the plains, its streets were filled with thousands of volunteers waiting to be allocated to brigades. Aileen does not comment on the conditions there to her parents (on the whole, her letters are resolutely positive and uncritical of the communist regime) but Joan Purser, one of the nurses newly arrived from England who was to become a close friend, did later record the lasting impression the reception at Albacete made on her: 'Albacete was a seething mass of people who had come from all over the world, and who were being sorted out in a big barracks. We were briefed and threatened and generally initiated into the International Brigades. You were in the army and if you didn't behave yourself you were shot'.

Aileen, along with Joan Purser and her companions from Grañén including Kenneth Sinclair-Loutit, Thora Silverthorne and Archie Cochrane, were assigned to the *Service Sanitaire* of the XIVth Brigade, the French–Belgian contingent.

A few days later, on 8 January, they were ordered to depart for locations along the Madrid front. The brigade travelled two days and a night to the village of Villalba in the foothills of the Sierra Guadarrama where the medical team set up a hospital. They arrived on the eve of an attack, and all the theatres had to be arranged and the goods unpacked before they could sleep. Dropping exhausted in the early hours of the morning, Aileen shared the dining-room floor with several others. The next morning the casualties started to arrive. *Wounded pouring in from about 10 in the morning – the grim zoom of cars up the long drive to our new villa*, Aileen noted in her diary. It was the same the next day: *terrific congestion in narrow passages & inadequate rooms of house. Evacuation & more evacuation.* That afternoon Aileen was *hauled away* to interpret for the two Polish doctors leading the unit, who spoke French but little English, in conversations about starting a new hospital. The following day they loaded the truck with equipment and moved over to a villa at Torrelodones, just twenty-eight kilometres from Madrid. Soon the wounded were pouring in there at around fifty a day.

By the end of January, Aileen was clearly exhausted, having been working on the frontlines for five months straight. She was also suffering from having to adapt to a new regime and new people, especially as she was called upon frequently to interpret between the French- and English-speaking members of the service itself as well as helping to perform triage on the wounded soldiers who came from a variety of countries. In her Spanish diary's *Resumen de Enero*, she writes: *A slack & uninspired feeling due to change over to a new set of people, & not yet developed sufficient interest in any of them. For the first time, it really occurs to me to want leave, but we find it is not possible.*

During February, the unit moved to several different villages in the region of the Jarama valley, south-east of Madrid, where the International Brigades fought one of the major battles against Franco's mainly African force of Moors and Legionnaires. The single word *Attack* often constitutes the daily entry in Aileen's diary. Other volunteers from Australia were scattered through the various brigades along the Jarama front, including two of the four nurses Aileen met in Barcelona the previous December, May MacFarlane and Una Wilson. While Aileen never described the visceral details of her work in her diary, let alone her letters, Una recorded a chilling account of the days receiving wounded survivors of the Jarama battles at the hospital in Colmenar de Oreja. She told of the ambulances having to unload the dead and dying outside the gates for lack of space and the staff having to step over them to get inside. After days of almost non-stop work, she was overcome with despair: 'Never in my life have I felt so utterly tired, miserable and unhappy. I would be grateful to be caught by one of the machine guns which play about in the air. We seem to wade about in a river of blood without a break'.

After the sustained effort of the months since they joined the XIVth Brigade, the medical team returned to rest at the end of March in the same place at Torrelodones they had stayed in earlier. The buildings in which the hospitals were set up were often disused mansions; the Marquis's mansion that dominated Montgat where the Palmers had rented their villa only a year before was one such. Although grand, they were dilapidated: the lavatories often didn't work and the hot and cold water laid on in every room didn't run. One villa had a pianola and impressionist pictures on the walls, but, as usual, not enough beds for the tired workers. Their base in Torrelodones was one of the summer villas of the rich that reminded Aileen of *some posh outlying suburb of Sydney or Melbourne. There are times when I actually am homesick*, she told her parents.

Scenes that reminded Aileen of Australia often brought on pangs of homesickness as she crisscrossed Spain – the brown and sunburnt plains of Aragon and even, during the La Granja offensive in late May 1937, a former alpine ski lodge in which they were based high in the Guadarrama mountains: *a curiously beautiful place*, she told her mother, *like a more majestic Kalorama, that would be perfect heaven if it were not for the war.* Waking to see a flowery hillside from her window, she felt *much more homesick than usual.*

The depression she had fallen into at the end of January had dissipated; however, in the ensuing burst of work and from Torrelodones she assured her parents: *there is no question of my leaving*

Spain, even if I seriously wanted to. Once you are in a thing, you stay in it. On the whole, this is the most interesting life I have ever led…

When they arrived back in Australia in late 1936, Vance and Nettie began working intensively to make the apathetic and complacent majority aware of the situation in Spain, speaking at gatherings and giving radio broadcasts and writing newspaper articles. Nettie was particularly active on the Spanish Relief Committee, raising funds to send personnel and foodstuffs to Spain to aid the Republican cause. It was through the Committee's auspices that the four nurses seen in the photograph with Aileen in Barcelona were sent to Spain at the end of the year.

Though Nettie and Vance held deep concerns for their daughter, they were proud of her decision and do not appear at first to have given voice to thoughts about her safety. Nettie, who had left London for Australia five weeks before Vance, wrote to him from the ship with a kind of determined resignation: 'It's bewildering to think her time there has only just begun: it may mean years almost & nothing whatever that we can do'. When Vance's plans to visit Aileen in Barcelona before his ship sailed were thwarted because she had already left with the unit for Grañén, he wrote to reassure Nettie, and perhaps himself, that the venture might do their daughter good, casting her almost as if she were a schoolgirl off on an excursion: 'They're making an old house over into a hospital, and taking it all as a jolly adventure. I imagine there'll be a good deal of sheer dullness later on, when they've settled down – a little village in arid country, with nothing to fall back on except their own resources. I can't quite make out where it is, but it seems to be a good distance from the frontline…Perhaps a little bit of blank dullness would be good for her just now – she's had plenty of larger excitements, and probably the other girls will make her play games in her leisure & keep herself fit'.

Nettie moved to Ardmore when she returned to Melbourne to look after her mother who was becoming increasingly frail. She was worried about Helen's behaviour towards her grandmother as the university student tended to be impatient and short with her and the situation was becoming, in Nettie's words, 'grimmish'. Soon after

Vance arrived home in mid-November, he and Helen left for Sydney for an extended trip while he did a series of radio talks on Australian writers living in London. From their letters to each other around this time, Nettie and Vance seemed to be going through a period of adjustment themselves. Some of their old difficulties resurface and Nettie once again berates Vance for his lack of emotion. He tries to explain about his need for 'privacy' and 'reverie' and she attempts to understand it. Nettie is also wont to complain about Aileen's guardedness in her letters and doesn't seem to realise that her own neediness might be a contributing factor. On board ship returning to Australia, she had been shown a letter by an Australian acquaintance whose daughter had been at university with Aileen and who was now working as an *au pair*. 'Such a crowded, girlish letter', Nettie tells Vance, 'quite intelligent but crammed with all the jolly details affectionate parents like to hear...In its subjects & flow it was the kind of long, excited, detailed letter Aileen *might* have been likely to send us from Vienna during her first weeks there'. 'I think with you', Nettie concludes in a statement that reveals that the topic is not a new one, 'that Aileen's reticence & spareness is partly due to her feeling that she is a writer, not a mere spiller of ink: & partly', she continues cryptically, 'to her preoccupations'.

Nettie's anxiety about her daughter increased as she sailed back to Australia and the weeks wore on. News of the situation in Spain dribbled in via the newspapers and she constantly asked Vance if he had heard from her. Her anxiety was also mixed with annoyance as she needed information for the relief work she planned to undertake when she arrived home: 'If only she had sent me some Barcelona newspapers during those days she was there! Or asked her friends to send some. I could have made great use of them'. Vance started to display anxiety too, even though he had warned Nettie before he left London that it would be difficult for Aileen to get letters through. When they finally did hear from her in early January, he was still concerned: 'It was very cheering to get that long letter from Aileen, though it doesn't clear up the question of whether she's been getting our letters, and whether she's written before. And why was it posted in England? It's all difficult: she writes as if we knew something of her background, as if she'd written at least sometimes before'.

We know now that Aileen *had* written to her parents and that the reason many of her letters were posted from England was that she sent them with people who were returning to London where the mail was more secure. When she joined the brigades and was constantly on the move, the situation became even more difficult as mail was dispensed via the International Red Cross in Albacete and Aileen, for her part, complained that incoming mail didn't get through to her for weeks. When it did, it was often censored, as was hers. It seems that Nettie and Vance simply had no idea of the conditions under which she was living and were quick to fall back on blaming her for being a recalcitrant correspondent.

The letters from Aileen that do survive – some written in the early hours of the morning after gruelling shifts, some written by candlelight as she camped in open fields – are informative and friendly. She adopts her sister's predilection for funny nicknames, addressing her parents as *Dear Angelfaces* or *Dear Fishies*, even *Dear Old Bastards*. She writes about the day-to-day happenings and conditions in the medical service, gives her own assessment of how the war is progressing and political changes within the government, as well as responding to the situation in Australia, particularly Nettie's move to Ardmore to look after her mother (*It seems a pity that you have come back from Europe only to be more tied to grannie and the right and the wrong way of doing things than ever*). She also writes cheery letters to her sister who is at university, often asking her for information about members of *my Mob* and hoping they have not become too bourgeois. Through Helen, Aileen hears that some have married, including the group's leader Dorothy Adams, whose husband Ken Coldicutt, a former editor of *Proletariat*, would become an influential left-wing filmmaker.

It is hard to imagine today, when communication is only an email or a text message away, how the weeks between letters must have dragged for Nettie and Vance with a daughter on the frontlines of a war. But in some ways Aileen was put in an almost impossible position – expected to be both a 'girlish' adolescent writing 'jolly details' *and* a responsible adult. Vance and Nettie both relied on her for their information about what was happening in Spain, in fact the widespread effort they made in Australia on behalf of the Spanish Republic – in print, in speeches at gatherings and on radio – was largely dependent on Aileen's letters and the newspaper cuttings that she sent. Her view was always partisan, of course, and could certainly be contested in hindsight. She told her parents, for instance, that the government crisis and the deadly clashes in Barcelona in May 1937 between anarchists, communists and the POUM were the result of *the dirty work* of the POUM and not *that the Republic was torn by internal dissension*, as the bourgeois press reported. It was clearly rent asunder by internal dissension to the point where those who were officially on the same side were fighting and killing each other.

Occasionally, Aileen managed to send tiny snapshots of herself and her comrades and several survive that were taken during the period when the medical team was resting at Torrelodones around April 1937. Ironically, these snapshots taken in wartime show an unusually relaxed Aileen. In one, she is striding towards the camera along a tree-lined path, smiling, her arm raised as if she is about to throw something playfully at the person taking the photo. Another sees her perched on a stone wall in a white medical coat with one of the chauffeurs, Issie Kupchik, who is grinning and holding up a small dog to the camera. A photo taken in the garden with the villa's white arches and balustrades in the background shows the group 'sunbathing' around the laughing figure of their revered 'Chief Spanish Surgeon' Dr Moises Broggi, who lies with his head on Thora Silverthorne's lap. Aileen, being clasped around the neck by English nurse Joan Purser, is among the young women sprawled on the grass, while some of the men, stripped to the waist, lean over their shoulders laughing towards the camera. Interviewed in 1987, Dr Broggi recalled the few weeks of rest at Torrelodones, saying (in translation), 'I feel a strong brotherly tie of friendship with all these people. I feel sure that a book could be written around the lives of many of them'. He was to continue his work as a surgeon after the war, never renouncing his political affiliations. In 2011, aged 103, he stood as a Catalan separatist for a seat in the Spanish Senate election and died at the end of 2012.

Aileen went to Madrid several times on day leave during the Torrelodones period. She usually had a list of things to buy: *ink, folders, whiskey, socks, brassiere, suitcase.* A snapshot Aileen sent home from one of those trips shows her enveloped in a huge coat that almost reaches her ankles, hands in pockets, standing in the street with the cheerful-faced driver, Issie Kupchik. The city had been under siege since the previous November when Franco had boasted that his generals would soon be drinking in the *Puerta del Sol*. But Madrid had proved more resistant than he expected. Bombardments still continued, but the rate had slowed down while the frontline fighting dragged on at the *Casa del Campo*, the university area on the city's outskirts.

When Aileen visited on 27 April she noted that the atmosphere was different from a couple of weeks before, that there had been a recommencement of heavy bombing, that there were not many people on the streets, and that those who were there were moving very fast. That day she heard that seven people were killed in the street in the course of their daily business. When she first arrived that morning she went to the Hotel Florida on the *Gran Via*. Most of the foreign journalists stayed there, including Ernest Hemingway, who, like those in the know, had suites as close to the ground floor as possible where there was less danger from airstrikes. Aileen's diary notes that she had a long bath while she was there (in whose suite I do not know – one of the journalists she knew perhaps, like Sefton Delmer from the *Daily Express* in London), then lunched in the basement restaurant of the hotel with nurse Ada Hodson, Reggie Saxton, a surgeon from the unit, and an American journalist, possibly Virginia Cowles, who later wrote a book about her experiences in Spain, *Looking for Trouble*.

The shelling started towards the end of the morning, paused, then recommenced at about 4 pm when Aileen was in a barber's shop on the top storey of a building on the *Gran Via*, the most frequently bombed street in Madrid. *When the first shell came*, Aileen reported later to her parents, *most of the people scurried around and shifted their clients further from the windows; a mirror in the room was cracked with the shock, though the bomb had fallen in the street down below. I was going to look out of the window, to see if anyone was hurt, but the girl who was doing my hair stayed in her place and kept saying to me keep your head back until she had finished washing my hair and put some fijador on it; by the time she had finished another had fallen, also very close, and the other people had scurried out of the room, and were doing their clients on the top of the stairs. 'Falta el otro', the girl said – they always fall in threes, apparently – and the last one was not slow to follow.* Further shells rained down when Aileen and Issie went to the Picture Palace further down the *Gran Via* and saw Charlie Chaplin in *Modern Times*.

Aileen's reports to Nettie and Vance are always matter-of-fact and cheerful, aware of the danger she is in but not overwhelmed by it. She often said in later years that she never considered she would be killed in Spain; perhaps it was partly her youth and her inbuilt stoicism that protected her, and also her intense commitment to the cause she was fighting for. That said, she became keenly attuned to the different sounds of war and what they meant, which she elucidated to her parents on this occasion in a way that may well have struck fear into their hearts: *Shelling is much more horrible than street-sniping or serial bombardment, as we have known it so far. You can generally hear the aeroplane, or if it drops a surprise bomb near you, you know it won't drop another till it has turned round and come back, which it probably won't do: but you never know when the shells are coming, or when they will stop.*

Shells crashing over as we waited in the dawn. Slept all morning on the edge of the forest, Aileen noted in her diary a month after that visit to Madrid. The unit she was with had spent most of May travelling at a bewildering pace, held in reserve wherever a fascist attack was feared and ready to go into action if required. They set up and transplanted seven hospitals, but there were occasions when Aileen and her comrades had time to fossick around their surroundings. Reporting back to journalist John Fisher from one *sunny village* that had formerly been a religious centre, she tells him: *Yesterday we explored a large convent, containing the mummified corpses of one James Stewart, Duke of Alba and Berwick, and the founder of the Dominican convent here. We explored endless underground passages with wine-barrels along the walls, but unfortunately previous explorers had emptied them all. The place must have contained hundreds of inhabitants once and would have been a magnificent fortress for the fascists at the beginning of the war.* Countering the charge that the Republicans had burnt churches and then walled them up, which certainly did happen in Barcelona, she wants Fisher to make clear that in other parts of Spain, church buildings were used as storehouses for village provisions, or hospitals, or barracks for troops.

While there were occasional lighter moments, much of the time was spent in the large tents the unit set up as they waited for fresh orders. This existence soon palled and Aileen once more became frustrated by the extended quiet periods, waiting around to be needed on the ever-moving frontlines. She also felt that she and a few others, including Thora and Kenneth, had been exiled from the rest of the English personnel who had left to form a base hospital for three brigades.

By late May they were at the beginning of the La Granja offensive in the Guadarrama mountains, which was intended to take the road to Segovia and, if possible the city itself. They set up a hospital in a former ski lodge and Aileen's diary for the next few days reads simply:

30 May: Attack – 150 wounded.

31 May: Attack – 250 wounded.

1 June: Attack – 250 wounded.

2 June: 150 wounded.

3 June: 60 wounded. Issie and Wogan.

The two chauffeurs, Issie Kupchik and English aristocrat and artist Wogan Phillips, had spent day and night ferrying casualties back from the frontline to the *Club Alpino*. Then, during a lull in the fighting, their ambulance was hit by a shell, targeted because of its Red Cross. Wogan was only slightly wounded in the arm, but Issie's wounds were severe and a few hours after being brought to the hospital he died. It was Aileen's first experience of the death of a close comrade. To her mother she wrote, resorting at first to the impersonal second-person 'you': *Somehow it is impossible to imagine he is dead now. You grow so terribly impersonal about death at a front-line hospital that you are incapable of associating death with anyone you have known well for a long time. Issie was a bloody fine kid. I had a photograph of him, taken with me at Madrid, which I sent you some time back. If it reached you, please keep it for me.* But to her friend Glen Mills in England she was more forthcoming about her feelings: *One should be used to this sort of thing, but somehow it has taken the heart out of me for the moment. I want to drop what I am doing and get away. Of course, I could not bear to leave Spain permanently before this war is finished, especially after the sacrifice so many comrades like this one have made. But for the moment I feel terribly unstable, introverted and irresponsible, incapable of concentrating on the day to day jobs, and I think I now definitely need some sort of a change.* Years later in Melbourne, Aileen was to say how she was silenced by people who said being in Spain must have been *a wonderful experience.* How could she explain to them *what it's like to become only too familiar with death?* After writing that one morning she had *to wrap up Izzie* [sic] *Kupchik in a winding sheet and send him away to the cemetery near Madrid,* she comments: *I didn't cry over the death of Izzie. I don't think I ever cried when I was in Spain.*

The nine months of war without more than a few days' leave was starting to take a heavy toll on Aileen's spirits, and Issie's death acted as a catalyst for a severe depression. In her diary she simply wrote: *Strange how one still goes on. But I do want to fling this all up & start writing.* The war that the young volunteers had set off for with such high hopes that it would be over in a matter of weeks was stretching forward interminably and becoming ever more intense. Aileen and her companions often felt powerless and when the unit retreated from the mountains to the heat and flies of Torrelodones in mid-June, her frustration at their inertia overflowed: *And the fascists are in the streets of Bilbao. It is the same thing – like November in Granen: fiddling while Rome burns. Why, oh hell, Why?*

Everyone was on edge and even her closest comrades, Kenneth and Thora, were getting on her nerves: *At moments I almost hate them for their childish egoisms, & petty concerns for their own well-being; also for certain snobberies – despite their declared hatred of all these things.* Her diary over this time is peppered with French phrases – *Anything to get away – n'importe ou* (it doesn't matter where); *Je m'en fous* (I don't give a shit) – as well as the repetition of the more sinister German word *Selbstmord* (literally, self-murder). She plunged into escapist reading to stop thinking about suicide and suffered a *crise de nerfs* when told she discovered she was fourth on the list for leave: *I am growing battier & more desperate every day; am doing nothing of value & have recurrent moods of self-pity & feeling that there are no comrades in this bloody world.* Even her renewed desire to write is thwarted by the lack of privacy: *Writing again.* T[hora]*'s temper unbearable – she swots flies all over her patient friends, & objects to the noise of my typewriter in the room. There remains nothing to do but smoke & think.*

Early July brought Aileen out of her despair as the unit was ordered to move to the historic town of El Escorial to provide support for the most intense battle of the war so far – the Battle of Brunete. Afterwards, Aileen wrote an unusually vivid letter to her mother describing her time on this front, graphically indicating both the conditions they worked under and how the war was escalating: *Our last hospital was at Escorial, which you will find on any map to the north-west of Madrid: the wounded from the Brunete sector nearly all passed through Escorial, where there were three hospitals, the gravest wounded being sent to ours. We had five operating theatres working day and night. Altogether, during the fortnight I was at Escorial, we had about 1300 wounded. Julian Bell, the nephew of Virginia Wolf* [sic] *who had just come out to join the unit, was wounded by a piece of schrapnel from a bomb that fell on the lorry he was driving; he was brought into our hospital, and died that evening. He was a very popular chap with the drivers, and though he had only been out a short while, he was replacing the chief of transport who was down with 'flu at the time of his death.*

Archie Cochrane, whose job it was to decide which of the wounded were beyond help, initially categorised Julian Bell that way as his wound involved the heart. But upon recognising him, he ordered that he be taken to a separate room where Reggie Saxton gave him a blood transfusion. Bell recovered enough to have a conversation with Saxton but soon lapsed into unconsciousness and was left to die as nothing more could be done. Virginia Woolf wrote a short memoir about her nephew at the end of that fateful month of July in which she posed the question of why Julian would go to Spain knowing how it would torture his mother, Virginia's sister Vanessa, whom he adored: 'What made him do it? I suppose it's a fever in the blood of the younger generation which we can't possibly understand. I have never known anyone of my generation have that feeling about a war'. Virginia's sentiment was one with which Nettie and Vance might well have concurred.

Aileen continued her letter to Nettie: *These days at Escorial were the most intense experience we have been through yet. Every night the aeroplanes were over us, usually the electricity was switched off at the main and the theatres had to operate with candles and torches, until we established our own emergency lighting. In any case, most of the hospital was in darkness, and the large classification room, where most of the wounded were brought, had to work with only one light. The wounded were Spaniards, Germans from the Thaelmann and Edgar Andre Battalions, and a sprinkling of English. I believe the losses of the English battalion were high, but as there were not many severely wounded they did not come through our hospital. Incendiary bombs were a new feature that we had not come across yet. We were used to the thud of bombs in the distance, sometimes close to us, but this time you would not hear the bombs falling, only going out in the small hours of the morning you would see a glow as of bushfires all round the horizon: fire-bombs dropped among the forests and the crops. To the personnel in the hospital, though, the risk was of the slightest: the people who suffer are the drivers, going up to the first-aid station at Brunete and driving back, sometimes the 'planes would follow the ambulances, swooping down and machine-gunning them. Two of our ambulances were put out of commission by bombs.*

This letter was written in London at the end of July where Aileen had the time and privacy to concentrate on it in a way that was never possible in Spain. When her long-awaited leave had finally come through, she had been reluctant to take it while she was needed at the front, but was given no choice or she would lose it. Meeting Thora and Kenneth, who were also returning, at the Hotel Florida in Madrid on the morning of the 22 July, she and her comrades set off on the long and complicated journey to England, on trucks via Albacete to Valencia, train to Barcelona, then boat and train via Paris to London. Aileen's homecoming at Victoria Station on 28 July could hardly have been more different from the day almost a year earlier when the British Medical Unit was farewelled there with such fanfare. Disembarking at six o'clock in the morning, she lugged her baggage round to the digs of two of her friends only to find they were away or had gone from those addresses. She eventually trudged off to the SMAC headquarters where she was welcomed by Isabel Brown who, to her relief, proved to be *friendly & assuring & terribly mother-to-the-waif.*

Nettie and Vance were understandably relieved that Aileen was out of danger and cabled her immediately to suggest that she should stay in England for the winter and they would send her money to write her novel. While remaining calm in their letters to their daughter, they had each separately confided their anxiety to their friends. When she got the news of Aileen's leave, Nettie crowed to Leslie Rees: 'Aileen's now in London, praise-be, on long leave at last. All our heads are like bubbles on top. Astonishing how long you can bear a weight without quite locating it'. Vance, the man famously reticent about his emotions, had confided to his friend Frank Dalby Davison a few months earlier that he was finding it hard to concentrate on his writing: 'I'm desperately concerned, inwardly, at what's happening abroad: particularly in that corner of a foreign field where my own personal affections are so deeply involved that some vital part of me would die if the worst were to happen. One tries to hide these private fears, even from oneself, but they affect the inner energies and make life just a business of filling in the days'.

Aileen thanked her parents for their offer, but after a few weeks during which she *slept a hellish lot*, visited friends and caught up with comrades who had come back to England, she was ready to return to Spain. Each daily entry in her diary from 9 August begins with the words *I MUST GO BACK*. On one of those days she got drunk at the pub with Thora and Kenneth, who were not going back to Spain. Kenneth would finish his medical degree and the pair would get married and start a family.

The diary finishes mid-August, and with it access to Aileen's more intimate feelings during the war. To Nettie and Vance she explained reasonably: *After four weeks of England I begin to feel that life in Spain is in many ways more comfortable mentally, as one is getting on with the job in one's own corner, and here you have to sit and read about the world going up in flames.* Perhaps feeling a little guilty that she would disappoint her parents and aware that they must be anxious about her returning to the war front, she promised to send them a copy of the first two chapters of her novel – *as an earnest that I have done something in this direction and in case I have to surrender or lose my copy in Spain.*

12

'Call Aileen'

Aileen returned to Spain at the end of August, travelling with her nurse friend Joan Purser, who had also been on leave in England. As usual they journeyed by a circuitous and eventful route, shepherding precious packs of cigarettes successfully through customs on the French–Spanish border. There they waited in a long queue to buy tickets for a train crowded with peasants bringing produce, including live ducks, down to Barcelona. When the pair arrived in Valencia from Barcelona, they found a parcel waiting for Aileen from Glen Mills in London, containing *Craven As, shorthand book, Russian vocabulary and clothes.* Aileen wrote to her Australian friend: *The clothes could not have come at a more opportune time, as we had left all our luggage at the station, the unit's villa at Valencia being some distance out of town. We had been travelling all night and morning...were as dirty as hell, and appreciated a change of blouse muchly. I am wearing a silk one from the parcel and Joan has donned an embroidered one with Hongkong stamps on it.* The parcels from Glen came about because Nettie and Vance sent regular sums of money from Australia to London for her to buy provisions to make life a little easier for their daughter on the frontlines.

On their return to duty, Aileen and Joan were sent to the English Hospital inland at Huete that served as a base for the Madrid, Guadalajara and Teruel fronts. *Huete*, Aileen told her parents, *is on one of the treeless, eroded plains that seem characteristic of inland Spain, apart from the pine-clad Sierras. Here and there an olive-field crouches behind a jutting ledge of rock, here and there is a small wheat-field; but the rest is bare, brown and grey.* However, the Spanish landscape, while seeming to be uniformly brown and dry, still held some surprises. Aileen had passed through Valdeganga on her way to Huete, where another English Hospital was used for the convalescence of long-term patients. She wrote that Valdeganga was in *a little pocket in the hills beside a river. It used once to be a watering-place: there are mineral springs there, and a fine, clear bathing-pool. The country around it is very like Australian bush: only a few wandering poplars give it an idyllic and tamed look.*

The conditions at Huete base hospital, established in a ransacked monastery six months earlier, were vastly different from the frontline hospitals Aileen was used to in terms of facilities and general comfort. The building had been renovated and the lighting and plumbing fixed. It had an operating theatre and sterilising room, an X-ray department, a pathology laboratory and a pharmacy. But it was the food that most impressed Aileen: *There is butter and decent bread, not the bricks you get at the front; fresh meat is scarce, but bullybeef stews are better than most fresh meat you get in Spain, anyway. Vegetables are quite plentiful at present, and there is some variation in the fruit – apples, melons and grapes.* She found the work there less exacting than when stationed in frontline hospitals and told her parents: *If I am not required for work at the front soon, I shall get quite a decent slice of my novel done, though it's apt to turn out rather mechanical being done in these conditions.*

But such hedonistic pleasures as butter and grapes and time to write turned out to be short-lived, as within a few weeks of her arrival Aileen and her comrades were ordered to move to the Aragon front where she had begun her time in Spain almost exactly a year before.

On the Aragon front, Aileen was based with the 35th Division at the *Jefatura Sanidad*, a central headquarters for the hospitals scattered through the villages familiar from her stint at Grañén in 1936. She met up there with other members of her équipe, including Dr Leonard Crome, who had been appointed to replace the Polish commandant of their division, Dr Domanski-Dubois, killed just a month earlier by a sniper when the town of Quinto was taken. Writing back to Thora and Kenneth with the news (and with desperate requests for cigarettes), she related *a lovely story* Len Crome had told them about a visit from one of the senior figures of the Spanish Medical Aid

Committee, Dr Hyacinth Morgan: *When the old boy appeared, Crome took him round and showed him some of the work, told him how many hospitals we had set up, and how many wounded had been dealt with. All Morgan could say was 'Is that all you can show for all our money?'*

Aileen slept at the old hospital in Grañén where most of the English were stationed and walked two miles to the office every morning, hoping that it might have some effect on her (rather solid) figure. Once again, the situation in the village (*and what a hell of a place it is*, she told the Sinclair-Loutits) was one of stagnation on the fighting front but stretched to the limit in the hospitals scattered around the villages, which were full not with the gripes this time but with flu and typhoid: *We have had about 600 sick from the division since the middle of October.* Complaining again about the lack of *bloody fags*, she told Thora and Kenneth: *We have never been as badly off as far as the physical amenities of life go. Even in the bad old days on this front, there were fairly regular supplies of Favaritos and Elegantes.* Archie Cochrane had recently sent a thousand cigarettes from London for herself and her nurse friends Joan and Ros, but as no one else had any they were dispersed at once.

It is hard to overestimate the importance of cigarettes to all the workers on the frontlines – men and women. Everybody smoked, not only to relieve tension and allay boredom or hunger pangs but also as a way of helping to overcome one of the most pervasive accompaniments of war – smell. George Green, whom Aileen met when he was recovering in the hospital at Huete, described the atmosphere in one of the battle dressing stations in a poem: 'Here the sweet smell of blood, shit, iodine, the smoke-embittered air, the furtive odour of the dead'. No wonder Aileen's pleas grew louder and her language more colourful as the weeks wore on and she received no replies to her letters to Thora and Kenneth. One she sent in early December begins: *Dear Loutits, You are a pair of shits. You have never written to me, nor sent me any cigarettes. A pox on you both.* She finishes: *But send me some fags and write to me, you pair of bastards*, signing the letter with her nickname from the first period at Grañén, *Eagle-Eyes.*

Aileen wrote that December letter sitting in Thora's old theatre at the hospital, where she often spent her evenings, sometimes smoking the pipe lent to her by Len Crome's adjutant, the young American,

Bill Pike. (*You have to learn to make the best of every situation,* she told her sister about her pipe-smoking. As a child she enjoyed being told she was the spitting image of her father, except for the pipe. She might have reflected that now the resemblance was complete.) As she sucked on the pipe and wrote to Thora, she remarked casually: *The place was bombed, as you may have read in the English* Daily Worker *and other places. However, the operating theatres are still intact, and we have an emergency theatre here, as well as one in another village.* The war had escalated dramatically from when the first British Medical Unit had set up the hospital the previous year; then there had been little danger from the air. Blatantly disregarding the non-intervention pact they had signed in 1936, Italy and Germany had for months been supplying Franco's forces with aircraft.

To her friend Glen in London, Aileen described the *nine big planes (Capronis) and clouds of little escorting chasers* that flew over the village where the office was situated *and went down to the other village where the hospitals are.* The bombs hit the railway line (and wounded the station master who died a few days later) and also a garage. *From our village I could see a huge column of black smoke soaring up from the burning garage, and a smaller column of smoke from a truck that was burning on the railway-line. I got on to the first ambulance that went down to see what had happened. I saw them dragging cars out of the garage, hauling out beams of wood and plunging them in water, all with a movement as swift and coordinated as a lot of ants restoring an upturned nest. The wounded had already been taken to the hospital. Our people were operating. The planes did not return, though everyone was expecting them again. They flew very low over our village, but dropped nothing.*

To her parents, Aileen simply wrote: *I started to write to you a few days ago, but there was nothing to write about. We are still in the same place. There has been no action here recently, and all we have had has been epidemics of sick.*

A couple of weeks later Aileen was with her comrades in a train, travelling, and as was often the case, she knew not where. General Franco had planned a massive winter assault on Madrid and, to forestall this, the Republicans launched an offensive at Teruel on the

Aragon front in mid-December. The town was taken on the 17th by Spanish brigades, who fought their way up the mountains through ice and snow, taking the rebels by surprise. Teruel was the destination for the train in which Aileen and the medical unit were travelling. They had been ordered there as part of the 35th Division to join the International Brigade backup for the Spanish troops to make sure the front was held. To her parents, Aileen wrote: *The fascist radio stated that Teruel had been taken by 24 International Brigades (!) and that operations in these conditions would never have been carried out but for the instigation of the Russians, who wanted to experiment on war in the extreme cold. It is probably well known by now that there exist only six international brigades who by now are largely mixed with Spaniards, and that the taking of Teruel was not due to the International Brigades but to the veterans of the centre front, the Spanish brigades of Lister and Campesino.* English journalist and communist Winifred Bates reported back to London: 'The untakeable city is taken, and the Spaniards are holding their own'.

Bates sent regular reports to London for the *Spanish Information Service Bulletin,* and a pen snapshot of Aileen can be found in her account of the work of the medical units published by the *Bulletin* in the February 1938 issue: 'An ambulance driver goes in and reports the position of an ambulance to Dr Crome, the Commander. "Call Aileen", he says. She comes in looking very rosy and well; dressed in corduroy trousers, and an enormous old sheepskin coat, she reminds me of one of the Lost Boys in Peter Pan. "Write letters in Spanish to so-and-so about such-and-such", he says. She goes to a cupboard under the stairs, which has been turned into an office by the fixing of an electric light bulb and the addition of a table, a chair and a typewriter. Dr Crome calls "one of our most reliable drivers" and gives them the letters. "If the ground is not in fascist hands fetch that ambulance back", he orders. They step out into the night'.

Teruel, smallest of the three provincial capitals of Aragon, is situated 900 metres up in the Sierra Palomeras where the lowest winter temperatures in the country are registered. The sheepskin coat Aileen was wearing in Winifred Bates's vignette may not have been as old as it looked, just well worn, as the hospital at Huete had received a large consignment of Australian and New Zealand woollen goods while she was stationed there a few months earlier. Aileen noted then that they would serve them in good stead for the coming winter in the unheated Spanish buildings, not knowing just how necessary the sheepskin would be in the ice and snow of Teruel in one of the bitterest winters on record.

Aileen was now secretary to the Division's Chief Medical Officer Dr Leonard Crome, a surgeon with whom she had worked at the Battle of Brunete and whom she liked and respected. Six years older than Aileen, he was a considerably more senior figure than Kenneth Sinclair-Loutit had been. Len Crome had been born Lazar Krom in a part of Russia that is now in Latvia, later studying medicine in Edinburgh. Aileen described him as *a tall, genial, comforting figure* and he had attributes of character that would have appealed to her. He was highly efficient but easygoing and, unlike some of the senior brigade figures for whom uniform was a matter of pride and status, Dr Crome always looked dishevelled. Nan Green, who succeeded Aileen as Crome's secretary, was to say he had 'a devastating irreverence for bureaucracy and liked to surround himself with eccentrics and oddballs'.

Some of the members of his team were comrades of Aileen's from the early days of the war, including Keith (Andy) Andrews, who was in charge of the sterilising van, Catalan surgeon Dr Moises Broggi and English surgeon Dr Reggie Saxton, who pioneered the use of blood transfusions for the badly wounded while in Spain. He knew the blood groups of all the team and they were called upon to give blood in emergencies, which Aileen said always made her feel sick and sorry for herself. The Australian nurse Una Wilson was also in Teruel with the Belgian surgeon Dr Dumont, whom she worked for throughout her time in Spain. She was not a particular friend of Aileen's, who described her as *extremely capable* but *mentally unenterprising.*

Aileen tended to prefer the chauffeurs and the doctors – her male comrades – to the nurses she worked with in Spain, *though*, she told her mother, *you know it isn't a particular characteristic of mine to think more of men than of women.* The nurses she found generally to be lacking in political conviction and, with a few exceptions, *stodgy and brainless, emptily flirtatious, or temperamental and pettish, or all of these.* At the same time she acknowledged that they were *all bloody good when it comes to a tough job of work.* One of the reasons she gave her rather pointed assessment of the nurses to Nettie was because her mother had been on the interviewing committee of the Australian and, later, the New Zealand nurses who were funded by the Spanish Relief Committee. Aileen found two of the New Zealand nurses she worked with to be *quiet, capable, reliable sort of girls* and the third, Millicent Sharples, *pleasantly cracked.* Millicent was the cause of much amusement, wanting to buy a car for her personal use and very concerned about her appearance: *She has developed a crush on a Spanish doctor of porcine appearance, and of course whenever we have a fiesta she is terribly worried because she has absolutely nothing to wear. (Yours truly appears, if at all, in corduroy uniform trousers and hobnailed boots, and many of the other nurses likewise.)*

Several nurses became her firm friends, however, and they kept in contact intermittently for years afterwards. Thora Silverthorne was one. Among those she counted as friends at Teruel were Spanish nurse Aurora Fernandez and the English Joan Purser. Joan later wrote to Aileen: 'You kept me half-sane in Spain'.

Several hospitals with British personnel were set up around Teruel. Aileen was stationed with Len Crome's hospital in the village of Cuevas Labradas, just north of the city on the Saragossa road, treacherous for the ambulances to reach as they had to negotiate snowbound roads and hairpin bends over precipitous drops. It was at this hospital that Winifred Bates came across Aileen in her sheepskin coat. It was also the time when Aileen confused the officer of the Assault guards who interviewed her in Teruel when she accompanied an ambulance to collect medical equipment for the hospital: *'Eres hombre o mujer'*, he kept asking.

Conditions around Teruel were more severe than any previously encountered during the long and bloody war. Wounded Spanish soldiers poured into the hospitals in a terrible condition, many with frostbitten limbs that had to be amputated. Blankets were hung over glassless windows in an attempt to keep out the rain and snow. Aileen reported that she had taken a much-needed bath in Sister Una Wilson's operating room when it was off duty: *Here one washes as one eats and sleeps – when there is time and opportunity.* Aileen didn't mention another hazard to her parents – lice – which had troubled everyone at times; in Teruel, with little opportunity to wash, the itching became unbearable. Her friend Aurora Fernandez recalled finding it so difficult to sleep that she poured a little ether on herself to anaesthetise the lice, until it was pointed out that those smoking around her could cause her to go up in flames.

The brigade divisions holding Teruel were preparing for Franco's counterattack which they knew would start when the appalling weather conditions eased and the bombing could begin. The Nationalists and their allies deployed at this time over 400 aircraft, a vastly superior force to that of the Republicans. The New Year brought a contingent of ninety Italian aeroplanes and forty-two German, including twelve Messerschmitts and other bombers, to Teruel.

Aileen didn't hold back on news of the bombing to her family this time and wrote vividly of the initial attacks: *A few days back, when the snow had thawed, the fascists counter-attacked, gained a couple of hills but not what they were after. The attack began with an almost incessant bombing and strafing of all villages within the vicinity of Teruel. They came up at about 9 o'clock in the morning, streaming back and forwards across the sky, till it was almost covered with the white circles drawn from the smoke of their exhaust pipes. They dropped some incendiary bombs round us, but none of them did any damage. We thought they were marking out the pitch for a later bombardment, but the other bombs they dropped only made holes in the ground, not touching the hospital. The village was churned up a bit – some houses bashed in, streets encumbered with shards. There were no casualties. We wondered rather at first why our village had been singled out for a display of aerial gymnastics on the fascist part, but we soon found that the bombing had been universal. Ambulances were put out of action with machine-gun bullets in the course of these days, and two of our drivers had to go to hospital with light wounds. We had three surgical teams working in a hospital close to the front, others working in hospitals further away along the evacuation route.* There was only dry bread and marmalade to eat that first day as the cooks had fled too. Len Crome, who did not run away, told her *the main thing is to convince yourself that they can't get you: they may get the other person.* It was a lesson she learned well, in Spain and later working in the East End of London during the Blitz.

Many years later, her raw account honed to more literary prose, Aileen wrote again of her memories of that first day of the savage counteroffensive. This time the German aeroplanes appear both beautiful and menacing: *They came over, early, one fine still sunny morning, steel-grey, and nicely patterned against the sunlight.* Some of the doctors ran off into the hills; one, whom she does not name, *scampering off to his hole, with his white surgeon's apron flapping around him, like a rabbit's tail.* She returned to one particular event during that day several times in her later writing. It occurred towards sunset, after the bombers had all gone and the skies were clear. Suddenly a team of Messerschmitts appeared, diving low and strafing the village with bullets: *One of the nurses exclaimed in surprise: 'Look! There are men in those things!' as she had seen one of the pilots leaning out. This was long before the days of Hitler's pilotless planes, that were afterwards to make havoc in London late in World War II, but, at the end of a day like that, it was queer to realise that those brutal machines that came over were directed by human beings.*

The Nationalists retook Teruel in February and on 9 March Franco launched a major attack on a fifty-mile front in Aragon, close to the river Ebro. As the Republican forces began retreating from the Aragon front, the medical units took to setting up hospitals anywhere they could, in olive-green tents. Aileen told Glen Mills in London to reassure her family that she was *safe and sound* as rumours had got around that they had all been captured when their hospital was bombed. In a piece by Aileen in the SMAC Bulletin, called a 'diary entry' but more polished than her real diary entries, she describes the way they are forced to operate: *Our front hospital is in tents now, it's not safe to work in villages any more. The tents are pitched in an olive field, surrounded by hills. The ambulances come down by a rough track and disgorge the wounded into the first tent, which serves as a classification room. The worst wounded are sent to the second tent, which is an operating room, and the lightly wounded are dressed and evacuated rapidly. The third tent is set up as a ward. Most of the work is at night. To-day the sky is alive with the continual menace of wings. The bombs fall close. We crouch or lie on the floor. Then one falls just outside the tent, shrapnel pierces the thin canvas, and the place is filled with dust. No one hurt? Then get on with the evacuation, that ambulance shouldn't be standing there a moment longer. To-night the hospital is to be moved further back...*

As the retreat continued across the Ebro, the Republic was eventually cut in two by the Nationalist forces, isolating Madrid and Valencia from Barcelona. On 2 April the International Brigades base was moved from Albacete to Barcelona. The same day Aileen also arrived there with her unit.

The next day she wrote to her parents from the magnificent garden of a mansion owned by a Catalan poet who had given it over to the exhausted medical unit. She could see a fountain playing in the square in front of the house and hear frogs croaking in ponds teeming with goldfish. Inside, the *lofty mansion* presented *a quaint picture reminiscent of scenes early in the war. It is somewhat the atmosphere of a ship or a smart hotel, you almost expect to see people moving about sipping cocktails. Stretcher-bearers and first-aid men are playing billiards, others are looking at magazines in the library, tired doctors, nurses and stretcher-bearers have fallen asleep on the plush lounges that are still protected by spotless linen coverings. But instead of cocktails, people are having their supper of bread and garbanzos.*

Looking from the terrace at the top of the winding stairs over acres of blossoming orchards, she found it hard to believe that not far off there was a war, with bombs hurling destruction. But she could not forget the refugees who were their constant accompaniment on the roads out of the battle zone: *All along the roads we have seen the pitiful pilgrimages, – peasants driven from their homes by the annihilating bombs, uprooted Spaniards trekking eastward to the coast with their flocks and herds if they have any, with their ramshackle mule-drawn carts piled up with mattresses, bits of furniture, bits of food, sometimes taking their hens and chickens which are all they have, sometimes people who have nothing at all to eat, women carrying children and making the long trek on foot, not knowing where they will get anything to eat but placing their faith in the relief organisations till they get to some more tranquil town where they have a relation or someone and they will be able to find a corner to settle down. They are mostly people who have never moved from the villages where they were born and have grown up, and who have suddenly seen the whole world they knew turned into a heap of dust and crumbled shards...It is a long, painful journey for all of them.*

Despite what seemed to be a disastrous situation for the Republicans in Spain, Aileen still pinned her hopes on Europe waking up to Hitler's actions and coming to their aid. She felt there was a reawakening in France, with political strikes demanding that armaments be sent to Spain. Above all, she felt there was a general movement to put pressure on the governments of France and Britain to abandon their disastrous policies of non-intervention. We know now that those hopes were misplaced.

By early May, Aileen was seriously considering leaving Spain. *After a very mobile existence, in cramped ambulances or in tents*, she told her parents, *I have settled down to a bureaucratic life in a spacious office with four assistants, including a drawer of maps*. She hardly saw her colleagues from the hospitals. Such a life, away from the action, would not have suited her at all, no matter how important her desk job was. But before she could apply to leave, she needed to find a replacement who would have to be bilingual (with good spoken and written Spanish) and who could type. On the subject of going back to Australia or staying in England she said she was divided.

Having made the decision she moved quickly to secure a replacement and at the end of the month arrived at Victoria Station in London as she had done ten months before when she returned on leave. This time she did not go back to Spain; after almost two years on the frontlines of the war she was no longer 'on call'. She told her parents: *My intentions are to make a prolonged stay in England and do some writing*.

From London, Aileen heard about the last great campaign by the Spanish People's Army – the re-crossing of the Ebro – in July 1938. She was replaced as Dr Len Crome's assistant by English communist Nan Green, with whom she would remain in touch intermittently for years after the war. From London, Aileen heard in September that the International Brigades were to be withdrawn from Spain in order to persuade the League of Nations to pressure Germany and Italy to withdraw their troops. But on 29 September, in an act of appeasement towards Germany, the United Kingdom and France signed what became known as the Munich Agreement, allowing Hitler's annexation of Czechoslovakia. From London, Aileen heard about the farewell parade through the streets of Barcelona by the remaining members of the International Brigades on 29 October. Franco's troops entered Barcelona in January 1939 and took the city. At the end of March, Madrid surrendered. With the defeat of the Republic, the Spanish Civil War was over. Spain was to remain under the rule of General Franco until his death in 1975.

13

Prelude to a New War

On the evening of 19 March 1939 an unusual performance took place at the West End's Savoy Theatre, where the comic operas of Gilbert and Sullivan were the customary fare. Instead of swashbuckling pirates or Japanese maidens entertaining the audience with satirical lyrics and toe-tapping melodies, the bare stage was peopled with black-clad Andalusian peasants performing a tragic tale of violence and death. The occasion was the English premiere of Federico Garcia Lorca's play *Bodas de sangre*, later known as *Blood Wedding*, but translated on this occasion as *Marriage of Blood.*

Mingling with the usual West End theatregoers at that Sunday night performance were well-known actors of the English stage and people curious to see the latest production mounted by the Stage Society. These productions were usually of plays that were not likely to be performed in the commercial theatre, and many were first performances of foreign plays in England, like this one, which was first produced in Madrid in 1933. *Marriage of Blood* was directed by French director Michel Saint-Denis and the central role of the Mother was played by Martita Hunt, who would give a memorable interpretation a few years later of another fated figure, Miss Havisham, in the film of *Great Expectations.*

Stage Society productions were performed only once, in commercial theatres that were normally closed on Sundays. Although it was not known at the time, this would be their last production as they would not survive the war that was then on the horizon. Critic James Agate, of *The Sunday Times*, commented favourably on the 'surrealistic production' of Lorca's poetic drama of an arranged marriage, in which the characters of Moon and Death, as forces of nature, play their parts in the fates of the bridegroom, the lover of the bride, and the bride, who is widowed on her wedding day.

Aileen was in the audience at the Savoy that night. Lorca's influence on her as a poet was profound and would endure throughout her life. She sent Nettie a volume of his poems for her birthday that year. As well as admiring Lorca's poetry, Aileen had also been appalled and saddened by his execution at the age of forty at the hands of the Nationalist rebels in Granada in the early days of the Spanish War. He was in Granada visiting his parents when the uprising began in July 1936 and, although he went into hiding at the house of his friend Luis Rosales, on the afternoon of 16 August he was arrested and detained by the Civil Guard. During that month more than 500 men, many of them intellectuals and academics, were shot by firing squad. The daily executions were mostly carried out at dawn at the municipal cemetery situated among the beautiful hills and olive groves surrounding the Alhambra. Late on the night of 18 August or in the early hours of the 19th, Lorca was taken from the civil government headquarters, driven to the chosen place of execution and shot by the side of the road at the foot of the Sierra de Harana. His death certificate, drawn up by the new Franco regime in 1940, stated that he died of war wounds, his body being found on 20 August 1936 on the road from Víznar to Alfacar.

Aileen was in sombre mood as she sat among the theatregoers at the Savoy. On 1 January, in a scrappy diary kept on pages torn from notebooks, she had noted: *Suffering still the terrible inertia of exile and silence.* She had been devastated by the increasing dominance of the Nationalist forces that led to the withdrawal of the International Brigades from Spain the previous October. By the time of the performance of *Marriage of Blood* in March 1939, Franco's forces had captured Barcelona and he was on the cusp of victory. I found the draft of a poem among the scraps of Aileen's diary for 1939 that reflects the kaleidoscope of emotions she experienced that Sunday night.

It begins with echoes of Lorca's poetic language as Aileen writes of the human tragedy brought about by the violence of warring families and the pain experienced by those who survive:

A woman mourning for her murdered son
A woman mourning for her murdered lover
Bring in the dead
Their eyes like broken flowers

She then decries the shallow, bourgeois audience in a scathing tone that prefigures her despair at the complacent Australians (*comfortable, cushioned people, stuffed men*) she would encounter when she returned from Europe after the war:

Lights up. There's Sybil Thorndike over there
Against the wall. Just three rows behind Phil
Raising her hand now. She looks quite ordinary.

And two by two the audience oozes out.

Darling, I've got a programme.
The historical parallel is metaphysically possible...
But aren't the Spaniards rather cruel?

In the last section she compares the unfeeling audience to those who murdered Lorca and poses a stark question about the apathy of a society that remains unmoved by such distant atrocities as the Spanish War:

In the afternoon they murdered Garcia Lorca,
They burnt his poems in the square of Granada.
Here he is published in de luxe editions;
And they produce his plays at the Savoy –
But what do they care, the bovine audience
Ogling at Sybil Thorndike through binoculars,
(The historical parallel is metaphysically accurate)
Are they one whit less cruel in their stolid indifference
Than sadistic legionnaires or fanatical Carlists?

Within days of her return from Spain nine months earlier, Aileen had set about honouring her promise to her parents to work intensively on her Spanish novel, telling them, rather airily: *I have brought back any amount of typed and jotted notes which the censor in Barcelona was good enough to let through; writing is merely a question of giving a form to the subject. I shall probably begin with a short novel, of which the beginning*

& the end are already rather patchily written, which will deal with certain aspects of the war, and which will be more or less romantic in form – in the sense that it will be told more or less all by one character, & centre on three or four. Later on, I want to embark on a more complex work. Aware of the strain she was putting on their finances, she also assured Vance and Nettie that she would try to live on £2 a week. She remained involved in political work as well, selling copies of *Daily Worker* and taking part in 'Arms for Spain' rallies, but when Nettie worried that she was spending too much time on committees and meetings, she assured her that she set aside a definite writing time for herself every day and that most of her meetings took place after 4 pm anyway.

Aileen moved digs several times over the next few months, mostly in the Bloomsbury area, including a lengthy stint at the flat of Edith Young, her parents' Irish friend who had so impressed her on a visit to Emerald when Aileen was a child. Always an 'arty' type, Edith was now known as 'Mother India' because of her interest in the country and her association with Indian writers. It was while she was lodging with Edith in Charlotte Street that she was asked to sit for Australian artist Madge Hodges, the result being the intriguing portrait ('conducting the world with a cigarette') that Glen Mills delivered to Nettie at Ardmore on her return to Australia in 1940. At other times Aileen shared digs to save money, at one stage renting a large room in Finsbury with her nurse friend Joan Purser for fifteen shillings a week. Moving required no great effort as her meagre belongings fitted into her Fordite suitcase, the only other essential being her typewriter.

To earn a bit of extra money, Aileen also accepted a job typing up chapters of the book the Australian nurse Una Wilson was writing, based on her Spanish diaries. She wrote to her parents about it, complimenting the nurse in backhanded fashion by saying her writing was *quite lively, and she is sweating over it quite a lot*, but adding that *she can't sweat herself into a good choice of words.* Aileen even sent a few pages to her sister Helen, fully aware of how unethical she was being, to show her how *pedestrian* Una's writing was. Was there perhaps a smidgin of rivalry involved, given that both women were trying to turn their experiences in war-torn Spain into books?

After three months Aileen had completed a draft of her manuscript. She told her father that if she had continued with the more ambitious novel she had set out to write, she *would probably be still sitting smoking and chewing the end of my pen like I used to in the old days.* She had decided to cover *the period of the war from August 1937 to March 1938 and the scene is viewed from the point-of-view of members of the medical service.* She did, however, complicate the writing by having four of the characters narrating sections in the first person. As she wrote she showed her work in progress to several people, including Edith Young, Glen Mills, a friend of Glen's who was a reader for Heinemann, and another friend of Glen's who had recently published a book. It appears she may even have shown it to Justice 'Bert' Evatt, who was in London and who knew the Palmers. He wrote to Vance that he had met Aileen and that she had promised to let him read the manuscript of the novel she was writing. At the suggestions of these various readers, Aileen rewrote as she went along. *I should perhaps have worked out a more tightly-knit plan at the beginning,* she told her mother ruefully as she struggled to deal with her well-meaning friends' comments.

Before Nettie settled down in mid-October to read the rough copy Aileen had sent them, she confided to her diary that Vance was 'anxious' about the manuscript and hoped it would not be published as it stood. But the next day, after reading it herself, she wrote: 'Much impressed. Certainly she is writer! Endless material in what she has experienced, this book obviously being one of many she could have written. Anxious for her to do it full justice'. Over the next few days, the three Palmer family members in Australia discussed the manuscript 'a lot'. Vance wrote Aileen a detailed list of suggestions, including the rather substantial one that she should recast the first half of the novel in the voice of one of the characters, Stephen. He told her he was willing to pay for her to stay in London while she rewrote. Helen agreed with his suggestions, saying that Aileen was lucky to have such a critic as her father.

Over the next few months, new versions of the manuscript from Aileen crisscrossed the ocean with letters of suggestions from Vance, followed by letters of suggestions from Nettie regarding the recast chapters. During those months Aileen sent versions successively to Gollancz, Faber, Curtis Brown, Creswich Press and Dent's. Some sent back useful feedback, but all rejected it. *I think there's rather a slump in books about Spain at present,* she told her parents apologetically.

Bad timing may have been one of the reasons publishers were unwilling to take on her novel. The Spanish War had ended in defeat for the Republicans and people had moved on to more pressing concerns about the volatile European situation closer to home. Eventually, Aileen appears to have become disillusioned about her prospects for the novel that was then called 'Death in the Olive Grove', which she had planned to publish under a pseudonym. In July she wrote to her parents that Edith had suggested sending the manuscript to someone she knew at Methuen, *so I will do so; but I won't break my heart if nothing ever happens to it at all. It's only from your point of view chiefly that I am sorry.* Unlike many young adults who might expect resistance if they told their parents they wanted to become novelists, Aileen suffered the opposite problem. Having been brought up by two formidable writers and critics who valued writing above all else, publishing a novel represented for her a badge of respect in their eyes.

The only version of the 'Spanish novel' that survives in Aileen Palmer's papers is called 'Last Mile to Huesca', named after a line in one of her favourite poems by John Cornford, 'Heart of the Heartless World', written in the early days of the war on the Aragon front near Grañén:

On the last mile to Huesca
The last fence for our pride,
Think so kindly, dear, that I
Sense you at my side.

The surviving version is not a complete manuscript, but rather a disparate collection of notes gathered together under characters' names. It was probably partly written after she returned from England to Australia in 1945 and builds on the earlier novel, covering the period from pre-war Vienna (drawing from Aileen's experiences there in 1935) through the Spanish War and during World War II in London. The messy and rambling structure of this later version, written from several points of view, justifies Vance's earlier criticisms regarding 'form' and contrasts strongly with 'Poor Child!', the carefully structured manuscript Aileen wrote when she was seventeen years old, the action of which took place over one day. That manuscript she showed to no one and it displays a confidence that is lacking in 'Last Mile'. Perhaps the responsibility of showing that she was an adult novelist following in her father's footsteps proved just too onerous. Many years later, in a section of 'Pilgrim's Way' titled 'How Dutiful are thy Feet?' she was to write, with typical self-deprecating irony: *I'd never want, exactly, to walk in my father's footsteps, as Blake Pilgrim had always a very neat, tidy foot, which my own foot wouldn't fit into, at any price.*

However, Aileen also seems to have been conflicted about the type of novel she was writing. On the one hand, she was trying consciously to write a 'potboiler', a romantic novel that would sell well, as Vance had done throughout his life, separating his money-making writing from his serious novels. (Shades of the young Aileen's aspirations in 'A Feminist's Heaven', the play she wrote when she was fourteen, in which the heroine makes millions writing thrillers under a pseudonym.) And yet, because the Republican cause and the defeat of fascism were more important to her than the romantic involvements she devised for her characters, she was surprised to be advised by the publishers' readers to whittle down the political conversations and make them more personal and to avoid what the Gollancz reader called 'heavy local colour'. This is just one instance of the ongoing tension in Aileen's life between her political activism and her desire to become a writer.

In the frustrating absence of a manuscript of the earlier version, a section in the rambling collection of fragments, 'Pilgrim's Way', written more than two decades later, may give us the best clue as to the content of the novel that was rejected by Gollancz and other publishers in 1939 and which covered the period from August 1937 to March 1938. Aileen reminisces that she *suddenly saw the shape of the story* when she was leaving Spain in 1938, which would finish with an episode she had already written after the Republican forces had retreated back across the Ebro from the intensive bombing near Teruel to Catalonia. It would culminate with the suicide of the main character to avoid capture by the enemy, a concept she later felt was wrong even though it prefigured a similar ending in *For Whom the Bell Tolls* by Ernest Hemingway. *Because I had written the ending and knew where the story would arrive, the book was finished not long after I went back to London; but afterwards I wasn't sorry all publishers to whom I offered it saw fit to reject it. It comforted my pride a little, of course, that a Gollancz reader compared it favourably with a work by T. C. Worsley on a similar theme, but after my first eagerness to complete it had worn off, it seemed to me only a piece of mullock to add to that large heap into which I would delve in years to come.* (Interestingly, T. C. Worsley's novel, which the author 'Cuthbert' Worsley describes as a memoir not a novel, was eventually published in 1971. Worsley had accompanied his friend, the poet Stephen Spender, to Spain in 1937 when Spender was looking for his ex-lover Tony Hyndman who had volunteered for the Republican forces and was in danger of being shot as a defector. The characters in *Fellow Travellers* are based on Spender and Hyndman and others from the time, and the book prefigures another novel *While England Sleeps* by gay American novelist David Leavitt, first published in 1993 and withdrawn after Leavitt was sued by Spender for the unauthorised use of his 1951 autobiography *World Within World*. Leavitt's novel was later reissued in a censored version. Spender raised no objection to the publication of *Fellow Travellers* by his English friend.)

While Aileen accepted Vance's criticism of her work seriously and respectfully, an underlying twinge of resentment was also present, particularly regarding his assumption that he could rewrite her work without her approval. When Aileen read the published version in late 1938 of 'The Olives Are Not Plucked', a short story she had sent Helen as editor of *Melbourne University Magazine*, she must have reacted with annoyance at sentences like this one: 'All right, let us stay then. But when the 'pavas' come they will certainly kill me, as they will make you the bride of the Moro Juan!' She remonstrated, albeit gently, in a letter to her family: *Thanks for M.U.M. It's a fine production. Dad has certainly improved it. But did I use the word 'pavas' in exactly those places, or did he pick up the word from somewhere that I had used it, and give it wider circulation? Because 'pavas' literally means turkeys, and it is the graphic description of planes because they lay eggs (not a description of fascists in general).* She later read the story aloud (presumably restricting the word 'pavas' to its proper usage) at one of Edith Young's weekly 'séances' at her flat in Charlotte Street and told her parents proudly that it had appealed to their friends Joyce and Hedley Metcalf, who were visiting England, *more than anything else that was read because it was more concerned with actualities.*

Even at this stage, Aileen regarded poetry to be her more serious writing. Given her admiration for such poets as Lorca, Cornford, and Aragon, whom she would later call 'Poets of Liberation', it was likely she felt that in this medium she could use her literary aspirations to serve a larger political purpose. Soon after she returned from Spain she sent some poems under a pseudonym to the journal *New Verse*, which published the likes of W. H. Auden and Dylan Thomas. Not surprisingly, her poems were rejected. But a year later, she had more luck with her poem about the German-speaking battalion she first encountered when stationed at Grañén, which was published in the June issue of a small, new left-wing magazine called *Poetry and the People*. The magazine's opening issues in 1938 had published articles by Australians John Manifold and Jack Lindsay extolling the ballad tradition, important in their country's literary tradition with its connections to the songs of convicts and pioneers. Aileen was to identify strongly with the way Manifold positioned his work as non-bourgeois – using vernacular not considered suitable for poetry and writing in the ballad style.

The rousing rhythm of her poem, 'Thaelmann Battalion', mimics the marching feet of the German refugees, marching not for Nazi Germany but for the Republican cause:

This is our moment,
You can hear us singing
Where the earth is brittle under the southern sun
Watch us marching in serried ranks to the death that is our homage
To the unbroken spirit of our dishonoured country.

The last verse with its chilling reference to Hitler (and written before the declaration of World War II) echoes the first, describing a part of Spain that reminded Aileen so much of the Australian landscape:

Here we have shown to the world our country's other face;
And not the face of the hangman with the sprouting forelock
But the face of the young men who march together singing
Through southern plains where the clay is brittle under the sun.

Aileen's poem has found new life in recent years, published in a book of Robert Capa's photographs, in a volume of International Brigaders' poems, and featuring in a stirring reading in Spanish on YouTube.

When Aileen returned from Spain in late May 1938, exhausted, she retained a vestige of optimism about the outcome of the Spanish War and still nursed the hope that fascism could be contained. By mid-June she was ambivalent about England's politics under Neville Chamberlain: *England has taken a firmer stand on the Czechish question than anything she has done for many months, but she lets Franco bomb on an average a ship a day without registering more than the most polite of protests.* By mid-September Aileen was more certain that Chamberlain would not stand up to Hitler over Czechoslovakia, telling her parents: *London has been in a state of jitters this week. Chamberlain – 'this grand old man of 69, for the first time in his life mounted in a plane' – has been on a special mission to Hitler, & the result will probably be some sort of sell-out on the Czechs.* She was right. On 29 September Chamberlain's policy of appeasement towards Nazi Germany culminated in his signing, with France, of what became known as the Munich Agreement, which accepted that the Czech region of the Sudetenland should be ceded to Germany. He believed that by appeasing Hitler he was assuring 'peace in our time'. Aileen was despairing: *The business of Czechoslovakia is about the lousiest thing that has happened since Hitler came to power. The only lousier thing that could happen would be some sort of a Chamberlain–Mussolini 'settlement' in Spain.*

She was not going to stand by idly. Early in the new year of 1939, when Spain was on the brink of falling to Franco, Aileen and an English comrade from the Brigades, Angela Guest, mounted a daring demonstration against Chamberlain's appeasement policy. On 1 February *The Times* carried a small article with the headline 'Red Paint on Downing Street'. It detailed the appearance of two young women in the Bow Street Police Court charged with throwing red paint on the doorstep of Prime Minister Neville Chamberlain's residence at 10 Downing Street. They were fined five shillings each.

After entering Downing Street by the back entrance through the park, Aileen and Angela had splashed the paint on the doorstep of No. 10 from innocuous-looking thermos flasks. They then strewed leaflets they had hidden in copies of the *Ladies Home Journal*, pointing out Chamberlain's guilt in signing the Munich pact and appealing for arms for Spain. The red paint was a striking visual metaphor for the blood spilled during the years of conflict in Spain and a warning against further bloodshed. Spreading it on the doorstep of the Prime Minister's residence suggested that Chamberlain had blood on his hands. Their action also connected with a huge 'Arms for Spain' demonstration that evening.

Aileen did not mention the incident in which she had been arrested to her parents until later in the month when she discovered that news of it had reached the Australian press. *I see the fat's in the fire,* she declared, *so I suppose I may as well give you all details.* She felt she and Angela had been let off quite lightly: *Because we both had fairly upper-class accents and kept pretty cool and collected during the whole proceedings, I think we were treated much better than the people who were arrested in the demo that evening.* Aside from the five-shilling fine, they had to undertake not to commit a breach of the peace for six months or they would forfeit another ten pounds. Aileen added a handwritten PS to the letter: *Hope you are not feeling, despite your fine brave letter, that I have mortgaged my future for a tin of red paint. I don't think I have. Love, A.*

Nettie had been trying intermittently to establish when her daughter might be coming back to Australia, especially after it seemed likely that her novel would not be published. In mid-July she sent a wire with an offer that the Australian Spanish Relief Committee would pay Aileen to take a short trip to some of the internment and refugee camps in France, particularly where Spanish refugee children were being held. She would then report back to the committee about the conditions and the possibility of adopting some of the children in Australia. The secretary of the Committee for Medical Aid to Spain, Miss Helen Baillie, had been going to make the trip but was unable to leave Australia. The expectation was that after Aileen had finished reporting she would travel on from Perpignan to Marseilles and pick up a ship sailing to Australia.

Aileen procrastinated for several weeks and was clearly ambivalent about the prospect, particularly about the prospect of leaving Europe altogether. She was still heavily involved in political activity and was helping some of her ex-comrades who had escaped from Spain or were returning to London from internment camps. Spanish nurse Aurora Fernandez, who had been with Aileen through many of the battles, was one who turned up with a friend, and Aileen and Joan Purser put them up and tried to help them settle in. But she eventually assured Nettie that she would go to France and then return to Australia: *Don't think because I said I'd like to do something else or see something else before I came back and because I've been a self-indulgent bitch for the last year that I'll be too proud to wash up and peel the potatoes.* Nettie replied, a little caustically, that she was glad to get a letter at last, even though there was not much in it to show the committee and that Helen was typing up a few passages to show Miss Baillie, but 'not the bits where you say you're a she-dog'.

Aileen arrived at the Hotel Select in Paris on Sunday 12 August, spending the day *seeing the Louvre and loitering a bit round Paris which I adore.* Her passage home was booked on the *Stratheden* leaving Marseilles on 9 September 1939, a firm commitment that delighted Nettie: 'I haven't said yet how much it means to us that you're coming home: not once! If you could know how it colours all the days'.

The feeling that she was a tourist in her favourite city was short-lived as Aileen began the series of harrowing trips to the camps that week. She travelled to civilian camps in the Paris region in a lorry that carried beds, mattresses, shoes, powdered milk and footballs for the women and children there, catering for their material needs and providing the children with some means of exercise and amusement. The refugee camp at Châteaudun held fifty-two Spanish women and twenty-eight children. An old prison, it was cold and damp, and the rooms in which the women and children were kept were windowless except for barred windows above the doors. Aileen's fluent Spanish made it possible for her to speak with many of the women – from as far afield as Bilbao, Lerida and Andalusia – and she reported back that morale was good and the food adequate.

Over the next three weeks Aileen visited a children's colony at Biarritz, the concentration camp of Gurs where members of the International Brigades and other Spanish men were interned, and travelled across to the east coast to inspect camps at Perpignan. During that time the mounting fear of imminent war infected the country and added to the horror of what she was witnessing.

In the southwest French resort town of Biarritz on the Basque coast the atmosphere was bizarre. Orchestras played through the night in the cliff-top cafes as wealthy Americans and English danced the tango and drank liqueurs, oblivious to the stateless Spanish refugees beyond the bright lights. There were 7,000 children in camps in and around Biarritz as well as around 700 in the various Fosterparent Colonies. Aileen visited the children's colony run by Australian Esme Odgers and funded with Australian money, and reported back to Miss Baillie that the children were well and happy, infinitely different from those in the camps, and that they were taken to the beach frequently. She also stressed that legally it was quite impossible for Australians to adopt Spanish orphans, one of the reasons being that it was difficult to establish who were actually orphaned rather than just separated from their parents.

The contrast when Aileen reached the Gurs concentration camp was stark. Seemingly endless rows of barracks surrounded by barbed wire stretched across bleak, windswept plains that would be freezing in winter and baking hot in summer. Friends and family members of the 18,000 men interned there lived at the civilian refugee camp in the town of Oloron-Sainte-Marie sixteen miles away, and the vehicle Aileen was travelling in passed a long pilgrimage of women and children walking to Gurs as they did on the three days a week when visits were permitted. Aileen took her place at the 'parloir' at 8 am to give the names of some ex-comrades she knew were interned there, then had to walk three-quarters of a mile to another entrance along the road skirting the camp: *You could see rows and rows of barracks and men walking about, but could not speak to any of them – several rows of barbed wire were between the men and the road.* After presenting her application to the office in charge, she managed to speak with just one of her friends, the Austrian Comrade Endler, who told her that the men were doing their best, in spite of the appalling conditions, *to organise their time, to study, learn, make things – keep going, and not let the present circumstances of their lives get them down. They are all*, she wrote home, *so desperately anxious to retain their hold on life and remain active, creative people.* Endler told her that if he had expected her visit he would have brought a copy of the review they wrote and promised to send it to her. He was true to his word and Aileen treasured her copy of 'A Little Book of Gurs' that the men had put together, with their own photographs, and bound by them in spite of their meagre resources. She worried about sending it back to Australia, afraid that the censor might think the photographs had military significance.

A few pages of handwritten letters survive that were sent to Aileen from 'Camp du conzentration, Gurs, 23 August 1939', a touching testimony to the friendships sustained between comrades from Spain. One is in English and signed with three German names; there are also notes in German from each of them and a note in Spanish from another comrade. They were sorry to miss her visit, saying, 'The nasty barbed wire prevents us from coming together. Despite us remaining already for six months in the camp, they could not break our antifascistic conviction and our confidence'. They thank her profusely for the cigarettes she brought them, the gift she knew would be the one most appreciated.

I don't know what happened to those comrades. After the declaration of war just over a week later, the Spanish men were given the option of fighting for France or returning to Franco's Spain, the 'neutral aliens' were given the option of fighting or remaining at the camp, and the 'enemy aliens' (Germans and Austrians) remained interned at Gurs. Many eventually ended their lives in concentration camps in Germany.

By the time Aileen arrived in Perpignan, war rumour had reached fever pitch. She wrote to warn her parents that if war did break out the situation regarding the Spanish refugees would change. She herself felt that it would not be an opportune time for Germany to strike as England and France had been mobilising and preparing for a fortnight, but added: *All the same, with all these elaborate preparations, censorship of telegrammes, postal and telephonic delays it feels less like last September than Barcelona in the first week of the war – minus the enthusiasm. This part of France is very Catalan.* To her diary, she confided that *because I am going away from it the tragedy of things becomes more oppressive. I want to stay in Europe & die.* But her mood lifted when she heard that boats were not going through the Mediterranean but were being deflected around the Cape, meaning that the *Stratheden* would not be sailing via Marseilles: *I begin to lose my sense of oppression for the first time. I'm mad, the things I let affect me, but still…*

When Germany invaded Poland on Friday 1 September (the day the *Stratheden* left London), Aileen decided it was time to head for England. *I left Perpignan on Friday evening*, she told her parents – *it took 24 hours to travel up to Paris, going dead slow without lights & changing several times. I'm glad Miss Baillie didn't come over, as it would have all been pretty hectic for anyone unused to travelling in war conditions. Trains were on the point of being commandeered entirely for military use & one travelled either standing up or sitting on suitcases.* Reading the *Paris-midi* on Sunday morning – 3 September – she realised that it was a dramatic moment in the world's history: the morning when war was *actually* declared. But as she walked through the silent streets of an evacuated Paris she felt despondent: *I had been living in the expectation of bombardment before any actual declaration – there was no excitement, nothing dramatic about the morning, only, as throughout my journey, a sense of accumulated tristesse, resignation to the catastrophe, & a dull, fixed determination in face of the 'guerre qui sera longue et implacable'.* The dripping trees on the Champs-Élysées showed her a different Paris from the last time she was there and she was reminded of the first line of a Paul Verlaine poem that echoed her mood: *Il pleure dans mon coeur comme il pleut sur la ville…*

Arriving in Dieppe at 11 pm that night, she walked through the dark city to the quay and boarded boat and then train to London, finding it looking remarkably normal despite the train being in darkness. Reminiscent of her anticlimactic return from Spain the previous year, she rushed to the house she shared, found no one home, climbed in a window and deposited her suitcase before heading out into the street again to gather news. Aileen was back in London, her passage home to Australia was null and void, and once again in her life it seemed that, through a twist of dramatic irony, fate had propelled her into war.

14

Love in the Blitz

Having had the foresight to wire to Australia House from Perpignan to cancel her passage on the *Stratheden*, Aileen managed to retrieve the money on her return to London. There had been no shortage of people wanting to get out of England in early September. Her main problem was trying to work out the most diplomatic way of explaining to her parents why she was not booking another passage on the next available boat sailing for Australia. In a letter that echoes her assurance to her parents that Barcelona was safe in 1936, she describes the first weeks in London after the declaration of war as *a rather muddled sort of picnic. People who rushed out of London in the first days are now coming back. London is supposed to be safer than anywhere else now as it is so well defended.*

The Palmers had many Australian contacts in London and Aileen was more than a dutiful daughter keeping up with them. Joyce Metcalf, in London with her husband Hedley, and Joyce's sister Doris Beeby were two that Aileen developed a friendly relationship with in 1939 when the three women were working in various capacities for Australian Spanish Relief. Joyce and Doris's father, Judge Beeby, was an old friend of Vance and Nettie's, although many years their senior. His daughters were more than a decade older than Aileen and she had some reservations at first about Doris's *carmine fingernails and corresponding fandangles* but found Joyce, who wore a black beret angled over her Eton crop and rolled her own cigarettes, more to her taste. Joyce seemed to treat Aileen with a slightly protective air, and when war broke out in September she urged her to drop in frequently to the Metcalfs' flat, which, she said, was 'becoming a sort of depot for Australians'. Doris and Joyce immediately applied for work as ambulance drivers with the Auxiliary Ambulance Service – full-time, earning £2 a week. A few weeks later Aileen joined them at the ambulance station at Stepney, in London's East End. Having secured a job, and one that was doing National Service, she felt more confident to make her case to her parents about staying in London.

I am sorry, darlings, Aileen wrote after explaining her job situation, *I am so wanting to see you, but I feel rather as the Beebies feel that I don't like clearing out at this juncture. I'm not afraid of being torpedoed or bombed at sea, but I feel that anyone as tough and sound in the nerve as I am (despite my novel) ought to stick around and try to be useful here.* Joyce had indeed written home optimistically that she felt she and Doris must stay as this was a war against fascism, not against the Germans but the Nazis: 'whatever turn the war takes, it is the beginning of other things, of a different struggle to make sure that there are no more wars. I know that was said in 1914. However, the situation is very different in 1939, and the mood of the people is very different; the mood of the German people is more than different. I'm not saying that this is the final battle – but it is the beginning of that wider struggle for a new social arrangement – and in that we greatly want to take a part'.

Aileen moved into digs in a share house in Finsbury with a friend called Phyllis, whom she had known in London in 1935. She immediately threw herself into wartime life again. Some of her time was spent on training exercises with the ambulance station, learning to drive the heavy vehicles and taking part in mock air-raid trials; she also brushed up on her first aid with Thora Sinclair-Loutit at the flat she shared with Kenneth in Great Ormond Street. In the evenings she gave English lessons to a Czech ambulance driver Joe Edenhoffer, who had been a comrade in Spain and who was soon to marry her Spanish friend Aurora Fernandez.

When Vance penned one of his infrequent letters to his daughter, trying to persuade her to return home (probably on Nettie's behalf), Aileen's reply was upbeat. *Personally,* she told him, *I don't feel nearly as depressed about things as I did a few months ago when Hitler was marching on unimpeded.* And she assured him: *I am terribly fond of you all; and I do want to see you again; and I think when I come back we will all have got so much nearer to one another, and I won't be as self-centred and rowish as when I was suffering from acute mental growing-pains.* Aileen was holding to the silent vow she had made in 1936 to move out from under the shadow of her parents, even though it was not easy and she did suffer guilt over it: *Am I being horribly callous and self-centred?*

The Palmers' associates in London always reported back to them about Aileen, almost as if she were an adolescent rather than in her twenties, but probably at Nettie's insistence. Glen Mills had sent Nettie and Vance frequent updates about Aileen since 1936 and when she returned to Australia in early 1940 – bearing Madge Hodges's fine portrait of their daughter – she urged Nettie and Vance to advise Aileen to return home, as did Joyce Metcalf from London. It must have been difficult for Nettie as many Australian expatriates were starting to drift back to Australia in 1940. Violet Beasley visited the Palmers on her way back to Queensland when her ship docked in Port Melbourne in July and gave Nettie a good account of Aileen: 'says she's attractive-looking now & oddly popular'. But when the Metcalfs and Doris Beeby returned late in 1940 (despite Joyce's fervent desire to stay and fight fascism a year earlier), Nettie reported in her diary: 'Joyce spoke about Aileen, saying she'd have been better here as she "acknowledges no obligation to anyone". Not selfish: quite generous but self-centred'.

Why were the Palmers' acquaintances so insistent that Aileen, who was then twenty-five years old, should be urged to return home to her family? At least Violet seems to have commented favourably on her new popularity, but that might also have worried Nettie. Aileen was fearless in the face of danger and had learned to enjoy drinking with her comrades in Spain – to allay both her natural shyness and the constant tension under which they all existed. Perhaps living under the heightened conditions of a new war appealed to her and she took what her Australian associates regarded as unnecessary risks. As she said: *The black-out certainly doesn't prevent me from getting around. I'm pretty good at getting around in the dark.* In one letter she comments: *I'm happy, oddly enough. Perhaps my tone sounds to you a little cold-blooded, but the necessity I have always had, which I owe in the first place to you, of always taking a positive attitude to things that happen, prevents me from taking what is happening now in a passively tragic way.* (A marginal comment, which appears to be in Nettie's handwriting, probably before she passed the letter on to Helen, reads: 'Please work this out, Hell!')

It is an uncharacteristically effervescent letter Aileen wrote to her parents in August 1940, however, that offers the strongest clue to what was happening in her life at that time. It begins with a cheery *Lord, dears, it's so near your birthdays, and I haven't written for ages*, then she chats for several pages about friends – Doris and Joyce in New York, Violet's news from Queensland, Edith in London with a Spanish friend. She also describes the tense local situation where the proprietors of the cosmopolitan cafes in Charlotte Street place placards in their windows saying they are British citizens or have sons in the British Army to prevent their internment as enemy aliens. She describes the view from the window of the ambulance station as she writes – of the bustling street in Stepney with its old Jewish housewives, fruit barrows and soldiers in khaki, noting: *It rather grows on you this part of the world, so unlike any other part of London, with its humming street-life, resembling more the 'barrio chino' of a Spanish town.* The typed text gives way at the bottom of the final page to a handwritten scrawl that meanders around all four margins, in which she repeats the line from her earlier letter: *I'm happy, oddly enough*, and continues, *in this chaotic world – happier, personally, than I've been for a long time – enjoying odd walks in the woods & Hampstead Heath, enjoying being in love as I never was before, enjoying contacts with a diversity of friends & all the odd people one runs into in London.*

For the young woman who never reveals intimate details of her life to her parents the statement buried in this sentence that she is in love is extraordinary, and I had to read it more than once to ensure that I was not making it up. Did Nettie miss it? She doesn't refer to it in the diary entry she writes about receiving this letter two months later, but her correspondence from that time does not survive so perhaps there is an enquiry. On the other hand, being reticent about such subjects, perhaps she discussed the revelation with Vance and waited to hear more. Aileen does not divulge more details in subsequent letters, but another of her spasmodic diaries does survive, written between 23 August and 9 November. The lover she refers to throughout it is coded only with the initial 'B', but occasional personal pronouns reveal she is a woman.

While Londoners experienced the strange lull that followed the declaration of hostilities in September 1939, the war continued apace on the Continent and, with the surrender of France on 22 June 1940, the balance of power in Europe radically changed. Aileen wrote to her parents that the talk in London (which happened to be enjoying *lovely, un-English weather*) was all about what was going to happen there. Her own, almost jaded reaction to the collapse of France was a contrast to the passionate fervour with which she had thrown herself into what she felt was a just war in Spain: *Somehow, I find the tragedy of France less overwhelming than the tragedy of Spain, because one never expected anything very fine to emerge out of the initial stages of this war.* Her main concern was for the people she knew in France, wondering what had happened to them. *So far*, she wrote, *the air raids on England, though quite a large number of bombers have been involved, have not touched us.* All that, of course, was about to change and the diary Aileen started in late August pulsates with the heightened emotions she felt for her secret new lover combined with the terrible experience of living and working during the Blitz.

I looked from roof-tops and saw London burn, she wrote on 8 September, the morning after the onslaught began and bombs starting cascading from the sky onto the city below: *All along the river, there was a chain of fires, reaching up to the sky, their red glow reflected on the fleecy clouds.* She had had the day off from the ambulance station on the 7th and *had felt rather melancholy, parting from B in the morning.* (From the diary entries it becomes clear that 'B' also works at the station and they must have been on night shift together.) The first raid started at about 4.30 pm and, after the all clear sounded at around 6.15 pm, Aileen kept a pre-arranged appointment at the theatre to see a play called *Thunder Rock* with a girlfriend who complained about *husband trouble* during the interval. It might have been an ordinary night out except that a siren at the end of the first act announced another raid, about which Aileen didn't think much during the play. But the two women walked into the night afterwards to a changed city *under a sky streaked with searchlights – aglow, on one side, with the red light of the fires.* When she got home, Aileen found the people from her share house huddled in the basement, but she went upstairs to read under the lamp in the kitchen as the light in her room was broken.

The new experience of having someone to care for, however, did affect her customary laissez-faire attitude to life in a danger zone, and she spent the next day hanging about the house, *reading rubbish*, in case 'B' might call in after her shift, not knowing whether to go and look for her or stay indoors. The East End where their ambulance station was located was the worst hit on the first night of the Blitz. Feeling *rather numb and inert* she pondered her situation: *It's no use thinking of death, and no use worrying about it. I took a chance, with my eyes open – thinking, at the beginning, that it was less than a 'Chinaman's chance' – and not wanting anything else. Since then, life got a tighter hold on me than it ever had before, and I would gladly have fled this Europe if I could have taken you with me; but any thought of that is impossible now, we're both in it up to our necks, and all I want is for both of us to come out sane.*

Of the few pieces of Aileen's writing that survive from this period, a poignant story called 'Ambulance Station' – carefully typed and addressed to Vance Palmer in Melbourne but never published – paints a vivid picture of what she experienced on 'call-outs' after raids in the industrialised East End, which continued to be the most heavily bombed part of London. The narrator of the story and a female colleague take their ambulance to a bomb site through air *thick with flying cinders and the smell of burning.* When they arrive at the destination given on their instructions, they can just discern the ruins of a block of flats through a thick black cloud of debris-dust:

A shape that might be human is sprawled on the pavement. Bending over it with my shaded torch, I recognize the garments of a woman and the torn body of an air-raid victim.

E. comes out of the darkness, followed by two men, who are carrying something on a stretcher.

'Let's get the stretchers out', she says. 'We've got to load the ambulance with stiffs. That's all they've got round here'.

The lump under the blanket quivers as we lift the stretcher aboard. Arms and legs detached from human bodies are added to the load inside the blankets that we are asked to convey to hospital 'for purposes of identification'.

'There's something over there on the pavement', I tell one of the stretcher-party men, 'that once was somebody'.

The body is lifted up and placed on a stretcher, beside another dead woman.

No time for any more words. More ambulances are coming to carry off similar grim loads. Everyone speaks with a harsh, dry utterance that expresses a kind of inner numbness. So much piled-up death, so much plain butchery – it is too horrible to be pathetic.

Aileen wrote a poem nearly twenty years later, when she was back in Melbourne and her mental health was very fragile, that echoes the sentiments of her early diary entry about her new lover combined with the visceral images relayed in her short story. Apparently triggered by fear for an unnamed friend who was departing for a war zone, mingled with the recollection of planes flying overhead when she was playing basketball on the oval at one of the institutions she was periodically sent to, the poem resonates with that time in 1940 when love had suddenly awakened her to what danger could mean:

Danger is never danger
till the blood running over the street
is the blood of your own heart's crying:
the love you were coming to meet…

A few weeks after the Blitz began one of the team at the ambulance station was killed on a call-out. *People re-act very differently to death when it suddenly touches someone they have been used to seeing every day. I wondered who would be the first among us to get it* was Aileen's response. Perhaps the death also revived the shock she felt when her first comrade from the medical team in Spain was killed – her friend, Issie Kupchik. Most importantly on this occasion, however, the casualty wasn't 'B'.

The anxiety took its toll on Aileen over the next weeks and months. When not out on the gruesome ambulance call-outs, she was either holed up in the dugout at Stepney or at home in the evenings on her time off, unable to move about freely. Her diary entries reflect her frustration: *Life is all boredom, irritation, weariness and hanging about. One is more and more confined to one's own hole, shut in, cut off.* The constant bombardment also set her nerves on edge: *Sitting at home last night, hearing the shells splash and ripple through the pool of the sky…Then shrapnel hail, rather than the bombs, being so all-pervasive, tends to keep me indoors, but I hate this living cooped up in holes.* She found it hard to get used to the fact that raids could continue in all weather, encouraged rather than hindered by grey skies, whereas in Spain they had only occurred when it was fine. But the most stressful element of her life at that time was being separated from her lover and constantly anxious about her well-being: *I can't do anything with myself in the evenings, except go to bed early and sleep; I don't know till morning what has happened to B, and separation tells on us both.* Nor could she communicate her anxiety about 'B' to her friends; as lesbians their true relationship was clandestine, a further stress she writes about poignantly in the last entry of the short diary: *Sometimes it's awful to be in love and be separated at night. Last night I envied for a moment the lovers, lying all unconcerned with their arms about each other, among the hordes of people in the underground. There were quite a few handsome young people among the weary mass. They had no privacy, but they were close to their lovers; and clasping each other round their necks, they slept…*

Early in the new year of 1941 a bomb fell on the Finsbury area where Aileen lived. Although damaged, her house didn't suffer as badly as those around it and no one in the household was hurt. She decided at once that she could no longer live there. *There was a hole in the middle of the ceiling &* [in] *part of the wall fallen down there was just transparent lattice-work between my room and the next. Of course the windows were out, but the shutters had been left open, & they had not been blown off; I could fasten them across & keep out some of the blast while I was working there, but it wouldn't have been a very pleasant place to spend the night in this weather.* She describes picking up lumps of plaster and taking bucketfuls out to the gutter to be collected by the dust-carts that went by every few hours. Edith's friend Peggy came around to help and they both worked for hours, Aileen complaining that *every part of my being seemed penetrated with fine dust.* After giving Peggy some of her books and provisions, she packed her things and moved out. To her parents she apologised: *This is rather a detailed description of what was really an unimportant episode in my life, but perhaps it gives you a bit of a picture of everyday life in London.* She remained silent on the subject of what was important about this episode: she moved into a flat with an unnamed friend who was almost certainly her lover, 'B'.

Details of her living arrangements emerge in letters home over the next few months: she lives in a flat in the East End with a friend from the ambulance station who was bombed out at around the same time; her friend *has a rather stabilising effect* and is *very practical*; when either of them are *laid up with a cold* they look after each other. The furniture belongs to her friend; they have a kitchen and Aileen even cooks a bit and she sleeps more regularly. Never before has Aileen given as much detail of her living arrangements in London in letters to her family – whether living alone or with Joan Purser or Edith Young or Phyllis. Yet, while she is free with the names of most of her friends, this flatmate is never given one.

In a letter around this time, Aileen discusses the fact that wars seem to have the effect of producing babies and not only accidental ones, but those planned for deliberately, like the babies of her friends from Spain, Thora and Kenneth Sinclair-Loutit, and Joan Purser, now Joan Gilchrist. She adds: *I think that if ever I do have a child it will be unintentionally; and I'll probably think it's a damned nuisance.* A red herring for Nettie? If so, she bites, perhaps suspicious about her daughter's mysterious friend's gender and wondering if 'she' is a 'he'. In late 1941 Aileen replies to one of her mother's queries by telling her flatly that she is not having a baby: *I have no intention of having one, legitimate or otherwise, and I'm not suffering from any inner compulsion to have one. I agree with you that present conditions are extremely unpropitious for having children, but that doesn't seem to impede lots of people. Many of my friends, like the young people you were mentioning, are bursting into babies since the war. But I never felt I was made to be a mother and the advancing years haven't increased my inclination to replenish the earth.* She neglects to tell her mother that she is not interested in men.

Nettie continued to go on fishing expeditions, undaunted by her daughter's ability to ignore direct questions when it suited her: 'Have you developed a Stepney accent? Fine, and certainly new to this family. And what sort are your friends? What sort of a girl do you live with? Rachel seemed to say she had had a beneficial effect'. Rachel Wallis, an English friend of Aileen's from the Palmers' time in London in 1935, had sent Nettie a letter giving her news of Aileen, which Nettie duly recorded in her diary: 'Says AY is more attractive looking than years ago, thinner and striking. Seems to find A[ileen] solid & clear-headed, a good friend'. But, while Rachel clearly writes about Aileen's flatmate, she does not seem to give her a name either.

Earlier in the year Vance had written to Aileen suggesting that she should find a secure place in the country where she could concentrate on her novel and that he would support her financially to do so. Aileen did not receive the letter until two months later in October and replied immediately, thanking him for taking her so seriously as a writer but telling him rather testily that it was impossible as she was now in a 'reserved occupation': *at one point some months ago, we were told that we could no longer resign from the ambulance service – we could only be released from it on production of a medical certificate showing we were unfit for medical service, which should be confirmed by a medical tribunal.* Moreover, she reminded him that, although she was Australian, she was now considered a British subject having been in the country for more than two years. As in Spain when the volunteers were co-opted into the International Brigades and lost the freedom to leave, Aileen was once more a conscripted part of a war that she had entered voluntarily and, once again, she experienced the familiar tension between writing and political action. She tells 'Vance', as she calls her father in this letter rather than 'Dear old Dad', that she would like a couple of months off just to write but believes that being in England *one should be a cog in the war machine*, adding in frustration – *if only I didn't sometimes feel such an idle & ineffectual cog.* Where Aileen had felt that her involvement in the 'war machine' in Spain had been right and useful, and had been critical of poets such as W. H. Auden and Stephen Spender who visited Spain and wrote poems about the war but who never committed themselves to action, she lacked fervour for this one and believed that England was taking the war *very lethargically* since they were no longer bearing the brunt of it by late 1941. *This is a very comfortable war, physically,* she said, *compared to the Spanish War; but mentally it is not so comfortable.*

It was not until August 1943 that Aileen managed to secure her release from the ambulance service. She had long become fed up with her *standing-by job* in the Auxiliary Ambulance Service where the workers were put on twenty-four hour shifts with five hours for sleeping, and she hankered to be put to some use during those shifts. Other women knitted or did handicrafts to while away the time, but that was hardly Aileen's forte or interest. She did use the time to write letters, but found that she could not concentrate on serious writing in the circumstances, especially with the influx of trainees during 1942. At one point she did some training for a factory job that she could take to the station, but didn't elaborate on what it entailed. She had also started to worry about her family's situation now that the war had extended to the Pacific region, telling them: *I'd rather like a wire from you now & then, now it is you who are in the Blitz zone.*

A month later, in late September, Aileen secured a job with the Australian Scientific Research Liaison Office at Australia House. Her 'boss' was a youngish Australian who had just started university when Aileen finished her degree, but she found him congenial and her work interesting: *My job is roughly filing and research, but it's rather difficult to define its ramifications, because it's the sort of job you can make into anything if you're keen on it, and I am, because our department's function is to collect and transmit all the expert knowledge on all matters relating to Australia's war effort. I thought at first it would be either deadly dull or quite above my head, because so much of the stuff we handle is concerned with realms of knowledge that are nowhere near my ken, but somehow I manage to function as a non-technical member of staff, keeping track of requests and seeing they don't get buried or overlooked, and so on.* The move from the ambulance station revived her spirits and gave her new energy, not only because she felt useful again but, sadly, because her relationship with 'B' appears to have soured. She moved out of the East End into an unfurnished flat, which she had to help furnish and decorate with her new flatmate, Betty, who does get a name.

It was to be a new chapter in Aileen's life in London.

15

Calling Aileen Home

During the years of World War II the correspondence flowed between Aileen in London and her family in Australia, but not freely. Subject to censorship and the vicissitudes of transportation across oceans in wartime – whether by sea or air – letters could take months to reach their destination, causing frustration at both ends. Helen was the only family member who wrote breezy, albeit rare, letters to her sister without complaint: 'It's nearly a year (!) since I wrote to you properly. What a swine I am'. Nettie, and occasionally Vance, complained that Aileen did not write frequently enough, leaving them in the dark as to how she was faring, who were the people in her life or, indeed, whether she was still alive. Aileen, for her part, spent much of the first page of nearly every letter explaining how many letters she had written and how she hadn't heard from her parents for ages. Sometimes she did apologise for the length of time since she had written last. Cables or wires were the only methods of quick communication and they were reserved for important occasions because they were expensive.

Aileen responded gratefully, however, to the many parcels of provisions Nettie sent her containing items such as tea, dried fruit, nuts, coffee, and, occasionally, cigarettes. She demurred about her parents' extravagance and took offerings from the parcels to the Palmers' Australian acquaintances around London when she made reconnaissance trips to check on them and report back on their welfare. These often-dangerous walks elicited some of Aileen's most vivid accounts of the devastating effects of the bombing, in descriptions that might not have reassured her mother. On a trip to check on journalist, writer and broadcaster Leonora Gregory, who lived in Central London, Aileen described the effects of *the heavy stuff – the land-mines – the type that come down with a parachute attached. People see the white parachute drifting down through the sky, & they rush towards it, thinking there is a parachutist attached to it – but there is a land-mine instead. It is a type of bomb that doesn't penetrate deeply where it falls, but does a terrific amount of damage over a wide area. Houses don't so much cave in as cave out; they look like skeletons blown out of joint, their walls lean out at precarious angles. Leonora's house had been more or less on the edge of a wave or several waves of blasts from various bombs. I wondered whether I would find her place still intact, but she thought once the cleaning up was done it would still be liveable.*

Presents of clothes from well-meaning relatives and friends were not as welcome as food and cigarettes and Aileen would thank the givers with polite notes, but when she was annoyed, as she was in the letter she wrote to Vance after he had urged her to go to the country to write, she could let fly. Esther Levy, an old friend of Nettie's (and someone of whom Aileen was very fond), had knitted her a beret and scarf and she tells Vance: *I never wear head-gear of any kind (except when occasionally I don my tin helmet for a moment if it's raining), I have several scarves, & everyone I've shown the things to says the colours would look awful on me.* She asks her father to tell Nettie to try and discourage such presents.

Through letters, Aileen learnt of the progress of the younger sister she had not seen since they were staying in London with their parents in 1935. Aileen had been in Vienna when Helen sailed back to Australia in January 1936 to take up her scholarship for an arts degree and Diploma of Education at the University of Melbourne. Since then she had graduated with Honours in French and done a stint teaching at Port Fairy in coastal Victoria. While there, she had written some short pieces about life in a small town (a subject after her father's heart) and one story about country school children was published in *M.U.M.*, the university magazine she had edited as a student. Though pleased, Nettie commented on Helen's story in a revealing note in her diary: 'Long argument with V as to where the pressure in it should be placed. She suffers from his restraint'. (Aileen was the daughter Nettie felt was 'essentially a writer' even though she conceded 'she may submerge it for years yet'.) When Australia became involved in the war in the Pacific in 1942, Helen joined the teaching unit of the Women's Auxiliary Australian Air Force (WAAAF), travelling around Australia for her work but still living with Nettie and Vance at their flat at Florida Mansions in St Kilda Road when in Melbourne. The plump schoolgirl with the wide smile had become a self-possessed young woman in uniform whose 'toughness' sometimes 'terrified' Nettie.

Vance and Nettie worked incessantly during the war years, although Vance had to leave his novel writing until more settled times. Among their many commitments, they gave lectures around Australia for the Commonwealth Literary Fund and the university extension board; they wrote articles for literary journals such as Clem Christesen's *Meanjin*; and their pioneering work on ABC Radio was so extensive it has been described as 'heroic'. Among their contributions to radio, Vance wrote a weekly article for *ABC Weekly* and presented a fifteen-minute session every second Sunday called 'Current Books worth Reading', reviewing five books in each programme, covering a vast range of Australian and overseas literature. Nettie took over his *ABC Weekly* column in 1943 when Vance was engaged by the Department of Labour doing war work; she also continued her work as a mentor and critic, editing collections of poems and short stories, writing introductions and doing translations. On the home front she had the responsibility of looking after her mother, who was becoming increasingly frail, and running the household at Ardmore.

Helen wrote to Aileen about Vance's departmental appointment in 1943, in jovial but not altogether complimentary terms: 'Vance is just becoming a sort of glorified Public Servant – i.e. he's got the job in Dept of Labour & Nat. Service, but isn't a civil servant. Though he's begun to speak of "Our Department" and "Our Minister"'. When he left the position in mid-1944 she wrote: 'Vance resigns on Monday from his status as an amateur civil servant. It'll be good to see him getting on to his own work again. Although I think he could have thrown his weight around a bit more where he was; he seemed a bit inclined to look pained and suffer when the red tape got in his hair'. By this time Helen, who was in her late twenties and had never lived independently, was finding it difficult to hold down a demanding job and be the sort of friendly, chatty daughter she was when younger and which her parents still expected her to be: 'I'm almost never home, and when I am I'm inclined to be glum, through nothing but carelessness! N & V told me off about it the other day. You can't tell them that you're not "expansive" because you belong to another generation, although that's the answer!'

Through letters, Aileen also learnt of her mother's declining health from the early 1940s, both from the letters' content and because of the increasing waywardness of Nettie's handwriting. Nettie, in her usual self-deprecating style, played down the seriousness of her illness when writing to her daughter: 'Darling AY,' she wrote in mid 1942, in an almost illegible scrawl, 'Having a holiday forced on me for a week by a funny little illness – just nerves for once, and at first I couldn't speak clearly or write either'. Her 'funny little illness' was the start of recurrent 'spasms' of coronary thrombosis – minor strokes that would leave her speech and writing affected. Undaunted, just two months after that attack she was off on a lecture tour to Brisbane. A year later, after a more serious episode, she did let her guard down in a letter to Aileen: 'As a matter of fact, this illness I've had lately – now much better – made me wish almost for the first time to cable mother-ill-come-home. Of course you wouldn't have done it anyway, so I had no real temptation. And I can get along quite well. But it was one of those vague things – a thrombosis in the head that made it impossible to speak clearly or write clearly, and brought attacks of violent fatigue'. Vance wrote more objectively to his daughter to inform her of Nettie's condition after the 1943 episode: 'She had a pretty bad breakdown about two months ago, which she probably covered up in her letters. It was a small clot, the specialist said, and for a while she couldn't articulate properly, but it's cleared up now and may not occur again if she looks after herself properly'. Helen's version was more flippant: 'As you've probably gathered, Nettie is just getting over what really amounts to a little breakdown. She's got to lay off public work, meeting people, etc. for a while. It was purely a nervous affair: you know the way she accumulates strain of various sorts until she can't cope with it any longer. Actually it hasn't done her any harm – physically, she's had a better rest than she could have had any other way'. A few weeks after these letters, Nettie travelled to Hobart to give a series of Commnwealth Literary Fund lectures.

Aileen's response to her family's accounts of Nettie's illness took the form of sympathising with her as well as (perhaps to assuage twinges of guilt) urging her parents in several letters to take a cottage by the seaside at Dromana or in the hills at Belgrave where Nettie could rest and Vance could get on with his serious writing. She also reiterated that she was planning to come home when the war was over.

The pressure for Aileen to return became more urgent after Nettie's mother died at the end of September 1944 and the Palmers moved to Ardmore, the large, rambling house in the suburb of Kew where Aileen and Helen had stayed with their grandmother whenever Vance and Nettie were out of Melbourne. It was also home to Helen during the time her parents were in England and Spain in 1936. Helen almost immediately wrote her sister a letter: 'I want to ask you please if you'd do something. The move to Ardmore is done, and one of the ideas behind it is to have somewhere for you when you come back. As I've been rather a pig about it, detesting the place for reasons too far back to count, would you let Nettie know that you think the move is a Good Thing, & that you believe Ardmore can be made into a pleasant, liveable place?' The subtext of this letter is clearly Helen's own desire to move out from under her parents' roof; she also felt that it was Aileen's turn to take some responsibility for their ailing mother. For her part, Nettie tentatively told Aileen: 'There'll be room for you to camp in Ardmore & make plans'. Then Vance added his voice at the end of the year: 'Dear old girl, we did hope to see you home this Xmas, but the war still seems to be going on: I'm afraid it won't be over till summer. We are finding what a comfortable house 'Ardmore' can be made into. N[ettie] is fairly well, but she has not quite recovered from her attack of a year ago, and gets tired easily. I suppose we're all getting a bit older. I wonder will you get shocked at our grey hairs when you get back'.

Nettie's health deteriorated further with another attack of coronary thrombosis in the new year, and on 12 February 1945 Helen took the serious step of resorting to a cable telling Aileen it was time to find any means she could to return to Australia. She also sent a letter explaining the severity of Nettie's illness, admitting that she was exaggerating a little, to ease Aileen's path through wartime travel restrictions. Still Aileen prevaricated, committing herself to her return and setting the lengthy process in motion, but remaining highly ambivalent about it.

Aileen's life had become infinitely more interesting since she had climbed out of the rut she had been in at the ambulance station. For one thing, she was following in her parents' footsteps, embarking on radio broadcasts – possibly through Vance's influence. In October 1944 she gave an engaging and personal talk on her time since arriving in England in 1935, including her trip to Vienna and her involvement in the Spanish War. It was broadcast on the BBC and then on the ABC. Helen was full of praise: 'What a spiffing broadcast! Apart from what you said, which was first rate, it's the way you said it. Your voice, albeit it's full of a thousand influences, from Nellie Stewart to Spain, is by far the nicest in the family, & that's saying something; & your style made us all feel amateurs! After that broadcast, the family are almost speechless with admiration for the wandering daughter'. Nettie sent to the ABC for a transcript of the broadcast and everyone was most amused by the stenographer's final mistake (after many) when she misheard the word 'critic': 'You've been listening to Aileen Palmer, daughter of Vance Palmer, Australian novelist and cricketer'. 'Vance', wrote Nettie, 'was swollen with pride'.

Around the end of April 1945, Aileen gave another talk for the BBC, this time about women's resilience during war. She spoke of the work carried out by her ambulance station, which was staffed principally by women aged from twenty to sixty, also of the women in the East End collecting blanket rolls for the daily trudge to the shelter, not knowing what they would find when they went home in the morning. She noted the *good deal of queer sense* in a remark by one of the women: *'One thing about these bombs is, they do take your mind off the war'*. (That had been Aileen's experience in Spain. When she was on her break in London, away from the front where there was plenty to do and no time to think too much, she agonised over the larger picture.) She then spoke of the life the women in France had been living during the occupation, of her mother's friend Jeanne who went around on her bicycle with her shopping basket, *an inconspicuous little woman of fifty-odd*, who was able to smuggle illegal ration books and identity cards to people on the run from the Gestapo. She spoke of the women returning from concentration camps now *with the Allied push into Germany*, one of whom was a young friend of Jeanne's whose 'crime' was sheltering Jewish children who had been forcibly separated from their parents by the Nazis and who was now *like a skeleton, tattooed, her hair quite white.*

The material about France in Aileen's talk was made possible by the invitation she received in mid-April to spend a weekend in Paris, much to her delight. It came about through Vance's friend, Bert 'Doc' Evatt, who was in London as Federal Minister for External Affairs in the Curtin government. On his recommendation, and in her capacity as writer Vance Palmer's daughter, Aileen was included in the ministerial entourage travelling to Paris. Between the obligatory formal functions she was able to make contact with Jeanne Billard, Nettie's friend from the days when she was studying philology in Europe before her marriage. The other extraordinary event that occurred that weekend was Aileen's visit as part of the official party to Picasso's studio where she found him, contrary to his reputation, *extremely amiable.* She reported to Helen: *On being told that he was greatly esteemed for the stand he had taken during the resistance, he said: 'What else could one do? Those who did not resist – c'était des cochons'.*

Aileen had started another of her intermittent diaries at the beginning of 1945. Written in a telegraphic, hectic style that is maddeningly cryptic and scattered with ellipses, she often speaks of her mood as being *elevated*, a kind of shorthand for her heightened emotions. So much was happening in her life. By April she was excited about the progress of the war and *scared crazy* about the unexpected trip to Paris (*no evening dress!*); she was anxious about the pressure to return home; she was busy campaigning for Labour in the coming elections, drinking till closing time in pubs with her friends in the evenings; she was in a demanding job – and she was falling in love again.

'B', Aileen's lover from the 1940 diary, is still mentioned in 1945, but not favourably. On her thirtieth birthday on 6 April, she noted: *For some inexplicable reason I was irrepressibly happy. Till I met B in the evening. Because I was rather more tense and elevated than usual, I couldn't just sit and let it pass when B started telling me what I ought to do. About going home. B of all people...The evening ended badly.* Aileen's new love interest does not even get an initial, but is referred to in the second person simply as 'you': *Today began well. You phoned. That gave to all the rest of the day, this Sunday which I spend so uneventfully at home with an accumulation of chores, a sense of expectancy, promise...*The entries are also dotted with exhortations to herself to be reckless, but then come the doubts: *There's only a month or so left of my current life. And I'm trying to shorten it as much as possible. The lilac by the road...Why not be mad? Why not be reckless while it lasts?* And later: *Perhaps it's better all the same that I'm going (coward...).*

A passage in wavering handwriting in a semi-autobiographical fragment written in the 1970s gave me pointers towards partially solving the mystery of the identity of Aileen's two lovers in London in the 1940s, while at the same time raising new questions. Using the same pseudonyms for her parents and sister as in her novel fragments, 'Pilgrim's Way', but written in the first person, she reflects: *After I came back from Europe, at the end of the war, the shadow of my parents seems to have impinged on my life, and I fell into one breakdown after another.*

As a child I saw Noni's life as drudgery, given in the service of her parents, Blake, and us kids, and didn't want to ever get married. Long afterwards, looking back on my life in Spain, and in London afterwards, I've thought I might have been happy if I'd married Lonya, who was my boss in Spain: but he didn't propose, and it didn't occur to me then, and eventually, I set up house with a woman – a bitchy, most damnable woman I ever knew, the way things turned out, although I've sometimes thought afterwards that it might have been different...

L—D—was in charge of the ambulance station, to which I went soon after the outbreak of war: making up my mind, while I was in the south of France, visiting camps of interned international brigaders, that I wouldn't go back to Australia then, after all, but see out the war in Europe.

Towards the end of the war, there came a cable from Gwen, telling me Noni had been very seriously ill, and urging me to try every means to come home. I wasn't living with L—D—any more then: we parted soon after I left the ambulance station, and went to Australia House, in about '44. There was a very attractive woman there, with whom I very impetuously fell in love.

So I had to tell L—: I had promised I'd tell her, if it ever should happen, but for a long time I did not, though L—was always suspecting me of having fallen in love with the various women I saw.

A photograph of Aileen from 1940 bears a statement on the back: 'I certify that this photograph is a true likeness of Miss Aileen Y. Palmer'. Signed Winifred L. Deller, Aux. Station Officer, L. C. C. Ambulance Service. 5 July 1940. This supports the suggestion that Winifred L. Deller was the L—D— of Aileen's memory and 'B' of the diary, although it does not solve the mystery of the code initial 'B'. From the fragment, it seems also that the 'you' of the 1945 diary was the *very attractive woman* at Australia House with whom Aileen *impetuously fell in love.* Surprisingly, she starts the reflection with the comment that she *might have been happy* if she'd married *Lonya* (Leonard Crome's nickname from his childhood). While she makes it clear in letters of the time and in later semi-autobiographical pieces that she liked and admired Crome in Spain, there is never suggestion of any closer feelings, nor does she seem to have had any contact with him after she left Spain. No diary survives from the period when she was working as his assistant in Teruel, however.

The most striking feature shared by the people whom Aileen loved (those that we know of) is that they were women; but another pattern also emerges: they held a position of seniority over her. Her first 'crushes' as a child were the much older Edith Young and Violet Beasley; she then fell in love with her French and German teachers at PLC. While the young women in the 'Mob' were nearer her own age, they were more established at university, especially the leader Dorothy Adams ('D'), who was a tutor. The nickname 'Twig' that Aileen was given by the Mob indicates her status in the hierarchy of the group. Winifred L. Deller (apparently 'B' of the 1940 and 1945 diaries) was in charge of the ambulance station, and in one entry in the 1940 diary Aileen complains: *B's telephone voice always seems to come from the person of months ago, kindly but remote, gladdening me but throwing me into confusion.* The unnamed woman she fell in love with at Australia House was also a person she looked up to. At one point she writes: *Sometimes I'm seized with a terrible urge to tell you everything – generally as to-night when you are not there. When you are there the talk is so sane and rational that my morbid thoughts could never dare utter themselves. I could* *learn more from you than from anyone else because you, more than anyone I have ever known, are what I would like to be if I could. The world is full of admirable people – that, with all my awareness of my own deficiencies, I would not wish to change into. But you...*The use of the word *morbid* is revealing with its suggestion of melancholy but also its meaning of 'unwholesomeness' when applied to the mind or *thoughts.* It suggests perhaps that Aileen was now thoroughly aware, in a way she had confidently and perhaps naively resisted when at school and university, that her lesbian desires were deemed by society to be sick or unnatural.

Aileen underwent an extensive period of psychoanalysis in the late 1940s following her first breakdown. Her sexuality would almost certainly have been viewed as a problem in that process and it seems that she might have been persuaded to recast her past in heterosexual terms. She did allude to her lesbianism in another semi-autobiographical piece around 1971, writing: *Any lesbian incidents in my life are long in the past.* In the sections of her unpublished novel 'Last Mile from Huesca' that were written after she returned to Australia, however, the person that 'Joan' the narrator lives with in London has become a man called 'Harry'. Harry also appears in sections of the rambling, fragmented collection of semi-autobiographical fiction pieces Aileen wrote in the early 1960s that fall under the general title of 'Pilgrim's Way'. In many ways the stories in which Harry appears follow the details of Aileen's life in the 1940s, with the important difference that, while Joan/Aileen works in an ambulance station in East London, 'B's' replacement Harry is not the head of the station but a factory worker. He is no longer in a position of seniority over his lover and the dynamics of the relationship as well as its gendered aspects seem different from those between 'B' and Aileen. Harry is jealous and demanding but Joan has the upper hand when he begs her to return to him after she leaves. On the other hand, another character, Mark, who also appears in both 'Last Mile' and 'Pilgrim's Way' and who replaces Harry in Joan's affections, is a doctor held in high esteem. He is also married and these two factors make him desirable but unattainable; perhaps the woman at Australia House was out of reach too, at least retrospectively.

In one of the rare sections of 'Pilgrim's Way' written in the first person, the narrator (in a passage that almost parallels the one Aileen writes about L—D— and the woman at Australia House) states: *And in London all sorts were easy to get on with, except Harry, to whom I'd given some rights-of-possession – without exactly setting out the terms on which I might (as I didn't quite foresee then) want to write it off.*

Give gold away and guineas,
But not thy heart away

as Housman said; and I certainly didn't give my heart away to Harry, though I may have slightly pawned it…and so he wanted to get back his assets when I told him I'd given it to someone else.

Then I broke off relations with Harry, but Mark didn't want my heart, particularly, and it's just as well it's in a fair state of preservation, even today…

So where does the reference to possible married happiness with *Lonya* (Leonard Crome) fit in? He was her boss during the latter part of the Spanish War and someone she admired enormously, but her statement that the idea of marriage came to her *long afterwards* and that it hadn't occurred to her at the time indicates that she may have been trying to recast her intimate history as heterosexual. That being the case, even if a diary had survived from the Teruel period it would have been unlikely to reveal cryptic comments about *Lonya* like the ones in the 1940 and 1945 diaries about the women she loved. Sadly, while Aileen was able to recast her past relationships on paper after psychiatric treatment, she does not appear to have had any more relationships in life after her return to Australia in her early thirties.

During Aileen's personally tumultuous month of April 1945, the long war was also nearing its end, at least in Europe. On 28 April Mussolini was executed and on the 30th, Hitler committed suicide in his bunker. Aileen captures the drunken elation of the VE Day celebrations in London on 8 May in her diary, but this is mingled with despair at leaving the woman she loves: *The purplish-white light in Piccadilly on Tuesday, the milling faces – not like daylight but like the floodlit brilliance of a midnight Blitz. Ron charging with the lamp, G saying cheerfully 'Remember Agincourt' and the wedge went forward, H behind me, regrouped…The lights across the lake and the park sown thickly with bodies. The other couples we lost. So I let things happen, do I? Perhaps if*

I hadn't let things slide for a while, it might have been slightly different – but not much. Home on our V-day feet. 'And if one green bottle should accidentally fall…'

And so we burn the debris of the past.

The rest of them I will meet again, of course. One always does meet the same people over and over again, with slight variations. Only you are not just a variation on someone else. You I won't find again anywhere. Unless I come back.

Throughout June and early July Aileen was kept busy *foot-slogging* for the election campaign (*pegging away – excursions into Chinese dens, back alleys*), all the time wondering when she would get notice of her departure date, expected to be around the end of July. Her farewell party was fixed for 14 July at Thora Sinclair-Loutit's flat (Kenneth had by that time fallen in love with another woman and moved on). It was attended by friends including many 'IBers', as her former comrades were known, and *a little elevated from beer-drinking* she was called upon *to make a speech and explain myself. And after that swifter and hazier to my eventual decline on the settee and nada.*

She saw the surprise landslide victory for Clement Attlee's Labour Party over Winston Churchill's Conservatives before eventually sailing on the *Empire Paragon* for Australia on 24 August. The day before she sailed she wrote in her diary: *It's been too pleasant in a way these last few weeks. An unreal life of irresponsible festivity, pursuing all my whims. And yet never having the courage to go straight ahead for what I wanted.*

'Come back, Aileen'…

Might Aileen have had more courage to pursue her desires if she had not been aware that her time left in England was so limited?

On board, she buried herself in books borrowed from the ship's library until the day she stood on deck as the ship passed the Cape St. Vincent lighthouse on the southwestern tip of Portugal and noted: *So I emerge out of the oblivion of reading in which I've been immersed the last few days, watching the sea blue-bright to-day white-flecked, the uneven patterns of foam over the ship's side, and space distance is piling up behind me…distance from you.*

Nettie and Vance had been waiting for months to hear when Aileen would get a passage home, Nettie with some trepidation: 'I feel I want to touch wood, in case after all you find you do not want to come. I want you to feel free to relent, or change your mind. There must be a dozen reasons for you to have a divided mind on the matter. I'm afraid that one strong reason for your return is that I turned turtle a while ago; but don't forget I'm very much better, and that doctor's letter to you is only a tool'. When they received news that Aileen would be sailing in late July or early August, they were both excited but also anxious. Nettie wrote: 'darling old soul. I'm beginning to feel nervous, in case you don't like the antipodes. Helen said the other evening (she was actually home & we were yarning round the fire): "But whaddle [sic] she talk about?"' Vance showed real perception about the difficulties Aileen would face returning to Australia after so many years: 'We hope you won't be disappointed in the set-up here. I know when I came back at the end of 1915, I felt at a loose end for a while. I hadn't been away as long as you in the one stretch, but since the beginning of 1906 I'd been out of touch with any of the people I needed to know and had to begin again in the matter of friends'. The Palmers' friends were also concerned in the months before Aileen's departure, Miles Franklin expressing what many of them felt: 'I hope Aileen gets home pretty soon. These homecomings to both parties are the sweetest thing in life'. Replying to a letter from Nettie when Aileen was actually on her way, Henry Handel Richardson wrote from England: 'So glad to hear you are getting Aileen home. Nine years – can it be possible?'

When the *Empire Paragon* finally sailed into port in Melbourne in October, Aileen saw a little crowd waiting at the docking point and *Dad's brown hat.* Days of talks with her parents followed; old friends of the Palmers dropped in and Helen arrived home a few days later to meet the sister she had not seen since she was a schoolgirl. Aileen was immediately in demand for ABC Radio talks and she started preparing her talk called 'Poets of Liberation' (Cornford, Aragon and Manifold) to be given at CEMA (Council for the Encouragement of Music and the Arts) in mid-November. To her diary she confessed some of her teeming thoughts: *Sorting out my impressions – feel this is after all a foreign country I've got to start learning all over again. Coming home – I'll always be a foreigner.* Her future was also weighing on her mind: *Whether to write – to establish myself as a writer – or whether my writing won't always have that weakness. Better to go immediately into some practical job and forget all that?*

In early December Aileen took some respite from the endless round of people and public commitments and took the train with her sister to the Dandenongs of their childhood. There, she started to let the peace of the Australian bush she loved seep into her tired being: *Sitting on the veranda at Molly Bayne's shack at Mount Evelyn smoking Helen's last 'tailored' cigarette and looking over amber-tipped gum saplings at smoke-blue Donabuang mountains of my youth. A magpie chorus and a few other birds and cicadas gently chirping. Came up yesterday with H – her first real holiday in ages. A real stepping back into the past (dipping the cake in the tea) – all of the bush sounds and colours, suburbs going on and on past the train and then only after Lilydale the sky bright blue as it only is above the grey of gums. Humped our traps from the train, H not quite knowing the way, and then saying, 'We'll try this one', and it was the shack, rose-coloured in front, somehow in its primitive prettiness reminding me of Edith. And the squawking of magpies at the back, sound of chopping wood, golden whistler, the way the rain-water tap turned on and the kerosene lamps…* Yet, unlike Helen, even in those peaceful surroundings Aileen was troubled: *I can't just bask in it all just as contentedly as she can (or appears to) – though – there's a context you can only know when you're working hard in a job and get a break from it. I haven't fitted – yet – into any slot, and till I do there'll always be this uneasiness at the back of my mind.*

The ability to 'fit in' in her home country was to elude her for the rest of her life.

PART III

A Life in Fragments

16

Mourning the Past

Aileen was given an upstairs room at Ardmore as her study, adjacent to the glassed-in balcony where Vance always worked, and was told she was free to write. Nettie's health was much improved since the attack of coronary thrombosis the previous February that had prompted Helen's cable urging her sister to return to Australia. Far from needing looking after, Nettie's main concern was the weakness in her arm that continued to affect her handwriting. She was delighted Aileen was home after so many anxious years and her friends noted how well and happy she looked. Writing to poet Hugh McCrae soon after her daughter's arrival, her tone was unusually ebullient: 'Aileen's a blissful visitant: I can't believe she's here much. She hasn't settled to a job of her own, but so far she has helped Vance – typing a long delayed ms [manuscript] and being much more than a mechanical secretary. If she can continue like that, she may even make me able to organise or mobilise some of my struggling masses of material'.

Of course, the Palmers' friends were all eager to catch a glimpse of the daughter who had been away for nearly a decade and who had been through not one, but two wars during that time. In one of his gossipy letters to his mother, writer Frank Dalby Davison filled her in on his unexpected meeting with Aileen and her parents in the entrance to the New Theatre League soon after her return. He related that she had been an interpreter in the Spanish War 'on the side of the anti-Francoists', told of her war work during the Blitz in London, even that she had been one of the women who 'painted Chamberlain's door red after the Munich business'. 'We are all wondering whether Eileen [sic] will not find Australia rather provincial after being at the centre of struggle for so long', he reported, giving his verdict that he found her 'a very agreeable person; one of those women who combine intelligence and considerable good looks with complete carelessness about dress'. Over the next few months he wrote to his mother of hearing Aileen talk 'on the air' and of attending her 'Poets of Liberation' talk, describing her as 'modest and retiring'.

Helen continued to breeze in and out of Ardmore until she was retired from the WAAAF in late 1946, after which she moved to Sydney to take up a job with a publishing firm. With that she achieved her desire to move out from under her parents' roof and establish herself as an independent adult, and Aileen, having spent years determined to free herself of the all-pervasive parental shadow, took her sister's place as the resident daughter. It was a decision that is hard to comprehend, but looking at Aileen's writings, both during that period and retrospectively, a picture emerges of someone who, after being completely inured to danger for so long, was in a paralysing state of shock.

I don't remember much what I thought about that first year home, except the double separation from Spain and England must have left me somehow numb, and nothing happened then to spark off any ability in me to write, she wrote in later years. What she did embark on was a serious study of Russian, taking Russian I and Russian II in 1946 and '47 as single subjects in the newly formed Russian language and literature course at the University of Melbourne. This was devised and taught by the charming and kind Nina Christesen, Russian wife of *Meanjin* editor Clem Christesen, who had recently moved the journal he started in Brisbane in 1940 to Melbourne. Close friends of Vance and Nettie's, although in fact only four years older than their daughter, Nina and Clem were to become important figures in Aileen's life back in Australia. Aileen passed with Second-class Honours and her study of Russian features in her ASIO file, not surprisingly given her family's reputation as pink-tinged if not 'red' in those early days of the Cold War. She had started to study Russian in earnest on the ship on the way home. Perhaps immersing herself in the language of her political heroes helped her maintain a tenuous connection with her immediate past.

Although Aileen was helping Nettie and Vance in their work rather than settling down to her own writing, several versions of an incomplete and untitled story (some handwritten, some typed) do survive in her papers from the time, probably written in 1947. The characters' names differ in each version, that of the central character being her usual pseudonym 'Joan' and, in one version, 'Kay'. The action takes place at a party in a Melbourne suburb and themes emerge, worked and reworked in the different versions, which illustrate Aileen's own sentiments on returning to Australia.

One concerns her sense of alienation. A typed, well worked-out version of this reads: *World of comfortable, cushioned people, stuffed men! That was how, in the detachment she secretly cherished, she often thought of them since she returned, a stranger – her mind walled off in its little cage of glass through which she saw them all with their outlines blurred, merged in each other, types – as though she were still on the ship and they were just fellow-passengers for an interlude, empty of any active association with past or future.* (The feeling of being in a 'cage of glass' would be echoed in Sylvia Plath's novel *The Bell Jar*, published in 1963, which, like Aileen's writings, is concerned with the madness of the world during war as well as the world of madness.)

All versions of Aileen's manuscript contain an account of the protagonist being asked to describe her experiences abroad, named in early versions as Spain and London. A typed version in which the protagonist is called Kay is less specific to Aileen's life abroad, better written than earlier versions and closer to the fiction she seems to be aspiring to, but still containing the essence of her experience: *She had had her chance to talk; they were eager to listen. They surprised her at first with their eagerness to hear everything. She was a newcomer just back from abroad, even a kind of heroine to some of them. But their notions of things related to an experience they had never visualised except in the crude, black-and-white terms of the newsreels. To their minds, overloaded with secondhand sensations, all she could say was generally disappointing.*

Another theme relates to the notion of people as 'types', types that she had encountered elsewhere, but with the realisation that now there were new types her memory couldn't put labels to: *Sign of old age, perhaps. She was thirty-two. Old enough to find that most of her school contemporaries had settled down into a formal pattern of living that to her seemed more alien and oppressive than any she had known.*

Alas, for the pretty women
Who marry plain men;
They settle down in the suburbs
And never come out again…

But if she had ever spoken these thoughts out loud, people would have said she was jealous; perhaps she was. Aileen had returned to Australia to find that the friends she had known, even some of those from the Mob at university, who had given her the courage to believe in herself and her love for women, had become wives and mothers.

In a relatively sustained piece of autobiography, written in 1961 when she spent several months in a small rehabilitation clinic recovering from a major breakdown, Aileen gave this account of her return to Australia. The style is more factual than the literary piece of 'fiction' she wrote in the 1940s, yet it is still distanced from memoir in its use of the fictional pseudonyms familiar from her writings from this period. Written in several titled sections, it takes the form of an extended letter to *Dear Louise* (Helen, to whom she sent it as she wrote) and echoes the sentiments of the earlier story with remarkable consistency. This is from Part II, entitled 'Idiot's World': *In 1945 I was to all appearances a fairly cheerful person. We have both of us always made a point of showing a cheerful face to the world. It's part of the Blake tradition in which we were brought up. I went to a lot of the lavish parties that abounded at that period, listened with apparent attention to Nora's long accounts of her really very valuable work among the refugees during the war, served the very simple lunches that met Blake's requirements and discussed with him books or politics or sometimes people: but when I look back on that year, it seems I'd hardly begun to tick again since leaving England. Part of me – the inarticulate part of me – was mourning the past from which I had cut adrift, but (outwardly attentive to what went on but inwardly withdrawn) my contacts with people didn't give me the required stimulus for bringing the drama of my past to life.*

Writing in 1961 with the privilege of hindsight, Aileen was able to describe the devastating consequences of the shock and numbness she had felt on her return home:

It's not usually what I've called 'frozen mind' that causes difficulties in one's relations with other people, though. The trouble begins when the unfreeze sets in. Far too late it occurred to me I'd probably made a mistake in settling down to live with Blake and Nora, as though it could be natural in our society for two generations to live under the one roof.

I saw very little of you, it seems to me, during my first couple of years at home. You went interstate a good deal, and then took a permanent job in Sydney. You were in Sydney in early 1948 when my way of going on began to worry Blake and Nora. You got leave from your job and came over promptly, to talk to me seriously, where I was lying out on the back lawn.

And that takes us back to Easter 1948 when Nettie and Vance became disturbed about Aileen's odd behaviour – sitting up all night writing, haranguing people at a party at the flat of the Palmers' friend, historian Brian Fitzpatrick – and called their daughter in Sydney to come over and advise them what to do.

17

In Hospital

Helen arrived from Sydney in the evening of 24 March 1948, just hours after she received the urgent wire from her parents, and procedures were set in motion that would profoundly affect Aileen for the rest of her life. Nettie and Vance had already started contacting doctors they knew through their circle of friends and, with Helen's agreement, it was organised that Aileen would be admitted to the private hospital that had been set up by psychiatrist Dr Reginald Ellery, only a mile or two from the Palmers' house in Kew. Helen accompanied her sister to hospital (*Of course, I didn't go quietly*). In later years, it was Helen whom Aileen blamed for that first incarceration.

Disillusioned with the repressive state asylum system, Dr Reg Ellery had resigned his position as Medical Officer at Mont Park Mental Hospital in 1931 and set up his own private practice in Collins Street in the city. Two years later, he opened Victoria's first private psychopathic hospital in a mansion called Alençon at 24 Mercer Road, Malvern. The Lunacy Department objected to mental patients being treated outside the recognised mental institutions, so the hospital, theoretically, admitted all medical cases. When nearby residents became aware that Alençon's patients were people with psychiatric problems, objections were raised and subterfuge was needed to keep the health authorities at bay and the locals pacified. Sometimes patients had to be hidden when a health inspector came to the front door; their illnesses were often 'euphemised' in the hospital's records; and occasionally staff were obliged to coax escaped patients in night attire back behind the hospital walls. But in spite of calls for its closure, the hospital stayed.

Reg Ellery's chief contributions to psychiatry were behind him by the time the Palmers called on him for help in 1948, but he still had influence over the small twenty-bed hospital, which he had passed on to Dr Guy Reynolds to run as an insulin clinic. Ellery had pioneered this treatment in Australia in the 1930s. Most of the cases he had treated in his hospital were those he diagnosed as schizophrenics, whom he described in his distinctive purple prose as 'those young and sensitive introverts who, like snails, had drawn in their horns at the touch of reality and shrunk into their encasing shells of fantasy'. Insulin coma therapy was one of the 'shock' treatments used in the 1930s, along with the other major somatic treatment innovation, cardiazol therapy, both of which were later superseded by electroconvulsive therapy. All were intended to 'shock' patients out of their disordered state and back into the real world. With insulin coma therapy, patients were injected with insulin (the drug used to treat diabetes), left to fall into a coma, often accompanied by convulsions, and then brought back to consciousness with glucose injections. It is recorded that they did not always regain consciousness. Ellery started with small injections of insulin, but after travelling to Vienna in 1937 to witness firsthand the levels used at the clinic run by the treatment's inventor Dr Manfred Sakel, he likened his tentative early attempts to 'toothpicks'. He wrote in his autobiography that at the Vienna clinic 'the schizophrenic rocks were blasted out with sticks of gelignite'.

Whether Aileen was diagnosed as 'schizophrenic' is not known, but she seems to have fitted the hospital's requirements for treatment and after her admission to Alençon in March of 1948, just before her thirty-third birthday, the young woman who had spent nearly a decade in European war zones was subjected to the 'gelignite' of insulin–glucose therapy. So intensive was the treatment in the early days of her incarceration, none of her family were allowed to visit her. During that time Helen returned briefly to Sydney to organise work and home arrangements in preparation for spending the next few months in Melbourne. Nettie described her to her brother Esmonde as 'Aileen's "buffer" against the world, private & public: wonderful'. She and Vance felt like helpless onlookers who could do nothing and she wrote that sometimes Vance felt like quoting the line from Banjo Paterson: 'A spectator's legs were broken – just from merely looking on'.

After a few weeks, when Aileen's response to insulin had not satisfied her doctors, electroconvulsive therapy, then in its infancy and administered without sedatives or muscle relaxants, was tried. Electrodes were attached to the scalp and an electric current strong enough to produce convulsions and short-term coma was passed through the brain. Restraints were used to prevent patients injuring themselves during the convulsions and they awoke confused and disorientated, often distraught at the short-term memory loss the treatment caused. Years later and in a different institution, Aileen wrote to her doctor to implore him not to give her any more ECT because of her *fear of losing my effective self (the self that has never been really effective, but has shown some evidence of being, this last year or two, particularly in writing, mainly poetry) if ECT treatment is continued...Most people have sometimes visions, images, of their awareness, usually relegated to the unconscious. ECT (in my experience) tends to wipe out memory, both of the real and of the imagined. The imagining can (given time) always be imagined again if desired, but the associated wiping out of awareness I still fear.*

It seems incredible today that a young, highly intelligent woman who had suffered a short-term change to her behaviour (though no doubt worrying and confusing to those around her) could be subjected to nearly three months of such extreme treatment. But Aileen's breakdown occurred during the period of intense psychiatric experimentation that had burgeoned in the decades after shell-shocked soldiers returned from the battlefields of World War I. Even though what had been previously thought to be a female malady (hysteria) had undergone revision to encompass male war trauma, women still continued to be singled out for deviations from what was considered to be within the 'normal' range of feminine behaviour. Aileen's drinking and aggressive outbursts before her hospitalisation, her cropped hair and lack of interest in her clothes and appearance, her lack of interest in the opposite sex, even her intellectual prowess would have all been negative factors considered in her diagnosis. And she was not alone.

While Aileen was undergoing intense treatment in suburban Melbourne, across the Tasman another young writer was incarcerated at the inaptly named Sunnyside Mental Hospital on the outskirts of Christchurch. Shy and socially awkward, Janet Frame had been diagnosed some time earlier with schizophrenia and subjected to a similar range of psychiatric treatments. She described her reactions to electroconvulsive therapy in a letter smuggled out of Sunnyside: 'I dreamed waking and sleeping dreams more terrible than any I dreamed before'. After one application of ECT, she smashed a window with her fist: 'I cannot remember why, maybe as an outlet for some strange feeling which had no other means of escaping'. Because of what her hospital notes described as a 'strong resentment' to electroconvulsive therapy, Janet Frame was later put on a prolonged course of insulin shock therapy, which left her drowsy and 'mentally numb'. Four years later, she narrowly avoided being given a pre-frontal leucotomy after the hospital superintendent read in the newspaper that she had been awarded the Hubert Church literary award for her first volume of short stories. When she eventually visited a specialist in London in the late 1950s she was told she had never suffered from schizophrenia.

Towards the end of the horror year of 1948, Nettie, who was working on a biography of the late Henry Handel Richardson, received a letter from Olga Roncoroni, H. H. R.'s faithful secretary/companion who had for decades laid a row of freshly sharpened pencils on her desk each morning. Olga related *her* experience of being 'incarcerated' in the psychiatric ward of the County Hospital near her home in East Sussex for nine and a half weeks after a breakdown at the end of July: 'I was first given Insulin Shock Treatment which made me feel worse than before. What finally pulled me out of the depths was eleven days of continuous Narcosis, which lessened the terrible nervous tension that had become unbearable. But, as a treatment, it is no joke, believe me! The nearest approach to it is the type of nightmare where one is trying to do something which *must* be done, but finds one's body is quite incapable of movement. However, it is over now'.

Although the treatments being administered to Aileen were painful and disorientating, they did offer the promise that they would fix her problems and enable her to leave hospital. It seems that almost the worst aspect of her incarceration for her (or at least what she admitted to in her writing) was the sheer monotony of her daily life. Her preferred artificial stimulants – alcohol and benzedrines – were forbidden and they were even cutting down her cigarettes. She was given sedatives to help her sleep, but the early dinner time and short visiting hours still made for long nights when she paced her room restlessly, pathetically grateful if the night nurse allowed her to help prepare the bread and butter trays and lay out the cups for breakfast. Gradually, every available surface in Aileen's room was covered with piles of novels brought in by visitors and loose sheets of poems she either asked for or which were offered her, and she would ask the night nurse to read poems to her as she took her temperature. Two that survive in her papers are written in pencil in Vance's minuscule hand: one is a John Manifold poem, the other a poem called 'Invictus' by nineteenth-century English poet William Ernest Henley, which begins:

Out of the night that covers me
Black as the pit from pole to pole
I thank whatever gods there be
For my unconquerable soul

Vance may have thought the last lines would offer his daughter some reassurance:

I am the master of my Fate
I am the Captain of my Soul

At the bottom of the sheet she has noted: 'written by Vance from memory for Aileen. 1948'.

Aileen wrote poetry herself while she was in Alençon Private Hospital, a place she referred to as *jail*. She recalled her experience there in a four-page piece of prose entitled 'My Apprenticeship', written in the 1960s, with '1948 (recollected)' pencilled at the top of the first page. A sonnet later published as 'In Hospital' is recorded here and she notes: *That I wrote, crying, to ease my mind, while I was there, in jail, as I felt, but having to accept jail, as better people had been in jail and had found ways of using their time to some purpose.* Referencing Baudelaire's 'Le Voyage' (1861) and Rimbaud's 'Le Bateau Ivre' (1871), Aileen's poem 'In Hospital' alludes to her fear but is also a plea for strength:

There are more peaceful places – ships perhaps,
whose timbers are well built to take the strain
of dashing winds and waves that wash like rain
on crowded decks and bulwarks…You can see
If now I think of ships it is that here
they leap into my mind when, restless still
(though knowing while I have to stay I will
no storm could break me now) I sometimes fear

How ships on other oceans madly dance
like Baudelaire's hull, tossed on a monstrous sea,
boundless, he thought, or Rimbaud, leaving France –
as though his drunken ship could travel free

Of Europe's ancient fetters. Let me think
of some frail ships no storm can break nor sink…

18

Twentieth Century Pilgrim

Less than two weeks after Aileen was forcibly escorted to hospital she began writing an extraordinary manuscript she called '20th Century Pilgrim'. *This may be the title*, she writes at the beginning – *it will do for now. And this is a sort of allegory – if you want to call it that – only most of it really happened, to some people, somewhere, in the 20th century. And a lot of it might just as likely happen to most of you reading it.* The manuscript ranges from descriptions of her daily life among the Magicians (hospital doctors) and Serfs (nurses) to convoluted discussions of Fossils, Owls and Dogs, to the state of the 'Intelligentsia' in a postwar world, to a debunking of 'pseudo-Shelley' English poet Stephen Spender, whom she met when she was in Spain. *I'm wandering anywhere in the 20th century that Pilgrim's been*, she tells the reader. Pilgrim is the narrator of the piece, but Aileen often lapses into first person, while in chatty parentheses she addresses the reader as 'you'. The sixty or so handwritten pages that survive – peppered with crossings-out and insertions – are only a part of the manuscript. Chapter headings range from 'Prelude' to 'Chapter 16', but there are many gaps and non-consecutive pages. A dense, cryptic, repetitive and often confusing document, '20th Century Pilgrim' is also fascinating – full of anger, sardonic humour and painful self-reflection. The further I went into exploring and decoding what appeared at first to be largely delusional raving, the more 'sense' I found in this richly allusive text.

The narrator Pilgrim is a person on a journey through the twentieth century, an *ugly century* in which conflicts that have occurred on a worldwide scale have created displacement and disillusionment among its people. She is on a kind of mission, as the term Pilgrim suggests, but, as a twentieth-century pilgrim, she is not on a religious journey but rather one in which she seeks, through writing and political action, to play her part in creating a world of peace and social equality despite adversity. The name Pilgrim puns on lines from Chaucer's *Canterbury Tales*, two that Aileen was fond of (mis)quoting throughout her writing life: *Then longen folk to go on pilgrimages,/ And palmers for to seek strange straundes.* She regarded her somewhat nomadic Palmer parents to be voyagers through life and, as we know, in later autobiographical novel fragments the family name becomes Pilgrim.

The central theme of the manuscript concerns the position (and composition) of the intelligentsia post–World War II, post–atomic bomb, now being gripped by the beginnings of the Cold War. Pilgrim is no longer able to read newspapers, encoded here as the *Poison*. The university she attended becomes the *Founts of Poison*, though she qualifies the term: *Yes, it doesn't have to be Poison you drink up there. And they don't all dish out Poison, the people who work there. They mostly do, though – the way they just keep drinking each other's same kind of Poison year after year, and the Poison of long-dead people...They just live in that world, if they work in it, drinking just about only Poison and nothing else. They don't grow up there but in the end become fossils. (That's what Rimbaud said, anyway.)* The reference to Rimbaud comes from his 1871 letter to Paul Demeny, part of his *Lettres du Voyant*, in which he envisions a world where poets will find a universal language 'of the soul for the soul' that will discover the unknown. These he contrasts to the 'academician – deader than the fossils'.

Pilgrim goes over the events of the party she went to where her behaviour was one of the reasons, she feels, that she ended up at what she calls *the Retreat*. This is the party that was held at the flat of historian Brian Fitzpatrick and his wife Dorothy, which Nettie also attended, the night before she and Vance wired Helen to come to Melbourne urgently. It is fascinating to compare Nettie's account, as 'a spectator', of Aileen's 'irresponsible' and bewildering behaviour at the party with Aileen's insider account and to observe how closely they correspond, except that from Aileen's point of view, her behaviour was entirely reasonable.

In the allegorical text, the party is described as being at *the flat of Two Nice People…where: Plenty to Drink was the motto at every party* (Brian Fitzpatrick was a well-known *bon vivant*). Nettie wrote to her brother Esmonde that Aileen 'was pretty unsteady & began chattering in a fatigued yet "enlightened" way, telling people how to make their lives go – asking a former poet if he was writing now, & so on'. Pilgrim says that during the evening she *earbashed just about everyone*; firstly, the *Might-have-been Could-be Poet*, then she *thought she saw a Fossil, a could-be, soon-to-be Fossil, a Fossil holding forth (the way they so often do) to two real people…and she probably started to tell him why he was like it and getting more like it each day.* The *Owl*, who she describes as *one of these people who puns in Latin (and the more so the more he is sozzled)* was another recipient of her earbashing that night until her mother *Brilliant*, who was also there and who *was really frightened to hear her own daughter earbashing*, urged her to go home with her.

Nettie said that the worst moment for her that night 'was when she [Aileen] was with a group, & said suddenly to one man, "Excuse me, er…what is your name?" "Partridge". Aileen half turned aside, & burst into laughter, feeling (I suppose) she had a right to ask such a [illegible] question'. An explanation for Aileen's rudeness to the *Owl*, Professor Percy Partridge from the History department at the University of Melbourne, can be found in a 1947 issue of *Meanjin* in which he wrote a critical review of M. Barnard Eldershaw's new novel, *Tomorrow and Tomorrow*, which Aileen described as *a 20th Century epic.* In it, Partridge takes the authors (Marjorie Barnard and Flora Eldershaw) to task for sharing 'the pessimism of many of the contemporary intellectual champions of the left in believing that capitalist society is in decay, destroyed by conflict and competition, its culture, institutions and values alien to the life of the masses'. This is precisely Aileen's point of view and one of the themes of '20th Century Pilgrim'.

Pilgrim later discourses on a figure she calls the *Dog…one rather sad dog much nearer home, who controls (or tries to) a semi-open space, though he lets all sorts of Owls and other strange birds just litter it up.* Pilgrim turns to discussing him because this 'dog' has just rejected a poem by her sister *Sensible* as he does not want to print poems about the war and her sister's begins: *Barbed-wire and gun-sites guard our beaches now* (in fact, an unpublished poem by Helen called 'Caloundra in War-time'). The Dog is undoubtedly *Meanjin* editor Clem Christesen, famous not only for his astute eye for a good writer but also for his irascible temper and general cantankerousness, which Aileen alludes to: *The Dog has fought hard for that Semi-Open Space, don't let's forget that, though you get a bit sick of it sometimes, if you listen a bit too much to the Dog and his troubles, when he's just in the whining mood. (He looks better in other moods.)*

Pilgrim regards the journal, which Christesen began as the small quarterly publication *Meanjin Papers* in Brisbane in 1940, to be a 'Semi-Open Space' for the expression of literary and political ideas, in contrast with the 'Poison' of the newspapers. He had brought the journal to Melbourne in 1945 in a bid to guarantee its survival after receiving an offer from the University of Melbourne to support and house it, an arrangement that was never properly established legally, causing logistical and financial problems that continue to plague it into the twenty-first century. As we know, his wife Nina was appointed foundation lecturer in Russian at the university. The insecure relationship with the university may well have led Christesen to publish more academic articles than he might otherwise have done, but he was also, like many non-graduates, apparently over-impressed with academia. Aileen writes: *I never know whether he goes round digging up Fossils, or whether they just happen to throw their (Bones) at him; but he does like living up there among the Fossils, so he's just about bound to run into them everywhere, whenever he moves, – and he does like Ready-Chewed Bones.*

'Ready-Chewed Bones' included articles reprinted from overseas journals, and the one Pilgrim took most umbrage against was an article Christesen had reprinted in *Meanjin*, in 1945, from the English journal *Horizon*. Aileen, in a rare instance, actually names both title and author: *'The Intelligentsia'. Chewed up and spewed by a Master-Poisoner, one Arthur Koestler, who's living in England now. Filled up a whole good acre of his precious Semi-Open Space, all Poison, the wickedest kind. And that got the Dog a bad name, if anything did.* In it, Koestler, a former communist whose anti-communist novel *Darkness at Noon* had been published in 1940, outlines his thesis, in the most inflammatory language, on the decay into irrelevance of Western intelligentsia after the collapse of 'the revolutionary movement' and its descent into neurosis.

Koestler's article caused ripples in Australia when it was first published in 1945. Kurt Baier from the Philosophy department at the university had offered a rebuttal in *New Masses* which Christesen reprinted in a subsequent issue of *Meanjin*, and a fierce rejoinder from Vance and Nettie's old friend and Aileen's mentor Katharine Susannah Prichard in the same issue was titled 'Koestler, the Irresponsible'. The article was discussed by Melbourne groups such as Realist Writers, to which Aileen belonged. Deirdre Moore, one of its members, relates in her memoirs the impact Koestler, one of the severest critics of Socialist Realism, had on the group and the heated discussions that ensued. Moore also relates how Aileen Palmer herself contributed to the determination of these young activists to resist oppression by bringing with her 'wonderful Louis Aragon and [Paul] Éluard poems' when she returned from Europe in 1945, as well as introducing the Melbourne scene to *Belles Lettres*, the organ of French left-wing intellectual writers, founded by Aragon and Éluard, and edited and promoted during the war by Jean-Paul Sartre and Simone de Beauvoir.

Tracking down Koestler's article in *Meanjin* helped me to make sense of the passion with which Aileen disavowed the term 'intelligentsia' as applied to herself. At one point in '20th Century Pilgrim' she reacts vehemently to a nurse who refers to her as one of the intelligentsia: *That word 'intelligentsia'!...But Pilgrim didn't fall in a swoon on the floor or fly at the Serf's throat as she might have done a couple of weeks before or even dealt her out a quarter of an hour's earbashing, because all that that word conveyed to Pilgrim just then (Pilgrim still attaches too much importance to words) wouldn't have meant very much at all to the Night Serf.* After Aileen asked the nurse if she called her that because she scribbled all the time or because she wore glasses, even in bed, she was told laughingly: *'It was because of the way you speak, of course'.*

Pilgrim's dilemma about conservative academic 'fossils' and those she called real writers and poets reflects Aileen's ambivalence towards the institution that she admits fostered her own intellect. Her attitudes had changed since her experiences in Europe, where she learnt from political poets like Cornford and Aragon that writers must speak for what she called the *Ordinary People.* Aileen's parents were not academics, although Nettie had a Master of Arts degree, and neither were most of the writers from their intellectual circle. The university English department had always been dominated by academics educated in England who taught across a range of subject areas, covering Anglo–Saxon connections in the Norse sagas and the likes of *Beowulf* as well as modern poets from Hopkins to Spender. Henry Handel Richardson and Christopher Brennan made it into the fourth-year Honours course, but there was no Australian literature course. It was up to guest lecturers like Vance and Nettie, funded by the Commonwealth Literary Fund (regarded as left-wing politically), to inject some Australian content from time to time, the importance of which had been deeply ingrained in Aileen since childhood.

Deciphering at least some of the layers of '20th Century Pilgrim' allows us a glimpse of the complex tensions and pressures that contributed to the 'breakdown' that Aileen experienced in 1948. Given the mind-numbing experience of the 'shock' treatments she was subjected to in her first weeks in hospital, it is extraordinary that she had the capacity to write it at all and the manuscript offers a rare opportunity to witness the writing of someone who has just undergone a psychotic episode, the nature of which is supposedly 'unspeakable'. Writers who have attempted to write their stories of 'madness' speak of experiences that cannot be constrained by conventional linear narrative, but must be made comprehensible through images or similes and which can only be described through metaphor and allegory. '20th Century Pilgrim' is a rich example of this form of writing.

19

Submerged Resentment

Two and a half months after her admission to hospital, Aileen went home to Ardmore into the care of her father and Helen. Surprisingly, her mother was not there to welcome her. Just a day or so before, Nettie had left by train to Sydney and then Tree Tops, the house in Caloundra to which she and Vance usually adjourned during the winter months.

Why was she not there after the ordeal Aileen had been through? It is true that Nettie had not been well, having suffered another of the 'spasms' that had afflicted her for several years. When preparing her journal *Fourteen Years* for publication by Meanjin Press a few months earlier, she had told Clem Christesen: 'Vance is much more hopeful about my book than I am. Much as I want to finish it, I am often limp and useless...Vance has had to help me immeasurably'. She was also working on her biography of Henry Handel Richardson and, no doubt, would have been able to concentrate on writing it in Caloundra more easily than at home. It seems probable that Vance and Helen conspired to keep the more highly strung Nettie away from Ardmore during Aileen's convalescence, possibly for everyone's peace of mind. Helen also obliged by taking over the care of her mother's Aunt Ina, who had become very frail.

Nettie's diary for 1948, which might have offered some insight into her feelings, is one of the few diaries missing from the papers held by the National Library. (It was still at Ardmore, however, when Aileen was looking after Nettie in her final illness in 1964 and she read it, noting that it *brought home to me the kind of worry people had on my account.*) In the absence of Nettie's own words, it might be speculated that one of the reasons for her inability to cope with Aileen's mental illness was shame; Aileen's drinking and outbursts would have offended the Higgins-family puritanism that was deeply ingrained in Nettie. She and Vance also held positions of respect in Melbourne intellectual circles, and have been referred to as 'inspirational tribal elders'. Nettie was clearly very disturbed by Aileen's behaviour at Brian Fitzpatrick's party in front of people from their circle of friends. She wrote to her brother apologetically about Aileen's attack on Professor Partridge, who was a friend of his, worried that he would hear about it from others. In the same letter she asked Esmonde to tell as few people as possible about Aileen's illness, offering him her understanding of the situation: 'It's clearly a case of deferred shock, very long deferred. When Aileen chose a life of action instead of a life of study, she tore herself up'. To friends such as poet and editor Bertram Higgins, and bush poet R. H. Long, she gave her reason for 'leaving Vance and the girls at home' as exhaustion after several years of looking after elderly relatives.

Inevitably, though, the news spread through the literary network and friends sent their condolences. Several gave their own views on the reasons for Aileen's breakdown as they sent their expressions of sympathy. Marjorie Barnard in Sydney, like Nettie, blamed it on war trauma: 'Poor child, a "crash" was probably the only way out from an intolerable burden – the cry for help that brought help'. Marjorie recalled her own shock at seeing a girl jump in front of a train at Wynyard station: 'for weeks afterward I'd wake three or four times a night to the inevitable rush of the train & it felt as if there was a raw track scored across my mind. I thought then of Aileen – though I did not know she was ill. I thought one incident can play such quiet havoc with my nerves what must it be for a girl like Aileen with a mind clearer and more finely drawn than mine, perceptions therefore sharper, realization fuller, to take upon her nerves all the shocks & ravagement just of the Spanish War & then the Blitz. I had a glimpse of what courage meant & the price of courage in strain'.

From Western Australia, Katharine Susannah Prichard wrote to Nettie about the young woman she had known since birth, showing her concern for all the family: 'Aileen…I am most concerned about. Have the greatest admiration for her, & a very deep affection. Feel sure that she will weather any storm with the hardihood she has always shown. But for you, & Vance, & Helen, I understand how dreadful this, being blown out of her course, must have been'.

Gossip was not entirely allayed either. Frank Dalby Davison wrote to his mother that Vance had confided in him that he had 'a brother whose nervous system was not equal to the strain of life, and he had to have institutional treatment; and it is a blow to Vance that it should have cropped up in his daughter'. He also wrote: 'The hard part for Nettie is that Aileen has some submerged resentment against her, and it came to the surface during her sickness; that explains Nettie's absence from home when Aileen came out of hospital'.

Enter the other treatment Aileen was subjected to after her breakdown: psychoanalysis.

In 1940, through the Victorian International Refugee Emergency Committee, Nettie had started teaching English to some of the refugees who were then pouring into Australia from Europe. Among her students was a small, plump, lively woman from Hungary. Describing herself as 'a reluctant immigrant', psychiatrist Dr Clara Lazar Geroe had come to Australia with her husband and young child through the sponsorship of a group of Australian medical professionals that included Dr Reginald Ellery, director of Alençon Private Hospital and friend of the Palmers. Dr Geroe had trained as a doctor in Hungary and then became a fully qualified analyst. During her training she became interested in the new field of child analysis and had close contact with Anna Freud and her group in Vienna. Clara was part of the vibrant psychoanalytic community in Hungary in the 1930s that was shaped by Sándor Ferenczi, whose psychoanalytic technique laid emphasis on child therapy and the early mother–child relationship. Historian Joy Damousi writes that 'Ferenczi also shifted analysis away from the Oedipus complex in favour of the separation of mother and child, and linked infantile sexuality to that of the mother–infant relationship', which gives us perhaps a clue as to why analysis may have brought out 'submerged resentment' by Aileen against her mother.

Nettie was fascinated by Clara Geroe, who she noted in her diary was 'a very high Freudian of international qualifications', and there are frequent mentions of lunching with Dr Geroe and inviting her home for coffee. She also visited the Geroes' flat, noting: 'Balkan embroideries & Freudian ideas'. The Melbourne Institute for Psychoanalysis was established in October 1940, with Dr Geroe appointed as the analyst, and its opening did not pass unnoticed in medical circles. Initially, her qualifications were queried and her status as an unregistered alien practising psychoanalysis questioned. Day to day, Clara was also frustrated by the restrictions placed on refugees' movements between suburbs, Nettie reporting in her diary: 'Agitated by stringency of police when she makes a slight blunder. "You say you're doctor, can't you read the rules!" Says it's plain hatred of the intellectual'.

When Dr Geroe starting practising as an analyst she worked with private patients; she also taught therapists who themselves had to undertake analysis as part of their training. The room in which she practised at the institute's headquarters on Collins Street was dominated by a couch covered with a brightly patterned Persian rug and embroidered cushions – an aesthetic reminiscent of Nettie's description of the Geroe flat. Clara would sit behind the couch where the patient lay, stitching a petit-point tapestry. One trainee therapist recalled that she would stitch the complex central motif when the talk from the couch was tedious and switch to the neutral-coloured background when 'the plot thickened'.

One of the first to undergo training as a lay analyst was Janet Nield, a friend of Nettie's who ran a progressive school called Koornong in Warrandyte with her husband. In 1944, Nettie had written enthusiastically to Aileen in London about Janet Nield's psychoanalysis: 'She looks so alert and she's so free from all personal worries and preoccupations that she's younger and more attractive and at the same time more intellectually interesting. Aileen, am I too old to be made over again and made different? What I have wanted ever since I can remember is some sort of regime to make me save time for the things I really want to do. When I sit down to work, the table always gets littered with all sorts of inconsequential things – one job, one person, one interest, reminding me of another. If only I could determine always to finish one thing before beginning another. I'd be sounder in all I call my nerves if I could do that. To think I ever tried to bring up children with my own feckless ways!' Aileen recognised how alike she and Nettie were, not in their 'good qualities' but 'weaknesses' and years later wrote to Katharine Susannah Prichard that it irritated her: *We have both, in different ways, led very disciplined lives at one time or another, and yet find self-discipline extremely hard: we have scattered minds, with farflung contacts and interests, and find construction on any scale very hard.*

Tacked on to the end of Aileen's '20th Century Pilgrim' manuscript are some pages of a letter, unfortunately without the first page. It seems, though it is not stated in the remaining pages for whom the letter is intended, that Aileen might have been writing to Dr Clara Geroe from hospital. In the letter she says she had been meaning to ask *the medical authorities (you, Dr* [Guy] *Reynolds, or the people who run this hospital)* if she could go home on the weekends as there was no treatment given on those days: *I had, off & on, intended to ask you this when I saw you next, but because there was so much left untold in the story I told you this morning (and that seemed worth your knowing) that I clean forgot to ask you about 'week-ends off'.* If left to her own devices during those weekend days, she writes: *I'm likely to be haunted by the person I was telling you about this morning. It's not because of anything I did or didn't do for her – though whether I could have done anything besides what I did does worry me sometimes, though I'm in no position to judge.* Pressing her point, she writes that she is inclined to think *that anything encouraging just now too much brooding on that particular episode I related part of to you this morning may be apt to delay my return to normal life.*

The letter is signed formally *Yours sincerely, Aileen Palmer.* It does not seem that Aileen's request for weekend leave was granted, but the content of the letter raises intriguing questions. The person to whom she is writing is a 'medical authority', and Aileen is confiding the kind of personal material that would be told to a counsellor or analyst, which suggests it may well have been Dr Geroe. If so, it would appear that she was undergoing psychoanalysis in the hospital at the same time as she was receiving psychiatric treatments of insulin-glucose and electroconvulsive therapy, which, according to a psychoanalyst from the time, were not usually combined. Of course, the most intriguing question of all is: who was the person she brooded over and was haunted by? Apart from the fact it was a woman, we have no idea.

20

Psychoanalysis

Letters flowed back and forth between Vance in Melbourne and Nettie in Caloundra after Aileen was released from hospital in early June 1948. Very soon after her release, Vance reported that Helen had been offered 'another small job by Dr Gero [sic] – typing private notes'. He warns Nettie: 'Don't refer to it in Aileen's hearing: Dr G. doesn't want her to know'. This supports the suggestion that Aileen had started seeing Dr Geroe while still in hospital. And what today might seem an unethical lack of confidentiality on the part of the psychoanalyst was then obviously not considered an issue, except for the concern that Aileen might find out and be disturbed by it. Indeed, over a year later, when Aileen was still having analysis, Vance reported to Nettie who was giving lectures in Tasmania: 'Helen was telling me about her visit to Gero, which seems to have been very satisfactory. Gero really does believe Aileen is making a good fight of it & as she knows a good deal more than anyone of what goes on inside A[ileen] we won't have to take too much notice of her apparent lack of responsibility'. Aileen's illness was very much a family affair. At thirty-three she was caught, not only in the loving family web she had tried to escape, but also in the close-knit network of Melbourne's artistic and intellectual community.

Vance sends optimistic reports to Nettie every few days throughout June and July about Aileen's behaviour: 'Everything is going swimmingly here'; 'A[ileen] surprisingly forthcoming, more so than she used to be. It's hard to remember that we were so worried about her a few weeks ago'; 'It's marvellous really how serene and placid she is'; 'she's very nice in the house and is taking her Russian seriously'; 'it's curious, by the way, the little interest Aileen shows in current politics now, though I suppose she hasn't changed any of her fundamental beliefs'. Nettie replies gratefully: 'I want to thank you solemnly, dear, for writing to me so regularly in these important days: if you didn't, I'd come home, and perhaps you know that! I'm just the opposite of Helen with her threat of "I'll leave home", if we say something she can't bear: but you've made me feel it's a good thing I came, absented myself, left you three together'. She does respond tensely, however, when Vance makes the mistake of saying Aileen was sitting too long at the typewriter and smoking too much: 'Can't help being a little frightened, though, when I hear she's still over-smoking & sitting to type in a fuggy room. Surely that's like walking hard on a lame leg. Can these doctors not minister to a <u>mind</u> diseased? If she had typhoid, they'd regulate her diet. But it's all dark to me; & I'll shut up'.

A thread that winds through Vance's letters to his wife suggests a shared anxiety about a subject that is never named or confronted directly, but which was probably of concern in Aileen's psychoanalysis; that is, her sexuality. The name 'Flora' occurs in nearly every letter: Aileen goes to 'Hamlet' with Flora; Aileen helps Flora shift to new lodgings. The comments also suggest that Aileen's preoccupation with Flora was part of her odd behaviour in the lead up to her breakdown. Vance says several times that Aileen 'is seeing a good deal' of Flora, always with a rider: 'but I don't think Flora has been overwhelmed by her' or 'but not with the same feverish compulsion behind her visits' or 'she doesn't seem as feverish about it as before'. In one letter he adds: 'I don't know Flora's point-of-view, nor does Helen'. The situation was obviously a topic of discussion between all three Palmer guardians.

The 'Flora' who is referred to is Flora Eldershaw, writing collaborator of Marjorie Barnard (M. Barnard Eldershaw), former headmistress of PLC in Sydney and a highly respected member of the literary community. She had served on the Commonwealth Literary Fund Advisory Board since 1939, of which Vance was chairman in 1948. The Palmers got to know her better after she moved from Sydney to Melbourne in 1942: 'Flora to dinner in the evening. She grows more satisfying as time goes on: there is something stimulating and yet restful about her. She draws on such reserves of inspired commonsense'. Aileen's 'feverish' attention towards her would have been seen by the Palmers as most inappropriate, especially as Flora's health was poor, but perhaps their anxiety was heightened too by the feedback they were getting from Dr Geroe's psychoanalysis.

Ironically, although I am privy to Aileen's predilection for women from an early age and more aware of her relationships with women in London than Nettie and Vance would have been, I would suggest that Aileen's feelings for the kind and intelligent Flora Eldershaw were more like the reverence she felt for other senior women writers in her life like Katharine Susannah Prichard than a romantic 'crush'. And it doesn't seem that Flora was 'overwhelmed' by Aileen or that she resented her attention. In fact, Flora had written a note to Nettie (barely a week before the breakdown) that might hold the key to Aileen's interest in her. Responding to reading Nettie's manuscript of her edited journal, 'Fourteen Years', which was eventually published in late 1948, Flora had praised the manuscript generously, beginning: 'It is lovely, Nettie, and so like you yourself. It is so rich and full and varied, moving so easily in so many worlds, not only geographically, but in literature, and art, and natural scene, and political movement, and above all, in people'. Later in the note she comments: 'I will ask Aileen to pick the ms [manuscript] up and take it home one evening. She looks in on me quite often these days & I am so glad to have got to know her. I found her quite unapproachable until she read T&T&T, which led her to take some interest in its (part) writer'. Aileen was very interested in the M. Barnard Eldershaw novel, *Tomorrow and Tomorrow [and Tomorrow]*, which was published in a censored version in 1947 because of its politics, and, as we know, considered it the epic novel of the twentieth century. She briefly mentions it in a fragment from her 1960s writings: *Towards the end of 1947, I read Fleur's* [Flora's] *novel, the Australian work that has had the most impact on me, and that set me both thinking and writing more about Australia and my own past.* She then ruefully observes: *Though this may all have been what Noni* [Nettie] *would have wanted me to do, the way I behaved then didn't suit her at all.* So Aileen's 'feverishness' to spend time with Flora may well have had more to do with the way the novel revived her desire to write than any inappropriate passion.

The friendship between Aileen and the woman who was eighteen years her senior mellowed into one of mutual support. Flora, who had financial as well as health problems, stayed at Ardmore in 1953 while Nettie and Vance were in Caloundra. As a help with her rent she sublet her flat to Glen Mills Fox, Aileen's friend in London who had married communist journalist Len Fox, co-author of Nettie Palmer's pamphlet *Australians in Spain*. (I said it was a small community.) At Ardmore, Aileen chopped wood, mowed and ironed while Flora made lemon marmalade and encouraged Aileen to go to Fellowship of Australian Writers meetings with her. After suffering a distressing bout of illness while she was there, Flora wrote to Nettie: 'Your darling daughter was the soul of goodness & responsibility, bless her'. After Flora died three years later in September 1956, Aileen published a tribute to her in *Overland*. Concentrating on the novels of M. Barnard Eldershaw, she described *Tomorrow and Tomorrow* as 'a penetrating imaginative record of the conflicts in Australia between the two wars' and elaborated on its themes.

Vance was privately so concerned about the 'problem' of Aileen's sexuality in 1948 that he wrote a letter to Edith Young in London, the writer and family friend with whom Aileen had shared a flat briefly in 1939 and who remained in contact with her through the war years. His letter does not survive, but Edith's lengthy reply in October of that year does, and it sheds light on how someone familiar with psychoanalysis might have understood what would then have been considered Aileen's deviance. Responding to Vance's queries about his daughter's 'personal emotional life', Edith suggests that she might have formed an 'emotional attachment' to 'a Dr Luted' for whom she worked in Spain and who Edith regarded as 'an attractive irresponsible adventurer type'. (This would have been Kenneth Sinclair-Loutit, but it doesn't seem Aileen was ever attracted to him.) According to Edith, Aileen 'made strong emotional attachments to women', possibly as a reaction to her presumed rejection by 'Dr Luted'. 'I know of two girls who were, what one might term, "in love with" Aileen for a time', she continues. But Edith admits that Aileen was always 'reticent' about talking about herself.

Later in the letter, Edith offers her interpretation of Aileen's situation: 'My own feeling is, that [for] some reason, she early made an emotional transference from the feminine to the masculine role – cutting her hair like a youth's, dressing in slacks in preference to skirts, cultivating an independent boyish attitude to other women – all seem to point to this. I have great sympathy with this attitude because, to a certain extent, I share a similar feeling. I am sure I have 'a masculine protest' as the psychologists call it. I have not easily been able to take the feminine role to a man, and that I think is one reason why my own emotional life has been, to a certain extent, unsatisfactory'. She advises Vance: 'Should this be tapped by her analyst, I feel that much good will be done...This emotional transference to the male would also be bound up with an identification with you, as a man, and as a writer. All this is a very delicate subject and I would much rather talk about it than write it. But my affection for Aileen is strong enough for me to want to be any help I can, and my sense of indebtedness to you and Nettie, the love I have for you both, strong still after so many years of separation, bids me not to be frightened to say all that is in my mind'. She also tells Vance that her son Michael's psychoanalysis estranged him from her for a time: 'I tell you this in order to warn you that the analytical process which Aileen may have to endure will probably arouse all kinds of antagonisms'.

Nettie's worry about Aileen's submerged resentment towards her, Vance's fear that he might be the cause of her 'emotional transference', and their combined anxiety about their daughter's mental health and 'psychic life' caused much pain for them, but they were not the only emotional undercurrents that were swirling about the Palmers in 1948. During that year, Vance's novel *Golconda* – the first part of the trilogy that is regarded as his strongest work – was published, with a dedication 'To Nina Christesen'. In a private note to the woman who was loved by everyone who knew her and who devoted many hours generously to teaching Aileen Russian, Vance wrote: 'To Nina: whose understanding and sense of truth are a touchstone for my writing; whose interest makes good work worth doing; and whose sweetness, radiance and human warmth gives me an image of ideal womanhood, this book is lovingly dedicated'. Ever since the Christesens had arrived in Melbourne from Brisbane in 1945, Vance had developed a secret passion for Nina, who was nearly three decades his junior, and wrote frequent notes and letters, even poems to her in which he praises her beauty and declares his love for her. The passion was not returned, but Nina managed with great sensitivity to remain friends with all the Palmers. To Vance, she appears to have fulfilled the role of muse, and several writers, including his friend Frank Dalby Davison, maintained that the writing in Vance's trilogy displayed a new level of emotional understanding. If Nettie knew of her husband's feelings for Nina, it did not dampen her affection for the younger woman and Aileen did not refrain from writing to Nettie about Nina staying at Ardmore (as she often did since the Christesens lived at Eltham in outer Melbourne). In a letter to Nettie in Caloundra in June, Aileen writes: *Your pa was in bed with a cold two days last week but he brightened up at prospect of Nina coming to stay the night on Friday. She came in her usual way about midnight on Fri., was up early in the morning & bustled about & then departed.*

Although initially willing to cooperate (as indicated in the letter she wrote before she left hospital, which was probably to Dr Geroe), Aileen's experience with psychoanalysis was not successful in the long run. She had become severely depressed during the second year of her analysis and her parents were deeply concerned. There were moments of respite and some grounds for hope, however. Vance was delighted when she unexpectedly visited him in hospital in September 1949 after he had suffered a heart attack. Writing to Nettie (who was away giving a series of lectures that Vance had been scheduled to present) he says: 'A great surprise yesterday. Aileen came in looking radiant, sweet, responsive – just as she might have looked years ago. Often lately I'd felt as if her very personality had disappeared, as if there was nothing left but her form. But today she couldn't have been better: it gives one new hope'.

A poignant entry in Nettie's diary at the end of the year shows a glimmer of understanding on her part of what Aileen had been through in her years abroad in war zones: 'Evening. Aileen at first rhetorical & restless, afraid we weren't listening to her dogmas on Shakespeare or Dostoevsky: then accidental question about Spain started A[ileen] talking & she sat down & told us quietly about many things she did & saw there. "The best part of life ever", she said simply. Bad complications of certain groups that attempted to join the British Unit before it was merged into the IB or the Spanish forces. Some crushing disappointments before the final defeat. Grief for France – couldn't bear to see it in 1939 facing a new war: less anxious about England although it was there she served over four years... Surprisingly direct talk altogether – we hadn't dreamt of [illegible] recovery for her – but mustn't count on anything definite in that way yet or even soon'.

Less than a year later Aileen was again hospitalised and Vance gave vent to his despair to Nina Christesen, uttering sentiments that he would never write to Nettie. There is no attempt to be optimistic here: 'I've been reluctant to you about Aileen, for I felt that you'd given up hope about her some time ago, while I, deep down, was expecting a miracle. Alas, none is likely to occur. After seeing her on Friday evening I felt crushed, and lay awake all night feeling that life was, at bottom, meaningless and that all that remained was to get through what was left of it with as good grace as possible. Sorry to unload this nihilism on you, Nina dear. It's not a normal mood. I see Frank [Davison] in the current 'Walkabout' credits me with an "inner poise that the buffetings of life have not been able to disturb". But it's when the buffetings of life operate on people you love that they hurt. And nothing on earth can be so heart-bruising as this kind of illness'.

Aileen herself recalled her experience of psychoanalysis much later in a piece called 'Notes of a Convalescent' when she was recovering from yet another period of hospitalisation and trying to write about her psychiatric history with detachment: *It would be very inconvenient and undesirable to go happy-mad again, but I'd rather go happy-mad than depressed-mad, as I'm sometimes afraid of going – like I went in 1948–50, off and on. I began happy-mad in 1948, and then couldn't pick up the threads of ordinary life when I came out of hospital after shock treatment, then had a stretch of being psychoanalysed, which only left me more depressed, so I went in for more shock treatment, then emerged to settle down to work in 1951.*

Despite Nettie and Vance's attempts to be discreet about their daughter's sexuality, rumours circulated in the literary community and continued to resonate years beyond their deaths, and Aileen's. Frank Dalby Davison had told his mother in 1947 that he and his wife were of the opinion that Aileen had 'limped home sorely wounded' from Europe after an 'emotional mishap'. To another writer he made more salacious comments about the 'mishap', along the lines that neither Aileen nor her lover could work out who was the man. David Martin, writer, CPA member and Palmer colleague wrote of Aileen in his autobiography published in 1991: 'Her attempt to write from within the Palmer constellation, her failure to escape. Chain-smoking her life away in Sunbury mental hospital, felled by her sexuality. Aileen was the poet'. In a scrap of memoir published by *Overland* in 2000, Dorothy Hewett recalls, rather theatrically, meeting Aileen in the 1960s – 'drunk, manic and dishevelled' – and recounts 'Aileen Palmer's story' as it was told to her by another writer, Frank Hardy: 'As a young girl she had fallen in love with the novelist Flora Eldershaw and kept running away to her house in the Dandenongs pursued by Vance. The monumental rows and confrontations between Aileen, Flora and Vance became part of the literary gossip of Melbourne'. This illustrates just how 'literary gossip' can take on a life of its own when small grains of truth are recounted and embellished through the creative talents of writers over years until the story itself becomes a work of fiction.

21

Peace Activist and Poet

In the years after the horror stretch of 1948–50, Aileen's life followed a pattern of periods of relative calm, periods of intense activity and then periods of hospitalisation. From time to time, she held down clerical jobs – at Australia–Soviet House, James Baird, Cheshire's and the Athenaeum Library – and once she lasted a fortnight in a teaching position. But mostly, in her well periods, she followed her two passions: political activism and writing.

While not turning her back on communism, she directed her energies more towards working for world peace, in particular the prohibition of the atom bomb and the fight against the development of nuclear weapons. Just as she had deplored those she called 'base-wallowers' during the Spanish War, she was not prepared to watch from the sidelines on this issue either. In early 1957, she announced that she was joining the so-called Peace Fleet, a fleet of small ships that was preparing to sail from Japan into the Christmas Island atom bomb test area as a protest gesture. Katharine Susannah Prichard was another who committed herself to joining the fleet in the knowledge that all who sailed into the test area risked a slow death through radiation sickness. Katharine explained in a press statement: 'I feel that it is my duty to support any effort to stop further tests of atom and hydrogen bombs...This appalling danger confronts not only living people, but the generations unborn – if we fail to stop the criminal madness of these tests. They constitute a crime against humanity'.

The Peace Fleet project did not eventuate, but a few months later Aileen was invited to become one of fourteen delegates from Australia to attend the 3rd World Conference against A & H weapons to be held in Tokyo in August. There, she aided in translating for delegates speaking in Spanish and French and a photograph from the conference shows her at the microphone translating for Martine Monod, a cousin of Simone de Beauvoir. With other conference delegates she visited Hiroshima and Nagasaki and what she saw there made a deep impression on her. A press article reported on a talk she gave to the Kew Peace Group after her return: 'Miss Palmer said she had seen the effects of air raids on civilian casualties in England and Spain, but nothing comparable with Hiroshima had ever before happened in human history'. Aileen made a passionate plea in her own press statement from the conference after visiting the bombed cities: *Not only had cities been destroyed and hundreds of thousands of people slaughtered, but still untold people were enduring what could only be described as a living death. Many of these, to whom I spoke, told us they had wanted to die when they realised the extent and nature of their injuries. Now they are kept going by one hope: that the sight of their injuries may help mankind to understand its own danger, so that another Hiroshima will never happen. If anyone doubts the necessity for the abolition of nuclear weapons, let them see the victims at Hiroshima and Nagasaki hospitals – a sight that will haunt you for the rest of your days.*

After the conference, on the invitation of Chinese delegates, Aileen visited China with five of the Australian delegates and was enthused by what she saw there: *After 30 years of Japanese occupation and civil war, the Chinese people appear actively and enthusiastically engaged in peaceful reconstruction. From my impression, the last thing they want is war of any kind.*

Aileen was also writing poetry, the kind of verse she believed in as *a poet of conscience.* In the same year as the momentous trips to Tokyo and China, Katharine Susannah Prichard paid for a small volume of her 'assorted verses' to be printed. A basic mimeograph production, *Dear Life* by 'Caliban', includes two of the sonnets Aileen wrote during her first hospital incarceration in 1948 – 'In Hospital' and 'The Swans'. As well as original poems, it also contains her translations of favourite poems by Pushkin and Heine and a poem that inspired her all her life, Aragon's 'The Poet to his Party'.

Other poems speak more directly to the political situation she found herself in during the mid-1950s. Intriguingly, one sonnet is simply titled 'To J. V. S.'. When I realised the initials stood for Joseph Vissarionovich Stalin, I was astounded. Aileen wrote this poem after Khrushchev's secret report of the 20th Congress of the CPSU was published in the *New York Times* in 1956, detailing the mass killings and deportations of the Stalinist regime. The CPA refused any discussion of the report and those who did not comply, including Helen Palmer, were expelled from the Party. Aileen's response was to write 'To J. V. S.', in which she mourns the dictator's deviation from the *dialectical way* and says *no one saw you clearly until today.* Yet she maintains her faith in communism, stating:

This brings no swift reversal of belief,
No discard of the works we once defended:
Whatever history holds of rage and grief
Our chances now are infinitely extended...

Poems such as 'Maralinga' and 'Straw in the Wind' reflected her recent preoccupation with the nuclear threat, the latter beginning *I am a straw in the wind / I have travelled far on the high winds of disaster.* Its conclusion speaks of the need to go on protesting whatever happens:

The wind stirred, but I would not go with the wind
Small and obscure and woven into the grass
I feared the voice in the wind.
There was death in the wind –
A new sort of death...
So I still must go with the wind
Singing my song down the wide lanes of the air
For where the new death rains no grass will grow
The grass, the intelligent grass, must keep on growing

A review of *Dear Life* in *Overland* praised the collection: 'Here is a poet who can take the shock of events that are contemporary and while they are still new, record an impression. The gift of musical line is hers and a natural, unstrained imagery'. The reviewer also noted a sense of misplaced self-deprecation: 'The personal note of suffering is inescapable in the verses but it is compensated by a passionate insistence on the soundness at the core of life. Also one gathers sometimes a sense that the work is offered apologetically – in the pen name – the dedication and such lines as "verse is the only parlour trick I know" but a poet with courage enough to face up to such subject matter as that of the lines "To J. V. S." is far from being tentative'.

Meanjin published one of Aileen's poems a year later. 'Song from a Distant Epoch' is a moving piece that evokes the effects of nuclear radiation on future generations and is clearly inspired by her visit to Hiroshima and Nagasaki. Even the ancient culture of the gypsies who overcame oppression by carrying their own 'iron house' refuge with them proves no match for the deadly poison (Aileen returns several times in her writing to the notion of the 'iron house' of the gypsies, which combines the 'firm house' she desired as a child with a nomadic life.):

Because your grief was an old lament without frontiers
the gypsies brought their caravans and their music:
each carried with him his own iron house
intangible as a rainbow, dim as a ghost
(you feared for the wasting child, the dream without eyes)

because the air was a cluster of deadly blossoms
the gypsies poured their melodies into your silence:
their tongue was an ancient babble of tinkling symbols
(child without hands, come and listen to the gypsies)

'we will give you eyes', they said: 'our eyes are invincible –
Come to the free, wide spaces – the world without clouds'
(child without feet, let the gypsies take you riding)

each carried with him his own iron house
intangible as a rainbow, dim as a ghost:
but the clouds of poison were massed on the low horizon
and you found no refuge there from the wind and the rain
(child without ears, have you no more strength to cry?)

Aileen became an active protester against the Vietnam War in the 1960s, declaring to Katharine Susannah Prichard: *I feel Vietnam is the Spain of the present moment.* But her interest in Vietnam started before that. Through her friends from the CPA, journalist Malcolm Salmon and his wife Lorraine, who lived in Vietnam in the late 1950s for two years, Aileen was asked to work on two unusual translations. The first was a volume of five long poems by the revolutionary poet To Huu, whose work was known by heart by many people in his native Vietnam. Aileen translated them from French and the small volume with its delicate cover design of bamboo leaves was published in Hanoi by Foreign Languages Publishing House in 1959.

The other translation Aileen was commissioned to undertake was published in Hanoi in 1962 and received a much wider audience. Reviewed in *The Times Literary Supplement* in England, it was later republished in the United States in the early 1970s and reprinted many times over the next two decades. This was the *Prison Diary* of Ho Chi Minh, President of the Democratic Republic of Vietnam and known to the people as 'Uncle Ho'. He wrote the poems during 1942 and 1943 when he was a prisoner of Chiang Kai-shek's police, picked up while he was on his way from Indochina to confer with him about forming a common front against the Japanese, but suspected of espionage. The 115 verses trace his journey as he is marched from gaol to gaol in South China, often in leg-irons, for over a year. He wrote them in a notebook in Chinese calligraphy rather than Vietnamese so as not to raise suspicion among his Chinese guards by writing in a language they did not understand. Aileen was provided with a literal translation of the Chinese word for word into English by the publishers and asked to provide a poetic rendering of the quatrains and Tang poems. She preferred to think of her work as a rendering rather than a translation especially when Helen, after she received a copy, queried whether Aileen could be called a 'translator'. Aileen did feel her work on *Prison Diary* was not as successful as the translation of the To Huu poems. As she wrote to Lorraine Salmon: *To have done a really good job, I would have had to know the music of the original, which you can't know, unless you know the language fairly well.* The apparent simplicity of Ho Chi Minh's verse does, however, create a distinctive music of its own:

Advice to Oneself

Without the cold and desolation of winter
There could not be the warmth and splendour of spring.
Calamity has tempered and hardened me,
And turned my mind into steel.

In an article American academic David Marr wrote in 1971 about Vietnamese sources on Vietnam, he remarks: 'If the recent stirring reception for The Prison Diary of Ho Chi Minh (Aileen Palmer, trans., Bantam paperback) is any indication, then readers have a real desire to find out what the Vietnamese have said, and are saying, about their country'. It seems Aileen was eventually starting to gain some international recognition for her political activism and skills as a poet and translator through her rendering of Ho Chi Minh's verse for an English-speaking readership. But her reception on the home front when she began her activist period in 1957, though also 'stirring', was much less positive.

22

Family Discord

When 'Song for a Distant Epoch', Aileen's poem about children deformed by radiation, was published in *Meanjin* in 1958, she was undergoing intensive psychiatric treatment in Sunbury mental hospital. Helen had been called from Sydney again by her parents and Aileen was admitted in April, for the first time as a certified patient.

She had spent a short time at Sunbury two years before being tested for the use of the relatively new drug, lithium. *I was not under insulin treatment, which until corrected I'm inclined to think of as a relic of barbarism*, she wrote about her stretch in what she referred to as *The Snake Pit* in 1956. *Drugs, lithium or largactyl or both, were administered at every meal, and I'm not altogether sorry I had one bout in the Pit, if it was the only way they could check on my allergy to lithium. This is a new drug... which apparently governs, that is, keeps at a practicable level, the speed of the mind: it is neither altogether a stimulant nor a depressant.* Although it was considered that patients with Aileen's type of recurrent disturbances could be kept relatively stable while taking their prescribed doses of lithium, many found that the medication made them feel dull and flat and Aileen was no exception. According to a letter Helen wrote to the psychiatrist at Sunbury after her sister's admission in 1958, Aileen had told her about a month before she left for Japan in 1957 that she had stopped taking her tablets 'because she no longer needed them' and Helen felt that it was unlikely she had taken any since.

The situation at Ardmore in the late 1950s was rather grim. Nettie and Vance were both over seventy and suffering indifferent health. Aileen was drinking heavily on a regular basis. As a child she had been shy and awkward, a listener and a writer rather than a talker; at university she had absorbed the atmosphere of the Mob and learnt through friendship to have more confidence in herself, but she still found being the centre of attention difficult. Like many shy people, she had found in Spain and later in London that alcohol loosened her inhibitions and she was able to talk and argue her beliefs in a way that she found impossible when sober. The trouble was that after her first 'breakdown' in 1948 and her subsequent treatment, Aileen's behaviour when she had been drinking took a different form with her family than with friends. In a sad letter from Vance to Helen while Aileen was in Japan, the difference becomes apparent. He tells his daughter: 'She's very heavily on N[ettie]'s mind. When she's herself she's very sweet to N, but as soon as she drinks a terrible change comes over her…N has come to have a morbid horror of the bottle'. Aileen had, he conceded, tried to control her drinking. But after she was invited to go to Japan, she was so excited she apparently, according to Vance, abandoned all responsibility around the house. He describes her departure: 'There are a lot of loyal friends around her but they haven't much sense. The night before she left was rather a wallow with all sorts of people coming to Muni's and bringing bottles. The truth is they seem to enjoy her when she's het up and pouring out words'.

Like many sufferers of mood-swing disorders, Aileen found the periods when she was considered 'manic' exhilarating and creative and, in common with many who experience those feelings, she sought to reproduce the heightened state through alcohol. It was always her family who manoeuvred her into hospital, and she developed a strong resistance towards them that manifested in drunken aggression. Helen explained to the psychiatrist the effect her sister's drinking had on her family: 'She then reaches a state almost identical with the manic state; she uses the same symbols and language, has the same key ideas, shows the same violent resentment against family and parents. The only difference is that she is apparently normal the next morning, having slept it off'.

Since 1948, Helen had been put in a similar position of responsibility to the one her father was forced to assume in 1912 when he returned to Australia to find his brother in a delusional state and his family unable to cope. Despite Vance's best efforts, Wob was institutionalised and never released, and his relatives were told that it was for his own good. Four decades later, though she was not relegated to a locked ward indefinitely, Aileen's intensive treatment certainly affected her ability to cope in the outside world. Helen had managed to create a life of her own in Sydney with a strong circle of friends around her. She was a teacher at Fort Street Girls' High School, she wrote a series of textbooks with her friend Jessie McLeod, making history accessible to Australian schoolchildren, and in the 1950s she founded and edited a socialist journal called *Outlook*. But she had also suffered difficulties during that decade. She had been refused teaching work for eighteen months after taking part in a peace delegation to China in 1952 and, a few years later, was expelled from the Communist Party of Australia to which she had devoted years of her life. Family friends such as Katharine Susannah Prichard reacted strongly against her stand with the CPA. As well, she was called upon to disrupt her life on several occasions and go to Melbourne to make decisions about Aileen's mental health on behalf of her parents.

Helen had a tougher character than her father and dealt with the responsibility placed on her with steely determination. A former school friend at PLC wrote of her: 'Helen had an extremely logical mind, precise in details, but able to draw on the *bon mot* when necessary and put everyone in her company at ease'. Comparing her to the 'more volatile' Nettie, who was inclined 'to collect lost causes', she said 'Helen just forged ahead to do what had to be done. I found her very rational, almost devoid of emotion'.

A long letter Helen wrote to her parents in May when Aileen was about to be sent from Sunbury to Kinkora Rehabilitation Hostel in Hawthorn seems to confirm her school friend's character analysis. She wants to prepare for Aileen's release and tells Nettie and Vance that it is 'essential that we underline to her that things are now different', that her sister 'has forfeited the right to decide for herself certain vital things such as whether she will or will not pursue what treatment is prescribed'. To that end, Helen wants Aileen to move out of Ardmore and for her parents to remove the 'props' that have cushioned her in the past. She insists that Aileen must get a job ('she's got to recognise the obligation that the world doesn't owe her a living') and that Vance must not continue to pay her bills. 'You may think I've suddenly grown a bar of steel in my inside', she tells them and her next tactic to lessen her sister's 'cushioning' is particularly brutal. 'I gather, V', she continues, 'that you've let her know that we incinerated some of her works because they were drivel; that seems to be the shot'.

Helen's following statement reveals her fear of the 'symbols' and 'signs' of madness she reads into Aileen's poems, but also her idea of what poetry should be. Like all her family, Helen was an occasional poet herself, but her best known poem 'The Ballad of 1891' (set to music by Doreen Bridges for the musical *Reedy River*) shows the difference between her style and her sister's. It begins:

The price of wool was falling in 1891;
The men who owned the acres saw something must be done:
'We will break the Shearers' Union, and show we're masters still
And they'll take the terms we give them, or we'll find the ones who will.'

Of Aileen's 'Song for a Distant Epoch' she writes: 'It's a pity in a way that her pome [sic] was published in Meanjin; it flows beautifully because it recognises no responsibility whatever to be coherent or to communicate with anyone (which isn't to say that it's just as coherent as much of the stuff published in Meanjin to my mind)'. Helen told Vance that Aileen's letters to her from Sunbury had been 'mostly preoccupied with where is everything? did we burn it?' Perhaps it is little wonder that Aileen in later years sent copies of her poems to receptive readers like Malcolm and Lorraine Salmon, Katharine Susannah Prichard and Christian Jollie Smith as soon as she had written them.

Some of Helen's stipulations did come to pass when Aileen was released from Kinkora later in 1958. She moved into a room in East Kew and got a job with the Melbourne Athenaeum Library. She was also active in helping Clem Christesen organise a special tribute edition of *Meanjin* for Nettie and Vance in 1959, although her assistance is not acknowledged in the published issue. Here I reproduce a substantial part of one letter from Clem to Aileen to show the extent of what he asked her to undertake: 'You might be able to help me regarding the following matters:

1) Kathleen Fitzpatrick wants to write a tribute to Vance, as broadcaster. She has asked for three or four of Vance's radio scripts.

Could you consult him and put a selection aside for me? I could call for these.

2) Tom Moore is writing an article about Vance and the CLF and covering his influence generally. He wants to have some concrete details (and dates) about Vance's 'extra-literary' activities in Melbourne – his association with various literary and other groups, with individual writers (and others); dates when he lived in this, that and the other place, and so on. Such information is not easy to obtain, but without it the story tends to be too general or abstract.

3) Has Vance copies of any radio plays? What of the play called (I think) The Sea Eagle? Keith Macartney, who is commenting on the published plays, would like to refer to unpublished plays and/or radio plays. Please see what you can do.

4) Some scripts have already been received. Please keep Esther Levy up to the mark.

5) Can you make any suggestions re the enclosed tentative arrangement of contents?

6) I'm afraid I'll have to rely on you pretty heavily once I begin work on the winter issue.

7) Bibliography. This is important, but who can prepare it in the time? I don't see how we can include a complete bibliography to date; but could you begin compiling a record more comprehensive than the Miller-Macartney one?'

It seems Aileen did follow up most of Clem Christesen's demands: Kathleen Fitzpatrick discusses some of Vance's radio scripts; T. Inglis Moore writes of Vance's association with groups and individual writers; among the plays Keith Macartney discusses is Vance's radio play *The Sea Hawk*; and Esther Levy does come up with an essay about Nettie. Clem also asked Aileen to chase up photographs of her parents and several are included in the issue, but he did not follow up her suggestion that, as Nettie was *far less photogenic than Vance*, he should use Lina Bryan's *very interesting portrait* of her. The cover photograph of a sour-faced Nettie is far less flattering than that of her genial husband in his customary bow tie.

Vance never saw the published version of *Meanjin*, No. 2, 1959, which included essays by many of his and Nettie's associates and friends, including Frank Dalby Davison, Brian Fitzpatrick, Marjorie

Barnard, Katharine Susannah Prichard and John Manifold. On the winter's afternoon of 15 July, Nettie was away in Sydney on holiday with Helen, Aileen was no longer living at Ardmore and Vance was at home entertaining Nina Christesen as he read a new play he had been working on that he thought one of her students might act. Standing up to put some more coke on the fire, he suddenly staggered back into Nina's arms and died of a heart attack. Clem's editorial for the tribute issue became an obituary: 'No writer gave more practical help and guidance to *Meanjin* than did Vance Palmer. I personally have lost a dear friend and mentor'.

Aileen wrote another version of her father's death that is less romantic, one that has both Christesens present: *Vance died smoothly and painlessly, chatting and laughing with Clem and Nina one minute, then collapsing and feeling nothing.* She wrote of Vance's death several times in her novel fragments, always in the context of the way he carried his carefulness and neatness through to the manner of his death and contrasting that with Nettie's impetuosity. *Blake died as I'd like to die, given the option, without any prolonged preliminaries, or pangs of dissolution extended over a period*, she wrote in one fragment. In another, she wrote a sardonic, but poignant pen portrait of 'Noni' viewing Blake's body after she returned from Sydney: *I went along with her, but stood in the background, while she hovered around his carcase with little quaint movements, then finally bent over him and kissed him. That was more than I could have done.*

23

Aileen and Nettie

In a rare photograph from the early 1960s Aileen and Nettie are pictured in the back garden of Ardmore, both wearing sensible printed cotton dresses and cardigans, but with Nettie's softened by a froth of lace at the neckline. Aileen is perched on the arm of Nettie's deckchair cradling her handsome tabby cat, Pushkin, who had arrived on the doorstep in January 1963. She is saying something to her mother, a half-smile on her face, while Nettie, looking frail and old, gazes up at her daughter, eyes quizzical, a typical questioning response seeming to form on her lips. It is a peaceful scene that belies the tension that existed in the household at that time. The close but intense relationship between mother and daughter had never recovered after Aileen's first breakdown in 1948 and now, with the help of a live-in housekeeper, the two women lived at Ardmore with Helen making occasional flying visits from Sydney. Perhaps Helen took the photo.

1960 had been a year of high creativity for Aileen but also a year of disappointments. In March she lost her job at the Athenaeum Library and soon after sat for the librarian's diploma without success. After applying for a number of library positions and being rejected because of her lack of a diploma, she found herself behind in her rent for her room in East Kew. Burying her anxiety in creative work she began writing a verse play. Based on the legend of Orpheus and Eurydice, it showed influences from her period of psychoanalysis combined with her typical desire to confront the ills of the world: *Eurydike* [sic] *was my mother and Orpheus my father, but I was also both of them. Related to their legend, I hoped to write a morality play, bearing on the main questions of our time.* Working intensively on the play, Aileen neglected looking after herself, even eating, with predictable results. With hindsight, she told Helen at the end of January 1961: *Where I probably went wrong last November or December was that my poetic knowledge probably went up the wall on its own, without enough continuous reference to people in this town – where I've never very much enjoyed living, except for brief periods that usually ended exceptionally badly, as you know. Last year was, up till about November when I think I called off the drink and began to be really intellectual and topspeed creative, a long way the best year I've spent in Melbourne, unless I did anything worse than I yet remember in the period I still don't remember clearly, just before I was whisked off to hospital.* After a stint in Larundel psychiatric hospital, Aileen recuperated for several months at the Malvern Clinic, a pleasant place far removed from the world of locked wards and punishing routines. She wrote to the matron at the clinic for years afterwards.

The experiment with independent living was over after Aileen's psychotic episode at the end of 1960 and Ardmore became her home again, now without her father's diplomatic presence. Still the dutiful daughter, she spent hours of every day typing (*donkey-fashion*) and sorting papers for her mother. One of her jobs was to type up Nettie's diaries: *bringing into legible form the compact and revealing little diaries she has kept over the years.* (Unfortunately for subsequent researchers, only the tiny notebooks in Nettie's increasingly impossible handwriting survive in the Palmer papers.)

Aileen also plunged into organising commemorative activities relating to Spain. Preparing for the speech she was to give for the twenty-fifth anniversary of Lorca's death in September 1961, she recorded the emotional effect his poetry still had on her and showed her resistance to writing *about* poetry: *This week I've been trying to prepare a talk on Garcia Lorca, but poetry is explosive stuff to touch... Poetry should be the place for those cumulations of knowledge we have that are a long way ahead of our intellect.* A year later, she was instrumental in organising the Spanish Festival that was held in Melbourne in late 1962. The brochure for the festival detailed it as *Festival Espagnol, Centro Iberico, Calle Bourke 169, 30 de Octobre – 2 de Novembre.* The festival included a display of art and handicrafts, including a reproduction of Picasso's *Guernica*, and posters depicting the Spanish struggle for freedom. (During the organising process Aileen wrote two letters to Picasso, whose studio she had visited in Paris in 1945, asking him if good prints of *Guernica* could now be obtained. There is no record of a reply.) Over the four days of celebration, poems were read and talks given (including one by IBers David Martin, Lloyd Edmonds and Aileen); the films *Spanish Earth* and *Goya* were shown and there was Spanish dancing and Spanish food as well as a call to support the Appeal for Amnesty for exiles and prisoners in Spain.

The situation at home became increasingly difficult for Aileen, however. She often had part-time clerical jobs as well as working for Nettie during the day, so the only time she could work on her own writing was in the evenings when Nettie was wont to complain about her typing late. In March 1963, Aileen wrote a letter to Dr Bell from the Malvern Clinic to ask if she would *write a few words* to her mother about the typing issue *that might help to eliminate further blow-ups between us.* Ardmore was a large house and it seems unlikely that a typewriter would have kept Nettie awake, but Aileen realised that the underlying issue was *that she has a recurrent notion that she must restrain me from working 'late', because she associates that with my past illnesses.* Aileen perceived the surveillance of her behaviour by her family, especially through Nettie's anxiety, to be *the most basic and continual problem of my life ever since my first illness.*

She revealed another sore point in a letter to Katharine Susannah Prichard. The writer whom she regarded as a mentor had always championed Aileen's writing and clearly did so in a recent letter to Nettie that Aileen read: *I feel very grateful when anyone reminds Nettie that my own writing is one of those things that matters. She'll never be very interested in it, I feel, but it still strikes me as extraordinary at times, after the way she impressed on me profoundly as a young child that writing was the thing above all others worth spending one's life on, and how she treasured and carted from pillar to post the exercise-books I filled with novels from the age of nine or ten, how little interested she is in what I have to say as an adult.*

Even Helen, who loved her sister and had her interests at heart despite her tough stance at times, felt that Nettie was not taking enough interest in Aileen's poetry. She wrote to their mother pleading with her to try reading Aileen's poems 'as if they were by a new poet you didn't know. Some of them – there's one about the Hammer and the Rock, for instance – I think are extremely powerful; and all, of course, have fluency. Many I don't understand at all, or merely get glimpses here & there. But the important thing is that what she wants most of all is to be accepted as a writer – principally of poetry – and in particular by you'. Helen had received a copy of Aileen's letter to Dr Bell and agreed with her. 'Aileen is very well', she wrote to Nettie. 'But she has a struggle ahead of her, and knows it. Try looking at it, not from her point of view, but from her position, for a moment: 48, a legacy of fifteen years of uncertain ups and downs behind her, a first-rate brain, society saying to her "we have no use for you, except part-time on a junior's pay to make the tea and answer the phone"; and then her last throw to get some recognition in the thing she values herself most highly, poetry, and the last people to give her any credit for it are her family'. Helen, in her direct way, then lays down Aileen's rights: 'She can't always be on tap and have a job and have some time to herself; but she's anxious to give you allotted times. But when she's not, her life is her own, and it is her home'.

Aileen's poem 'Lines Painted on the Wall of a Death-Cell', about political prisoners gaoled in Saigon, was published in the journal *Vietnam Advances* in August 1963 and Helen asked her sister if she might reprint it in the journal she edited: 'We seldom have the opportunity to publish poetry, but that would fit beautifully into our next issue'. The poem duly appeared in *Outlook*'s November–December issue and its clear message would have appealed to Helen. It begins:

For fear I go, and leave no trace
        of those I loved, and all I knew,
I learn my letters in this place,
        and pass this message on to you…

Publishing this poem was quite a gesture of reconciliation on Helen's part, but it doesn't appear that she was able to inspire in Nettie a rekindling of interest in Aileen's poetry.

Aileen's ambivalence towards Nettie seems to stem from the conflict between the huge sense of responsibility she felt towards her mother and her constant failure to measure up to her expectations.

In the guise of the teenage Vivienne Waller in 'Poor Child!' she had expressed her guilt for being born: *if only she could relieve her mother of all her burdens, she might be able to go back to poetry. What a pity she had abandoned it to have children!* Just prior to her first breakdown in 1948, Aileen wrote a rambling piece that was like a letter to her mother: *I just need the words to write to my mother – my mother too brilliant, just too honestly brilliant, to make allowances for the slowness of others, for what they can take at one time. It's the time that I've got to insist on – the piece for this afternoon, the peace for this afternoon. I need to write this letter, to start this story, but don't yet give it a name. It's a piece of my mind if you like – the pieces I can't give unless it's in a more whole form.*

In her fragments of autobiographical fiction, Aileen continued to try to write the story of her family. In 1961, she wrote to the editor of *Overland*, Stephen Murray-Smith, who was encouraging her to write her story: *What I am trying to clarify in my own mind is my relations with the members of my own family, and how these have stimulated or crippled my own abilities. This is about my forty-ninth attempt to put something of the kind on paper, but, thanks to the kind of things you have urged me to try and express, I may as well try again.* Her attempts continued intermittently until as late as the early 1980s, after which she fell silent. It was the relationship with her mother that was the most difficult for her to come to terms with and a passage in a letter to Helen at the end of the difficult year of 1963 is the most poignant, even chilling, statement: *As a child, and often since, including lately, even this afternoon, I've felt terrifically protective towards my mother (our mother), but I often also feel if there was ever a creature in history or legend (Medea, was it?) who loved gobbling up her own children, that's her. The Puritan (though also the poetic) mother...*

Nettie's health was deteriorating and in May 1964 she suffered a stroke. Helen arranged for her to enter a nursing home where she continued to receive visitors. Aileen read the many letters sent to her when she visited the nursing home and in September she wrote to Helen that her mother was asking her to tell Vance to write. Aileen promised that she would bring a letter next time she came and asks Helen to write *from Vance*: *This I feel you cd [could] more easily do than I can...as Vance has been to you (much more than he has to me) a master or a model.* Nettie died a month later on 19 October.

At the request of Stephen Murray-Smith, Aileen made several unsuccessful attempts to write an obituary for her mother. The most formal but unfinished draft was called 'Time and the Western Woman'. In it, she details Nettie's achievements but continues: *However, whatever her contribution to criticism, biography and general comment in essays, articles, broadcasts, and her active work on behalf of the people in Spain, and in aid of refugees arriving from Hitler's Germany Austria, I am inclined to think of Nettie Palmer above all as a poet. Nettie was both a potentially great poet, and a puritan, so, though she died peacefully, I feel she died feeling she had failed.* Thus, the constant theme in Aileen's writing about her mother was never to find a resolution. Her feeling of responsibility for the fact that Nettie had ceased to write poetry became combined with her belief that her mother's 'puritanism' held her creativity back and, implicitly, made it impossible for her to understand her daughter.

24

World without Strangers?

The publication of Aileen's volume of poetry *World Without Strangers?* almost coincided with Nettie's death in 1964. It is tempting to make satisfying claims about the significance of the timing: perhaps now Aileen could cast off her mother's shadow and fulfil her destiny as a poet? This *was* the most important publication of her life, but it was also her last poetry published and it did not bring her widespread recognition. Its value lies more in the fact that the slim hardback volume – with its sombre, olive-green cover illustrated with a shadowy globe above the uncompromising title and the urgent question mark – brought together most of the small oeuvre of Aileen Palmer, which had either been scattered through literary and political journals or had never made it into print. *World Without Strangers?* included poems that dated back to her first hospital incarceration in 1948, poems that had been previously published in journals such as *Overland*, *Southerly*, *Meanjin* and *Realist Writer*, those that were appearing in print for the first time like the unfinished verse play 'Variations to a Legend', and translations of favourite poets – Aragon and Heine – with new translations of Pushkin and Cuban poet Nicolás Guillén. Her mimeographed collection *Dear Life* had come into being through her mentor Katharine Susannah Prichard and this new volume was brought out by Overland Press through its editor, Stephen Murray-Smith, who had also become a kind of mentor.

It is perhaps curious that none of Aileen's literary family thought to mentor a collection of her work, but the problematic position her poetry held within her immediate family may have precluded that. Although in her early life Aileen appeared to be following the path of her father in becoming a novelist, we do know she was writing poems in the 1930s in London. But it was not until after her first breakdown in 1948 that poetry became the medium to which she was most devoted and through which she sought to express her most serious ideas. Inevitably, it became associated in her family's minds with illness, and a statement Helen made late in her life about Aileen's poetry may have spoken for Nettie and Vance as well: 'Anything that didn't make sense I couldn't comment on because I knew its hidden symbolism. There's a relation between the symbolism of poetry and the symbolism of madness. What other people saw as the symbolism of poetry, I saw as the symbolism of madness, and often it was so'.

The trope of the outsider, the stranger, runs through Aileen's diaries and prose fragments where she casts herself or her various alter egos as a person who does not belong, who is out of place in the world. In her diary after her return to Australia in 1945, for instance, she wrote: *I feel this is after all a foreign country I've got to start learning all over again. Coming home – I'll always be a foreigner.* In her poetry, however, her concerns are less personal and more overtly political and universal and her profound hope that there could be a world without conflict where people lived together in harmony is at the core of it – a world without strangers.

Some of the poems in the collection are written in a didactic style, using simple rhymes, vernacular language, and a strong rhythm that seems designed to be sung or at least read aloud. And indeed they were read, often with musical accompaniment, at gatherings in Melbourne in the mid-1960s when poetry readings and folk concerts were popular, especially among those with left-wing leanings; venues for such gatherings included the Emerald Hill Theatre and private houses on nominated evenings, sometimes at Ardmore. These are the poems that wear least well today, their satire appearing rather heavy-handed – the fate perhaps of verse written for a particular time and political ethos. 'Song from Planet 90', for instance, speaks of a planet yet unsullied by the effects of radioisotopes like 'strontium 90' used in nuclear testing. This is one of the nine verses:

They still have all ten fingers in
the Country of Methuselah:
with all their automation, they
they like using them for play:
the women all are lovely, and
the men are strong and handsome still:
the strontium-eating habit's not
progressed yet up their way

Another, 'A View of the Beach', begins:

The Distant Electronic Brain,
geared to remark the fall of sparrows,
cried: Holy Radioactive Arrows!
A whole damn planet's down the drain!

But one of Aileen's more didactic poems had been well received by the Director of the National Gallery of Victoria when it was first published in *Overland* in 1960. 'The Invisible Woman' was inspired by the huge Henry Moore sculpture of a featureless but expressive woman that had just been acquired by the gallery and which provoked cries of dissent at the time. More than fifty years later, she sits majestically, and peacefully, in the courtyard of the present National Gallery in Melbourne. Aileen's poem begins:

My muse may wear a thousand faces,
or, cast in bronze with none at all,
sit, near the Melbourne Gallery wall,
still, in her strong, immutable graces.

Of those who call, some flood the press
with 'What's gone wrong with modern art?'
Here sits no 'modern'; have a heart!
She came through time and wilderness.

Eric Westbrook wrote to 'Miss Palmer': 'I was most delighted to read your poem on the Moore figure which appeared in OVERLAND. I had despaired of anyone realising Moore's intention and putting it into words until I read your verse. Now I will be able to quote it to those who feel that there is something intellectually difficult about this piece. I think the trouble is that people always want an explanation and will not see it in human terms'.

War features strongly as a subject in Aileen's poems, often powerfully and movingly. The sonnet 'The Wanderer', written from her hospital bed in 1948, blends the classical figure of the wanderer Odysseus with her own war experience, culminating in her profound fear for the future of a world carelessly bringing about its own destruction. It is also a rejoinder to John Manifold's sonnet 'The Sirens'. 'A Sort of Beauty' was inspired by an exhibition by two Japanese artists called *Hiroshima Panels*, and one of the finest poems, 'Remembering Garcia Lorca', is a poetic response to Lorca's work that exceeds by far what she was able to say in the speech she gave on the occasion of the twenty-fifth anniversary of his death. It comes out of her own profound experience and begins:

You remember the streets with the oranges glowing like suns
in the leafy dark of the sidewalks; you remember the streets
where the cars were loaded with flowers – requisitioned vehicles
daubed white with initials of people's organisations –
F-A-I, C-G-T, U-G-T, representing liberty –
And the courage of the dark young men who would take Saragossa,
And the myriads of dark eyes, and the music, flamenco, –
That was the country of sunlight, the country of Lorca:
But the sky was loud with a prelude of German bombers…

Stephen Murray-Smith had started encouraging Aileen in her writing in 1961 when she was recuperating at the Malvern Clinic after her major breakdown at the end of 1960. She stayed at the clinic for six months but, at least in the later months, was able to visit Ardmore and go out with friends. On one occasion she went to see a production of *The Crucible*, which, she said, put her in a good mood. Yet she was still anxious about her mental state: *How far can I trust my good moods? How far is my illness real? While I'm writing I'm not alone, and the worst of my depression doesn't come on me.* She really needed the encouragement of someone like Stephen (she gives him the pseudonym 'Simon' in her writing) and she often shared a beer with him in town on Tuesday afternoons. He was, in her words, *one of the bright bunch of intellectuals who graduated from Melbourne university after serving a period in the second world war.* She received *a mild shock* when he suggested that she should write about her *own day* for the next generation, not having realised that the past that was so vivid to her was now history. He also suggested she should write about her experience of mental illness, and the notes she sent him are not only revealing of the inner workings of her mind during a psychotic episode but also show how closely related psychotic delusions are to a person's history and preoccupations and, in the case of literary people like Aileen, the influence of what they have read. In Aileen's case, her experience of war and her new fears for the world fed her manic state in 1961.

A few months after the event, she was also able to comment on her experience with wry humour: *Get away from Melbourne, was my thought last November. For once, find the courage to make a move on my own account, without anyone's urging: but it remained a castle in the air, without any practical steps worked out. 'A neurotic build castles in the air, a psychotic moves in'. In December I suppose I must have moved in.* (She left out the third part of the saying: 'and the psychiatrist collects the rent'.) During that November–December period she suffered from *alternating wish-fantasies and fear-fantasies.* The calls of bush-birds who had infiltrated the suburbs during the dry summer became mixed up with her wish-fantasy of a film on which she was collaborating. Reminiscent of Virginia Woolf's aural hallucinations of hearing birds singing in Greek, Aileen writes: *The birds had been trained by my collaborators and their calls were code, or cues directing me to action.* After she 'moved into her castle' the fear-fantasies took over. *Mixed up in it was Moses in the bulrushes and how you evacuate children to another planet from a collapsing world. Then there was the fear of atomic sickness, and the really ugly scene when I had to drown the cat for fear it would pass it on. Fortunately the cat was too much for me. There was the science fiction story about the electronic device set up in the Tibetan mountains to count the names given to god on different parts of the earth, and when all the counting was done the stars began to go out. Something made me keep looking at the stars to make sure they had not gone out.*

During the period leading up to Aileen's 'breakdown' in 1961, we know she had been *topspeed creative* working on her verse play. She never finished it, but parts of it were published in *World Without Strangers?* under the title 'Variations to a Legend'. Some sections are opaque and difficult to comprehend, but others are suffused with her experiences in Spain and World War II combined with her current fears about atomic war that would drive her to madness during that November and December. Greek mythology, art and poetry are also threads that feed into the rich allegory of a section like 'Treeless is the Land':

Pegasus is a wild horse running
Where I don't know: I hold the reins
Loosely: would these be Aragon plains?
Out of the sky a Nazi's gunning.

Bare, treeless is the land: they turned
Their beechwoods into conquerors' ships –
And suddenly, under their starved lips,
The sedge withered, the land burned.

Pegasus is a tired horse flying
Back from the shattered lands; flamenco
Wail in his ears: he'll murmur thank you
For the tongue stilled, for the stars dying...

Pegasus, the winged steed of Greek mythology, evokes the image of the screaming horse in Picasso's *Guernica*, which Aileen described elsewhere as possessing a 'strange beauty' born out of an 'ugly century'. The last line references a line from W. H. Auden's poem 'Spain 1937': 'The stars are dead; the animals will not look' (a poem she used to admire before Auden, in her view, fled to the United States instead of acting upon his convictions). The poem also reflects the delusions she recounted to Stephen Murray-Smith: *Something made me keep looking at the stars to make sure they had not gone out.*

Virginia Woolf's biographer, Hermione Lee, describes how Woolf, who suffered from a 'manic-depressive' or bipolar condition, responded to 'the competing narratives of mental illness – Darwinian, moralistic, Freudian'. She created 'an original language of her own... which could explain her illness to her and give it value' and she did it through writing that recognised 'the virtue of her illness, the happiness of mania or its creativity, as well as its terror and pain'. In the face of Aileen's knowledge that she might have inherited her illness from her uncle (the Darwinian narrative), Helen's moralistic attitude that she should just pull herself together and get a job, and her extensive, unhappy period of psychoanalysis under Dr Clara Lazar Geroe, she too created a language in her poetry that was inseparable from her illness. For Helen, a batch of poems arriving in the mail made her 'shudder'; for Aileen, poetry was a lifeline.

25

No Words

In the years following the deaths of Vance and Nettie, Aileen still worked in the service of her parents. Immediately after Nettie died, there were letters to write to friends and colleagues in Australia and overseas, as well as a flood of tribute and sympathy letters to answer from the many writers whose lives Nettie Palmer had touched – as friend, mentor, teacher, colleague and even critic. And then there were the years of organising, with Helen, her parents' papers for posterity.

Three years before Nettie died, when Aileen had been recuperating in the Malvern Clinic but making regular visits home, she reflected on a day she had intended to spend at Ardmore sorting her books and papers: *but it doesn't take long in the dark house to set me wishing I was never born. Helen fights off the same sort of feeling by ordering a new bath and getting the fence fixed; but I'd let the old bath do duty a while longer in favour of getting several filing cabinets or something that would help shift all that silted up history into more accessible forms.* Around that time in 1961, the sisters started discussing whether their parents' papers should go to the Mitchell Library at the Public Library of New South Wales or to the National Library of Australia in Canberra. After a period of negotiation, Harold White of the National Library secured the collection; Paula Fanning of the Library started visiting Ardmore in the years prior to Nettie's death and the process of sending papers continued until the mid-1960s.

Letters flowed between Aileen at Ardmore and Helen in Sydney about the collection; the sisters not always in agreement as to what should be preserved. There were disagreements over specific matters such as the wording on a book plate for the Palmers' book collection. They also had different conceptions of the collection. Aileen wrote to Helen: *You visualise it as a posthumous collection, paid for and finalised, whereas I should like to send them e.g. some of Flora's and Katharine's letters to me. I think it should be 'the Palmer Collection' rather than 'the Vance and Nettie Palmer Collection', and leave the door open for anything further to be depos[it]ed there, paid for or not.* She clearly wanted to leave the way open for her own papers to be preserved.

Aileen took in lodgers at Ardmore to help with expenses, up to three at a time, usually men, including two Malayan–Chinese students who were brothers. Ernest Chow was her favourite and she referred to him in letters to Helen as '*the importance of being Ernest*'. A cleaner was employed on an irregular basis to keep the place in some state of order, but she was never allowed to touch Aileen's room, which was usually strewn with papers. Helen made flying visits from Sydney to help with the sorting and dispersal of the fifty or so years of papers that had accumulated in the house, a practice that was not always appreciated by Aileen who in 1966 was trying to grapple with material that was left after the personal papers had been sent to the library: *The key problem for me in months to come, apart from having enough money to buy cigarettes, is how much history I try to preserve, as real history isn't much in what people have so far got into books, but in magazines N. has put by in 1936, and untidy files of stuff. However, don't come rushing over. Everything is under control, as far as it can be, and 'the one thing I hate more than sin is' the prospect of you rushing over, with few minutes to spare, to bulldoze me into this or out of that. Excuse my Spanish, but it's happened too often, and it need never happen again…*

Students and academics writing on one or both of the Palmer parents started contacting Aileen and Helen for information and access to papers. In the year before Nettie died, Aileen turned away Beatrice Faust (later a founder of the Women's Electoral Lobby) who was writing an MA thesis on Henry Handel Richardson, saying that her mother was too ill to see her. In 1965 Clem Christesen inquired, on behalf of Harry Heseltine who was researching a book on Vance, if there were still papers at Ardmore. Aileen said they had gone to Canberra but he could drop in and have a chat if he liked. Apparently answering queries from Aileen some time later, Helen wrote in her forthright manner: 'Nobody gave Heseltine permission to write on Vance (I've never met him, for instance; nor has he written to anyone). But he doesn't need it. Nobody needs anyone's permission to write about anyone'. Heseltine published a critical study of Vance's work in 1970. In the same letter Helen said: 'Will get on to finding out a bit more about V. Smith'.

On several occasions during the 1960s, Aileen entertained students who were writing theses on Vance. One researcher who was working on the Palmers and whose company she particularly enjoyed was poet and academic Vivian Smith, who stayed at Ardmore in January 1967. *Vivian and I had long discussions about the keeping of historical records and documents,* Aileen recalled, *which has been much neglected in Australia, especially in a period when everyone is moving from old family homes to more compact dwellings. This was interspersed, of course, with sips of beer, and Vivian going up to the Chinese cafe that has conveniently set itself up in Chatham Road to fetch us home our dinner.* As she took the year's Christmas cards off the mantelpiece, she passed them to him to look through for people he might write to about letters from Vance and Nettie. Vivian later edited a collection of their letters and wrote a critical study of their work. He also edited a collection of Nettie's poetry and essays as well as her diary *Fourteen Years*, which *Meanjin* had published in limited edition in 1948, thus ensuring that her stylish and elegant personal writing reached a wider audience. Aileen reflected that she would in due course have to part with her own papers, acknowledging that *Karin Piper* (the name she used for Katharine Susannah Prichard in her 'novel' fragments) did not want *her casual papers preserved anywhere, for fossickers, who could be as nice as Vivian, but could be Leonie Kramer, or something worse.*

Aileen had also continued campaigning against the Vietnam War during the 1960s as well as propping up the ailing Realist Writers Group in Melbourne. For the Sydney branch, she wrote an article on Spain and offered her poem 'Remembering Garcia Lorca' for the 'Spain Then – Vietnam Now' section of the summer 1966 issue of *The Realist.* The same edition carried an article by Malcolm Salmon on Aileen's translations of To Huu and Ho Chi Minh.

Towards the end of 1966, Aileen received a rejection letter for an application she had made to the Commonwealth Literary Fund (of which her father had been chairman) to write a novel. Preserved in her papers, the single sheet of thick, white paper is ripped in half down the middle. Sighting the two pieces with the jagged tear gave me what one researcher has described as 'the archival jolt…an assurance that we have connected with something real'. Suddenly Aileen Palmer was there before me, reaching across the years with an act of frustration that any writer immediately understands.

A few months later, she received a touching letter from the last of her 'Emerald uncles', eighty-year-old Guido Baracchi (her Uncle Esmonde had died in 1960), responding to reading her volume of poetry, *World Without Strangers?* Guido writes of the four 'moments' that for him make up Aileen Palmer. Part I, written in 'near-doggerel', relates to her Emerald childhood and finishes:

'You've got a will; you have a way
With you,' 'uncle' was wont to say.
You touched the heart, Aileen Yvonne:
Then turned the wheel – and you were gone.

He then describes the remaining parts:

'Part II would cover a single night in 1935 in Melbourne, when I sat beside you on the floor of a darkened room, listening to a talk with lantern slides, just before you were leaving for Europe – and Spain. Of all that evening, only you remain vividly alive in me. Part III would be represented by the portrait-painting of you that, during the later 'fifties and early 'sixties I saw hanging on the wall of the living-room in No. 7; that I greatly admired, as I told Vance or Nettie on each occasion I saw it, and that spoke poignantly to me about you. Part IV would be constituted by World Without Strangers? Which, even if you had done nothing else in life, I would think more than enough'.

The 1970s brought more periods of institutionalisation after a major collapse in 1968 and Aileen spent several years moving between Larundel psychiatric hospital and Ardmore. From Larundel she wrote to Matron Meyer, her ally from the Malvern Clinic: *You told me to keep my brain occupied, and take an interest in the things around me. Well, I'm afraid, for a long time, as I may have told you, I was very pessimistic & depressed & apathetic about most things. Most of this past year, though, I have been better, and gone back to reading quite a bit, of which I had done little. I've also written more intelligible letters (to my sister, mainly) and have written some kind of chronicle of my daily life. Since I left town about the end of '68 or earlier, I haven't written any verse...*

In 1977, Ardmore was sold and Aileen bought a small flat in the suburb of Reservoir, but within a year was in Mont Park hospital being treated for ongoing problems with her reaction to lithium. While she was there, she wrote to Helen: *H darling, When I lie down on the bed, and start talking to myself, I find I'm scared stiff you'll die before I do...so please don't!* But Helen, still working as language mistress at Fort Street Girls' High School, was ill, suffering a 'breakdown' herself in 1977, which she dubbed 'My Bad Year'. Through the support of her friends she was able to come through it and she did not tell her sister of it. She wrote about her experience in early 1979, saying 'For the first time I'll be able to help Aileen I think, because we're talking the same language'.

In a short piece simply called 'Aileen', Helen tries to write her 'concept of her'. She acknowledges that when her sister's poems were written, she felt them to be 'horrors' as 'words, words, words, were a sign of manic behaviour', but she now says: 'Slowly I've begun to realise the beauty and the moving quality of many of them'. Fearing that Aileen will die before she does, she plans what would constitute the 'occasion' to mark it, which 'must reflect Aileen the poet'. People from the literary establishment would be invited as well as her friends from the hospital. Helen would read some of Aileen's poems herself, 'particularly the Iron House one' (which is the very poem whose obscurity she had been so scathing about when it was published in *Meanjin* in 1958 as 'Song for a Distant Epoch', later published as 'The Silent Land' in *World Without Strangers?*). She also hoped people would stand up and give their memories of Aileen.

Sadly, none of this came to pass and Aileen would never have read of her sister's concept of her or her plans for a memorial service. Helen died of cancer just weeks after writing 'Aileen'. In the printed tribute that was read at her funeral on 10 May 1979, it is mentioned that 'Her sister Aileen is present with us', but no reflections by Aileen about Helen's death survive. She was now the last of the Palmers.

In the late 1970s, Aileen had been befriended by post-graduate student Deborah Jordan who was writing a PhD thesis on Nettie at the University of Melbourne, later published as a book titled *Nettie Palmer: Search for an Aesthetic*. Together they went to see Bruce Beresford's 1978 film of *The Getting of Wisdom* and, although Aileen does not write of her opinion of the film, she did lend Deborah the manuscript of her *school story*, presumably 'Poor Child!'. In January 1981, Aileen was taken on a holiday to Adelaide by Deborah, who invited several women to meet her, including feminist academic Susan Sheridan (then known as Sue Higgins), who remembered being 'emotionally exhausted' after the meeting: 'fascination with her life and pity for her institutionalisation...the vulnerability of a single woman who, I sense, hung onto her family – the mother she wanted to protect, the father she admired and resented – until they gave up on her'.

Deborah recorded an interview with Aileen during that time, in which Aileen speaks in a low, pleasant, slightly slurred voice. I found it poignant and difficult to listen to, especially when she spoke about the effects of her hospitalisation and psychiatric treatment: *Having spent large parts of thirty years in hospital I don't feel certain anything I may say may be a truth or a lie because in hospital I've had large parts of my life blasted out by...ECT, it's called – electric technology that ruins your memory in large slabs. So I can't talk from the moment I was born until the present day without needing to go forward and back.* The long-term effects of her treatment may explain, at least in part, why she obsessively wrote and rewrote certain incidents from her life and why she was unable to write a coherent account of it in what she called her *semi-fictional bits of egocentric writing*. After Helen's death, Aileen sent scraps of writing to Helen's friend Jessie McLeod, who was living in Melbourne and who visited Aileen frequently. Rambling and often incoherent, the fragments ranged over incidents in her childhood and she dwelt often on the subject of Wob, Vance's brother who spent decades in Goodna asylum near Brisbane. Living at Ward S14 for long-term female patients at Mont Park, Aileen was still receiving ECT weekly, telling Jessie that she felt that it *should possibly be discarded altogether, and possibly be replaced by insulin-glucose, which did me no harm in 1948.*

However, Aileen's attempts to write her 'novel' – an account of her life and her relationship with her family, which was fiction only to the extent of her practice of changing names of people and places – stemmed from more than a desire to overcome the effects of memory-obliterating psychiatric treatment. At its core was the desire to prove herself as a writer in the form that was favoured by her father and held in highest esteem by the mother who devoted her life to his success – the novel. Feminist historian Sally Newman uses trauma theory when trying to explain Aileen Palmer's obsessive autobiographical writing, suggesting that 'it was the "act of writing" itself that Aileen could not escape', that 'writing was arguably part of the problem and could never be part of the resolution that she sought'. This is a persuasive argument that would help account for the fact that Aileen kept on writing her 'novel' fragments even after her parents and her sister had died.

Yet, in the tangled web of the Palmer family's emotional dynamics, the situation proves even more complex. Beyond her personal writing about her family, Aileen wanted more than anything to be remembered as a poet. Nettie suspended writing her modestly successful poetry when her elder daughter was born in 1915, not wishing her to grow up with 'ink in her veins'. But war intervened and Nettie started to question the value of writing poetry in such a world, instead devoting her life to supporting Vance's writing career. Aileen wrote several times in her novel fragments that she thought Nettie had more of a touch of genius than Vance. She urged her mother all her life to cut back on her critical writing and lecturing and take up her creative writing, her poetry, again, but to no avail. Would her guilt at having been born have been assuaged if Nettie had done so?

Unlike her autobiographical fiction, Aileen did manage to complete many poems – and at their best they are powerful and moving. But she was unable to achieve recognition for them in her parents' eyes because they were inextricably associated with her mental condition and evoked fear and anxiety, particularly in Nettie. The tension in Aileen's life between her writing and her political activism found resolution in her poetry, where she became a *poet of conscience* writing about the state of the world, bringing together the two strands of her life that were most important to her. For Nettie, however, Aileen's activism was to the detriment of her writing and her mental health. 'When Aileen chose a life of action instead of a life of study, she tore herself up', she wrote to Esmonde after Aileen's first breakdown in 1948, blaming 'deferred shock' from her war experiences for her collapse. She held to that opinion for the rest of her life.

'Spain stands out in my own life like a beacon-light, as the time when we stood for "the cause of all progressive mankind"', wrote Aileen in 1962 to the Indian writer Mulk Raj Annand, whom she met through Edith Young and encountered in Spain in 1937 when he visited the brigade she was attached to in the Jarama Valley. She may have suffered 'deferred shock' (or what we might today call post–traumatic stress disorder) from her war experience after her return to Australia, but Spain also remained the highlight of her life. Through her poetry – influenced by poets such as Louis Aragon and John Cornford who combined activism with their politically charged writing – Aileen was able to continue standing in the light of that beacon while still living under the shadow of her parents.

Sometime during the 1980s, Aileen was moved from Mont Park to a small psychiatric nursing home in Ballarat where she died on 21 December 1988, aged seventy-three. Spanish Civil War historian Judith Keene visited her in both places. She recalled that at Mont Park 'I talked to her in a kind of visitor's room because we sat at a table but other people came and went. And the people who looked after her seemed quite fond of her in an instrumental-professional sort of way – though they certainly knew nothing about her as one of the male nurses said to me about her talking about the war'. They thought her talk was part of her delusions. When Judith visited her in the Ballarat nursing home (to which she was probably moved after the scaling down of psychiatric wards following the Richmond Report on Mental Health 1983) she found her 'in a kind of motel room and in bed...and my recollection is that it was quite sad because she barely spoke and I felt quite emotional about seeing her and knowing so much about her and that this could happen to her'. After Aileen Palmer's death, there were no tributes and no obituaries. But poet Colleen Z. Burke, who had admired her poetry and her activism, heard of her unremarked death and wrote a poem that was published in *Southerly*. 'No words' is a moving commemoration of Aileen's life. It begins:

In the end there
were no words you stared
endlessly into space
caught in the thin air – the
inescapable web of fresh
country air.   Shells bursting   cries/screams
of the slaughtered people always in your head
no more
the unbearable noise
within   no more…

On a mild, sunny morning in Canberra in December 1993, a memorial to the Australians who had served in the Spanish Civil War was unveiled at Lotus Bay on Lake Burley Griffin. Close by were planted young olive trees, a gift of the Spanish Embassy as a symbol of peace. During the ceremony, eighty-eight year old Len Fox (who co-wrote the pamphlet *Australians in Spain* with Nettie Palmer) read Aileen Palmer's poem 'Danger is never danger':

Danger is never danger
till the blood running over the street
is the blood of your own heart's crying:
the love you were coming to meet.

Death is not death till you
hear all planes pass in fearing:
not my own love they'll strike!
Not my own love they're nearing!

War is not war till you
find in the shattered stones
flesh of your own love's flesh,
dust of your own love's bones

A rare poem of Aileen's to combine the personal and the political, this became one of her most popular. Guido Baracchi, among others, thought it was the best of the *World Without Strangers?* collection. But it is not directly autobiographical, nor was it written during Aileen's time in Spain as was incorrectly stated at the memorial unveiling. There was a myth among the Realist Writers Group that Aileen had been traumatised by the loss of a lover (implicitly male) during the Spanish War and that the poem referred to that loss. As we know, she actually wrote 'Danger is never danger' in 1958, after a few whiskeys and just a day or two before she was admitted to Sunbury mental hospital as an involuntary patient. Aileen had suffered similar fears to those expressed in the poem when she was with her unnamed female lover in London during the Blitz, but she never lost a lover in Spain. The poem's immediacy is intensely moving, but like so much of Aileen Palmer's writing, it contains a layer of secrecy that she took with her to her grave.

Notes

Introduction: Portraits

a faded snapshot, Palmer collection, NLA PIC 885/1-8, 36a.

Meldrumite, AP to family, 25 July 1938, NLA MS6759, Box 1/1.

She didn't think, AP to family, 25 August 1938, NLA MS6759, Box 1/1.

'Remarkably good', NP diary, 9 January 1940, NLA MS1174, Series 16, Box 25 [all entries from NP's diary are at this number].

semi-fictional bits of egocentric writing, AP, 'Pilgrim's Way', 25 August 1959, NLA MS6759, Series 4, Box 4 [all further references are from this source].

several of her poems, J. Jump (ed.), *Poems from Spain.*

'Thaelmann Battalion', http://www.youtube.com/watch?v=OtP1BHCRJTM

'tragic daughter', D. Martin, *My Strange Friend,* p. 269.

'the one practical and matter of fact', Edith Young to NP, 8 August 1948, NLA MS1174, 7470.

A vast crowd, see J. Fyrth, *The Signal was Spain*, Chapter 4.

A convoy of Daimlers, L. Palfreeman, *Salud!*, p. 27.

The days passed, 'Barcelona Flashback', in 'Pilgrim's Way' [originally in 'Last Mile to Huesca' written just after the Spanish Civil War], NLA MS6759, Box 4/19.

their august and all-pervasive shadows, 'Coming of Age', in 'Pilgrim's Way'.

My mind is so full and following material in italics from manuscript by AP, 'March 13th 1948', NLA MS6759, Box 7/4/22.

'Aileen has had a breakdown', NP to Jean Campbell, Easter Monday 1948, NLA MS6759, Box 1/4.

1. Two Legacies

I grew up feeling ashamed, AP, 'Pilgrim's Way'.

Something had started them talking, AP, 'Pilgrim's Way'.

'I like to remember', VP to NH, n.d. 1912, NLA MS1174, 715.

'total abstinence', VP to NH, n.d. end 1911, NLA MS1174, 673.

'like two tense strings', NH to VP, n.d. 1912, NLA MS1174, 775.

Blake took religion lightly, AP, 'Pilgrim's Way'.

she was essentially almost cruelly honest, AP, 'Pilgrim's Way'.

'I am using it', VP to Mr & Mrs Higgins, Christmas Eve 1913, NLA MS1174, 1016.

'you seem to think', VP to NH, n.d. early 1914, NLA MS1174, 1019.

We have all been rather, AP, 'Day of the Voyager', '1.7.61', NLA MS 6083, Box 1.

'I've been nearly distracted', VP to NH, n.d. September 1912, NLA MS1174, 847.

'such a strange letter', VP to NH, 'Off Honolulu', 1912, NLA MS1174, 850.

'He remembers everything', VP to NH, n.d., NLA MS1174, 854.

'Your hussy', NH to VP, n.d., NLA MS1174, 889.

'I feel as if I'd crashed', VP to NH, 29 March 1913, NLA MS1174, 912.

'a very clever specialist', VP to NH, n.d., NLA MS1174, 909.

'The place', VP to NH, 5 April 1913, NLA MS1174, 914.

'There is no taint in our blood', VP to NH, 22 April 1913, NLA MS1174, 917.

'Wob is more important than I am', VP to NH, n.d., NLA MS1174, 923.

'we couldn't live here half as cheaply', VP to NH, n.d., NLA MS1174, 925.

devotedly ironing pyjamas, AP, 'A Clean, Well-lighted Place' in Dear Louise, July 1961, MS6083, Box 1.

2. Ink in her Veins

'bonzer', NP to mother, 28 May 1914, NLA MS1174, 1018.

'I'm beginning to understand', NP to mother, 7 July 1914, NLA MS1174, 1162.

'vigorously tanning', NP to mother, 24 June 1914, NLA MS1174, 1137.

'I do not feel life', EH to NH, n.d. April 1914, NLA MS1174.

'a big world to fill', VP to NH, n.d. March 1914, NLA MS1174, 1047.

'He seems much younger', NP to mother, 24 June 1914, NLA MS1174, 1137.

'War is officially declared', NP to EH, 5 August 1914, NLA MS1174, 1205.

'They say England', NP to mother, 5 August 1914, NLA MS1174, 1206.
'crumpling in all directions', NP to mother, 2 October 1914, NLA MS1174, 1256.
'slim and willowy', *Melbourne Punch*, 17 February 1916, cited in J. Sparrow, *Communism*, p. 64.
'Nettie had a distinguished', KSP, *Meanjin*, 18:2, July 1959, p. 243.
'I hope I know how to behave', NP to mother, 8 October 1914, NLA MS1174, 1267.
'She has been a splendid companion', NP to mother, 15 October 1914, NLA MS1174, 1270.
'But before I go any further', NP to mother, 29 October 1914, NLA MS1174, 1289.
'tremendously distressed', KSP to HP, 26 January 1961, NLA MS6083, Box 25.
'I quite realise that he's better', NP to mother, 6 January 1915, NLA MS1174, 1367.
'Dear scrapface', EH to NP, 9 April 1915, NLA MS1174, 1433.
'I meant to tell you some more', NP to mother, 14 April 1915, NLA MS1174, 1441.
simply decanted, AP to Jessie McLeod, 25 March 1980, NLA MS6759, Box 1/7.
'black hair but light eyebrows', NP to mother, 13 April 1915, NLA MS1174, 1440.
'I think she likes him to hold her', NP to mother, 21 April 1915, NLA MS1174, 1453.
'a slight little feminine song', cited in D. Jordan, *Nettie Palmer*, p. 115.
'Altogether it's enough to make', NP to mother, 21 April 1915, NLA MS1174, 1453.

3. Emerald

Conscription! Conscription!, AP, 'Black Bats and Speckled Fish', 'Pilgrim's Way'.
'the remote wavy blue wall', NP, *The Dandenongs*, p. 5.
'for many months afterwards', NP to Allan Edwards, 20 March 1954, V. Smith, *Letters*, p. 212.
Probably I was jealous of Gwen, AP to Jessie McLeod, 25 March 1980, NLA MS6759, Box 1/7.

The Hughes government, see J. Sparrow, *Communism*, Chapter 3.
'Aileen Yvonne, aged 2½,', NP diary, 7 November 1917.
'very broken-down', NP diary, January 1918.
'a band of brothers', D. Walker, cited in D. Jordan, *Nettie Palmer*, p. 153.
The tradition of masculinity, AP, 'The Women of Chilbrook', 'Pilgrim's Way'.
'horrible prospect', NP diary, 8 November 1917.
'Is this special or toy?', NP diary, January 1918.
Long served his jail sentence, AP, 'Thank goodness, grandmother', 'Pilgrim's Way'.
'Peace', R. H. Long, *Poems*.
'that mysterious depression', NP to VP, 11 June 1919, NLA MS1174, 2178.
'impersonal old blue-stocking', NP to VP, 24 April 1919, NLA MS1174, 2126.
'stabbed me a hundred times a day', NP to VP, 10 October 1919, NLA MS1174, 2244.
'This is our real home!', NP to VP, 10 October 1919, NLA MS1174, 2244.
settled in his deckchair, AP, 1959 diary, in 'Pilgrim's Way'.
'10 miles: Helen too, not yet 4!', NP diary, 6 February 1921.
Thinking people were the background of my childhood, AP, 'Black Bats and Speckled Fish', 'Pilgrim's Way'; quotations from the next two paragraphs are taken from various excerpts of 'Pilgrim's Way' and 'Dear Louise'.
'very sweet to the kiddies', NP diary, 6 May 1921.
the people who roamed in my thoughts, AP, 'Thank goodness, grandmother', 'Pilgrim's Way'.
A good many years have past [sic] *now*, NLA MS3044, Box 1/1.
'Aileen of course is writing furiously', NP to R. H. Long, 24 May 1925, V. Smith, *Letters*, pp. 31–2.
didn't have the least ounce of sense of humour, AP, 'Women of Chillbrook', 'Pilgrim's Way'.
'She had only one fault', Kathleen Fitzpatrick to Amirah Inglis, 10 March 1988, ANU Archives, A. Inglis Papers, Box 6.
'Vance dressed up as a Velasquez portrait', NP diary, 22 April 1925.
Gwen may not have done, AP, 'Have you got any atrocities then?', 'Pilgrim's Way'.
'Aileen made a country', NP, 'Alsia', 1938, MS6083, Box 2.
'Not Safe', NP, 1938, MS6083, Box 2.

4. Caloundra

AP, 'Diary, notes, etc. of Aileen Yvonne Flavia Denise Palmer', started Saturday 29 October 1927, MS3044, Box 1/4; her 'biography' is written on 6 April 1928 [subsequently cited as AP diary].

'rather restless', NP diary, 29 July 1925.

the Lord of Caloundra once, AP diary, 6 April 1928.

'with four rooms and no passages', NP to mother, 16 September 1925, NLA MS1174, 2672.

a beautiful place, AP diary, 6 April 1928.

'cantankerous crise de nerfs', NP diary, 20 October 1925.

'They take their lunch', NP to mother, 16 September 1925, NLA MS1174, 2672.

oldish, false teeth, AP diary, 6 April 1928.

'Aileen has developed a sudden passion', NP to father, 28 November 1925, NLA MS1174, 2697.

There wasn't much of that period, AP, 'Dear Louise', July 1961, MS6083, Box 1.

'trying hard to keep the family accounts', NP diary, 15 October 1927.

'lovely, cool house', NP diary, 25 January 1926.

an article on Henry Handel Richardson for *The Bulletin*, NP, 15 October 1925.

'it had published one on the lady', NP diary, 15 January 1926.

some feminist scholars, see Modjeska, Chapter 1, Vickery, Chapter 7.

'rather like cutting words', NP diary, 25 February 1926.

Dear old Adorable, AP to NP, 18 June 1926, NLA MS1174, 2795.

'well enough', NP diary, 21 July 1926.

Darling old Spooshable, AP to NP, NLA MS1174, 2827.

'rather bankrupt', NP diary, 6 December 1926.

'Juvenilia', NLA MS3044, Boxes 1–4.

Bertha stood motionless, AP, 'Simplicity', NLA MS3044, Box 2/2.

Aunt Constance is a thin, bony woman, AP, 'Cassidy's Farm', NLA MS3044, Box 2/2.

'a sprite and a comedian', NP to Esther Levy, 5 September 1928, V. Smith, *Letters*, p. 41.

'well cut – oh dear!', NP diary, 17 January 1928.

'Senorita' thrilling, AP diary, 17 November 1927, NLA MS3044, Box 1/4.

On the trip to Coolum, AP diary, 6 April 1928.

'A[ileen] romantically excited', NP diary, 12 May 1927.

'Violet Beazley came in afternoon', NP diary, 19 May 1927.

'Vance ought to inaugurate this diary', NP diary, 2 January 1929.

I wish you wouldn't be so 'umble, AP to NP, n.d. October 1938, NLA MS6759, Box 1.

'Spent wonderful afternoon on rocks', NP diary, 4 September 1925.

'(For the day, see Aileen's diary)', NP diary, 20 March 1927.

Wrote secret; Wrote secret in evening, AP diary, several references late 1927, early 1928.

'A[ileen] writing at some long stint just now', NP diary, 20 November 1927.

I am thirteen, AP diary, 6 April 1928.

'Aileen says Currimundi', NP to mother, 9 August 1928, NLA MS1174, 3185.

Around the stall would be gathered, AP, 'Coming of Age', 'Pilgrim's Way'.

Still, as always happened in our family, AP, 'At School', 'Pilgrim's Way'.

5. The Getting of Wisdom

'vast in its breadth', H. H. Richardson, *The Getting of Wisdom*, p. 77.

'To a Portrait of a Famous Woman', AP, Richardson Papers, NLA MS133/13/17.

'one of the poems', C. Probyn and B. Steele (eds), *Henry Handel Richardson: the letters*, V2, p. 203.

Judge Henry Bournes Higgins, John Rickard, 'Higgins, Henry Bournes (1851–1929), *Australian Dictionary of Biography*, Volume 9 (MUP), 1983.

'We feel it badly', NP diary, 14 January 1929.

'Helen is purring all the time', NP diary, 19 April 1929.

'Helen came home from school', NP diary, 27 June 1929.

'in a tartan rug', M. Tipping, 'Remembrance of Palmers past', *Overland*, 100, 1985, p. 13.

'She'll enjoy biting into something hard', NP diary, 22 April 1929.

'Aileen's whirling along', NP diary, 2 July 1929.

'Anxious to write a series', NP diary, 23 July 1929.

'seven times by Botticelli', NH, 1907, Commonplace book, NLA MS6351.

'Aileen, otherwise Pawpaw', NP diary, 24 August 1929.

'quite a charming, solid girl,' NP diary, 12 November 1929.

'very ambitious', NP diary, 28 December 1929.

'also doing a sudden', NP diary, 1 February 1930.

'A Feminist's Heaven', AP, NLA MS3044, Box 1/6.

'some entanglements', NP diary, 5 February 1930.

'A++ in BIBLE!'; 'I love life', HP to VP, 8 June, 23 July 1930, NLA MS1174, 3575, 3644.

'I must write to Brent', AP to VP, 16 May 1930, NLA MS1174, 3565–6.

'Dear old Helen', VP to HP, 25 August 1930, NLA MS1174, 3679.

'Keep all these letters', NP to VP, 18 June 1930, NLA MS1174, 3591.

'God knows I'm glad', NP to VP, 14 June 1930, NLA MS1174, 3560.

'need of assurances', NP to VP, 6 July 1930, NLA MS1174, 3608.

'I wish I could write', VP to NP, August 1930, NLA MS1174, 3665.

'Helen plays endlessly', NP diary, 20 May 1930.

'His friends are all prosperous', NP diary, 30 June 1930.

'I've told Mum about seeing H.H.R.', VP to AP, 18 July 1930, NLA MS1174, 3630.

'He struck me as perhaps', HHR to MK, 3 July 1930, Probyn and Steele (eds), V2, p. 195.

'People complain', HHR to MK, 16 July 1930, Probyn and Steele (eds), V2, p. 198.

'his women are of wood', MK to HHR, 20 July 1930, Probyn and Steele (eds), V2, p. 199.

'had a kind of a dare-devil mind', H. H. Richardson, *The Getting of Wisdom*, p. 164.

'the real romance', AP, 'Poor Child!', NLA MS 6759, Box 6/4/16; and NLA MS3044, Box 2/1.

'Very glad to hear', HHR to MK, 18 June 1929, Probyn and Steele (eds), V2, p. 122.

'active in mind & body', MK to HHR, 8 July 1930, Probyn and Steele (eds), V2, p. 196.

'I laughed at your description', HHR to MK, 16 August 1930, Probyn and Steele (eds), V2, p. 203.

'Your most entertaining letter', HHR to MK, 29 October 1930, Probyn and Steele (eds), V2, p. 213.

'The woman's a *born* journalist', HHR to MK, 8 September 1931, Probyn and Steele (eds), V2, p. 301.

'That book left an *arid* impression, HHR to MK, 8 September 1931, Probyn and Steele (eds), V2, p. 301.

'I'm so glad *Laura*', HHR to NP, 27 August 1931, N. Palmer, *Henry Handel Richardson*, p. 195.

'She was anxious', MK to HHR, 1 September 1931, Probyn and Steele (eds), V2, p. 299.

'She really is a picture of robust-ness. I always feel nervous about her frocks, they strain.' Michael Ackland quotes this in his biography of Henry Handel Richardson and incorrectly states that it is about Nettie, p. 235. This has since been picked up and paraphrased by Brenda Niall as referring to Nettie's 'plumpness': 'Ettie and Nettie', *Australian Book Review*, February 2013. Nettie Palmer was not plump; the adolescent Aileen was.

'make "The Getting of Wisdom" seem', NP diary, 17 August 1931.

'She has understood them well', NP diary, 25 September 1931.

'most devout in German', NP diary, 14 February 1931.

'You've been a noisy old windbag', NP to VP, 14 June 1930, NLA MS1174, 3560.

'Good excuse for doing badly', NP diary, 27 November 1931.

'Aileen very helpish', NP diary, 18 February 1932.

'writing something of her own', NP diary, 23 February 1932.

6. Poor Child!

'Poor Child!', AP, NLA MS6759/6/4/16 (1 vol); NLA MS3044/2/1 (3 vols) [subsequent references to PC from these sources].

Colour was ebbing, PC, p. 394.

bullying women, PC, p. 59.

'the *glamour* of their *ménage*', PC, p. 366.

This perpetual contact with S.S.D., PC, p. 372.

At tennis, of course, PC, p. 218.

'In those days school authorities', Henry Handel Richardson, *Myself When Young*, p. 70.

'*You poor child!*', PC, p. 21.

'*She's a Lesbian*', PC, p. 320.

remembering a scene that Clothilde had read her, PC, p. 214.

had no knowledge of this side, PC, pp. 220–1.

They wove themselves, PC, p. 62.

If she had been a man, PC, p. 72.

She had been a moody, PC, p. 35.

took her own awkwardness, PC, p. 36.

This is the way, PC, p. 363.

gateway *loomed up in the dim light*, PC, pp. 273–4.

Listening to her mother, PC, p. 275.

Vivienne had resolved, PC, p. 276.

'so they dashed into town together', NP diary, 5 October 1931.

'What a sibyl she is!', NP diary, 1 March 1932.

'Aileen's uncles at Emerald once', NP diary, 17 March 1932.

For with Helen's going, PC, pp. 207–8.

Phrases went round, PC, p. 223.

Her mother had written poems, PC, pp. 224–5.

But to her teachers, PC, p. 286.

Miss Jessica Gilchrist, see Kathleen Fitzpatrick, *PLC Melbourne*, pp. 156–7.

'Aileen to meeting', NP diary, 27 April 1931.

Alexia might be invited out to tea, PC, pp. 157–8.

the spirit of bathos, PC, p. 156.

Brunswick cable-tram, PC, p. 159.

and wore a kind, PC, p. 40.

there was something cruel, PC, p. 40.

Miss Garran reads it, PC, pp. 108–110.

Another exercise book, AP 1932 diary, NLA MS6759, Box 6/4/16 [subsequent mentions from this source].

D and I walked on ahead, AP 1932 diary, p. 54.

thought her too restrained, AP 1932 diary, p. 49.

Nellie and I hugged, AP 1932 diary, p. 16.

Shirley assured me, AP 1932 diary, p. 34.

She said she wasn't used, AP 1932 diary, p. 36.

a recent fictionalised memoir, Jill Golden, *Inventing Beatrice*.

'Gillie'; *Alexia took very little notice*, PC, p. 32 and p. 33.

horribly full of beans, PC, p. 78.

frenzied intuition, AP 1932 diary, p. 20.

Will I hurl myself again, AP 1932 diary, p. 20.

7. Young Communist

Aileen and Helen are posed, Palmer collection, NLA.PIC-vn4556901.

'like a flat hat', NP to mother, 21 May 1932, NLA MS1174, 3991.

'But where was there any chance', NP, *Fourteen Years*, in V. Smith (ed.), *Nettie Palmer*, p. 98.

'Granny is getting a teeny bit anxious', HP to family, 7 May 1932, NLA MS6759, Box 1/1.

'For the first time', *Proletariat*, Vol. 1, No. 1, 1932, p. 24.

'all noted as Communists', NAA, Series A6119, item A6119xr1; Aileen Palmer ASIO file incorrectly cites April 1934 as the date she joined the CPA.

'It's a very competent magazine', NP to HP, 'Green Island, somewhere around April-end 1932', NLA MS1174, 3961.

'centring around Mr. Samuel White', HP to family, 7 May 1932, NLA MS6759, Box 1/1.

'two sprouting daughters', NP to mother, 4 June 1932, NLA MS1174, 3994.

'Dearie mine Granny seems rather worried', NP to HP, n.d. June 1932, NLA MS6083/1.

'but what the dickens', AP to NP, n.d. [August] 1932, NLA MS6759/1/1.

'quoting Mr. Louis Esson', AP to parents, n.d. [September] 1932, NLA MS6759/1/1.

Am I a selfish little beast?, AP 1932 diary, pp. 21–2.

'gone off to some Labour Conference', HP to parents, 3 July 1932, NLA MS6759/1/1.

the same, but more subdued, AP 1932 diary, p. 3.

Blast! I feel utterly lazy, AP 1932 diary, p. 37.

'Horribly difficult', NP diary, 27 December 1932.

'to find a warm, sheltered place', NP, *Fourteen Years*, in V. Smith (ed.), *Nettie Palmer*, p. 117.

'as if glimpsed in a crowd', NP diary, 26 January 1934.

'very difficult', NP diary, 2 February 1934.

'oozed happiness', NP diary, 15 August 1934.

'Margaret shy & shrewdish', NP diary, 16 August 1934.

'clearly a literary man', NP diary, 13 November 1934.

'What a family!', NP diary, 3 January 1935.

'terrific assemblage', NP diary, 4 January 1935.

'A peculiar calm', NP diary, 28 January 1935.

'an extraordinary party', NP diary, 29 January 1935.

'the girls would be very fortunate', NP diary, 25 December 1934.

'sketching some protests', NP diary, 2 February 1935.

'making pounds', NP diary, 8 February 1935.

You remember when I cursed Dad, AP to parents, 4 October 1938, NLA MS6759/1/1.
'it seems', NP diary, 25 February 1935.
Aileen had been promised the job of translating, NP to FDD, 30 June 1937, in V. Smith (ed.), *Letters*, p. 151.
'maddish, whirling weeks', NP diary, 7 March 1935.
'an orgy', NP diary, 21 March 1935.
I hadn't come to Europe, AP, 'Pilgrim's Way'.

8. Europe in Turmoil

the spectre of Hitler, AP, 'Pilgrim's Way'.
'horrible and dear', NP diary, 30 April 1935.
We had no time, AP, 'Pilgrim's Way'.
'a laughable contrast', P. Sloan (ed.), *John Cornford*, p. 116.
'the poetry of revolution', in P. Sloan, p. 129.
'how can they sing', NP, *Fourteen Years*, in V. Smith (ed.), *Nettie Palmer*, p. 155.
'our common heritage', cited in R. Sullivan, *Villa Air-Bel*, p. 56.
'common action', AP, *Proletariat*, 4/3/Oct–Dec. 1935.
GB and KSP's visit to Russia, 1933, see J. Sparrow, Chapter 8.
'posher bar', NP diary, 21 July 1935.
'to cover ground', NP diary, 30 August 1935.
'a pocket-sized dynamo', *The Brooklyn Daily Eagle*, 25 April 1926, p. 93.
'full of suggestions', NP diary, 22 May 1935.
'restless like a cat', NP diary, 9 August 1935.
a charming city, AP, BBC radio broadcast n.d.
'heavy furs on their winter-mantels', AP to 'Grannie', 1 January 1936, NLA MS3044/2.
the Viennese habit, AP, draft of 'Last Mile to Huesca', NLA MS6759/4/19.
Helene Scheu-Reisz on Ocracoke Island, www.villagecraftsmen.com/news112908.htm, accessed 22 April 2011.
'feed her with European literature', NP diary, 9 March 1936.
'Horribly unsatisfying and disappointing', NP diary, 3 February 1936.
'quite at sea', NP diary, 25 January 1936.
'V rather shivery', NP diary, 20 May 1936.
had been depressed, AP, 'Pilgrim's Way'.
'Her alert talk', NP, *Fourteen Years*, in V. Smith, *Nettie Palmer*, p. 176.

'a very pleasant person', HHR to MK, 29 July 1935, Probyn and Steele (eds), V3, p. 120.

'I shall make a point', HHR to MK, 30 December 1935, Probyn and Steele (eds), V3, p. 145.

'A[ileen] would like to live in Bloomsbury', NP diary, 8 April 1936.

'brown and springy', NP, *Fourteen Years*, in V. Smith (ed.), *Nettie Palmer*, p. 202.

'Piled in, ready for anything', NP diary, 11 May 1936.

9. Barcelona – No Pasarán!

Excerpts from 'Barcelona Flashback' by AP, found in 'Pilgrim's Way' but originally part of her unpublished Spanish novel, written during and after the Spanish Civil War.

'When one came straight', George Orwell, *Homage to Catalonia*, London, 1938, p. 5.

'Dear Louse', AP to HP, 9 September 1936, MS6759, Box 1/9.

Notice how even the statues, NLA MS6759, Box 7/7:1.

'Unshaven men', A. Hodgson in J. Keene (ed.), *Last Mile to Huesca*, p. 94.

Hans Beimler had been a leading communist in the Reichstag and became the Political Commissar of the Thaelmann Battalion. He was killed defending Madrid in December 1936 and Aileen, who was on leave in Barcelona, took part in his funeral procession there with the other Australian nurses who had just arrived in Spain. Just two months earlier, Beimler had visited the medical unit at Granen to inspect it. Aileen wrote decades later that she had been 'kissed in the moonlight' there by Beimler, a comment quoted by Judith Keene and later picked up by Victor Pardo Lancina and mistranslated by him into Spanish as 'seduced'. Pardo Lancina also misread the previous sentence in Keene's article that quotes from a letter by Aileen to her parents saying that there had been 'various love affairs' at the unit; he wrote that Aileen herself had confessed to having affairs in Spain, one of them being with Hans Beimler. This is totally unfounded. His account was later drawn on by Linda Palfreeman and embellished further. See J. Keene, 'A Spanish Springtime', p. 81; J. Keene and V. Pardo Lancina, *A una milla de Huesca*, p. 239; L. Pafreeman, *Salud!*, pp. 45–6.

Els Segadors ('The Reapers') is the Himne Nacional de Catalunya; a version of it can be heard on http://www.youtube.com/watch?v=_muutTM66HM

10. Digging Shit

This chapter draws from Tom Buchanan, Chapter 3; Jim Fyrth, Chapter 4; and Shirley Mangini, Chapter 8.

rather lousy and stick in the mud, AP to parents ('Dear Parents'), Grañén, 11 November 1936, NLA MS6759, Box 1/8 [the letters to family are all in this file until further notice].

I went for a long walk, AP to parents ('Dear Old Bastards'), Grañén, 14 November 1936.

'the acronymic labyrinth of Spanish politics', K. Sinclair-Loutit, *Very Little Luggage,* Chapter 5, 'Spain', www.spartacus.schoolnet.co.uk/loutit5.htm, accessed 12 October 2011.

We long and painstakingly created, AP to 'Dear Family', 7 February 1937.

'We were a sort of pioneer unit', Thora Silverthorne, taped interview with Jim Fyrth, 7 June 1984, MML, IBMA, Box D-1:F/1.

Last night a mob of us slept out, AP to VP, Grañén, 14 September 1936, NLA MS6759, Box 1/8.

'The position of the medical service', Tom Wintringham to Harry Pollitt (head of the CPGB), 13 September 1936, MML, IBMA, Box C/5.

'There are some workers', P. Sloan (ed.), *John Cornford*, p. 226.

'the last mile to Huesca', John Cornford, 'Heart of the Heartless World', in P. Sloan (ed.), pp. 246–7.

'A Letter from Aragon', John Cornford, in P. Sloan (ed.), pp. 245–6.

'Heart of the Heartless World', AP, *The Realist*, no. 24, summer 1966, pp. 4–9.

Our work is, of course, very spasmodic, AP to 'Dear family', 8 December 1936.

terrible becalmed weeks, AP to parents ('Dear Angelfaces'), 16 December 1936.

spreading atrocity stories, AP to VP, Grañén, 14 September 1936.

'Idleness bred a fantastic web', letter from AC to 'Miss Martin', 15 June 1971, MML, IBMA, Box 3 Medical Personnel, B-3: COC/2.

'Secret Party members', AC to 'Miss Martin', 15 June 1971.

'our secretary, our interpreter', Thora Silverthorne interview with Jim Fyrth.

'a terrific quiet indefatigable worker', Kenneth Sinclair-Loutit, correspondence with Jim Fyrth, March 1984, MML, IBMA, Box B-3: SIN/1–7.

'Survey of a year's work with the British Medical Unit in Spain', K. Sinclair-Loutit and A. Palmer, 1937, RGASPI, Moscow, 545/6/88; my thanks to Dr Tom Buchanan for allowing me to see a copy of this document.

'smacked of Stalinism', K. Sinclair-Loutit, MML, IBMA, Box B-3: SIN.

'Radclyffe Hall was not yet', K. Sinclair-Loutit, MML, IBMA, Box B-3: SIN.

a lying little bitch, AP, Spanish diary, 2 January 1937, NLA MS 7162 [subsequent mentions from this source]; this diary survives because it was given by Thora Craig (formerly Silverthorne) to Judith Keene in the 1980s.

Viennese creature, AP to parents ('Dear Angelfaces'), 16 December 1936.

'She smoked a lot, no boyfriends', K. Sinclair-Loutit, MML, IBMA, Box B-3: SIN.

I am the only woman, AP to TS, 26 September 1937, MML, IBMA, Box D-1: G/2a.

The 'comandante', AP, 'Bury the Dead', 'Pilgrim's Way', NLA MS6759, Series 4, Box 4.

Aileen's worth was discussed – at a meeting between Tom Wintringham, Leslie Preger, Margot Miller and Archie Cochrane on 20 October 1936, MML, IBMA, Box B-3: COC/1.

as titular head, AP to Robson, 30 November 1936, MML, IBMA, Box C, File 7/5.

Actually everything I experience, AP to parents ('Dear Old Bastards'), 14 November 1936.

'was always snooping round', A. Hodgson in J. Keene (ed.), *The Last Mile to Huesca*, p. 120.

'shades of commitment', K. Sinclair-Loutit, MML, IBMA, Box B-3: SIN.

'a Marxist, but not a party fanatic', K. Sinclair-Loutit, 'Very Little Luggage', typescript, Rev. 5, 12/7/98; my thanks to Judith Keene for access to this typescript.

11. On the Move

'watery grey eyes', Hemingway, *For Whom the Bell Tolls,* p. 434.

internal differences, AP to parents ('Dear Creatures'), Albacete, 8 January 1937.

'Albacete was a seething mass', in L. Palfreeman, *Salud!*, p. 50.

Wounded pouring in, AP Spanish diary, 11 January 1937.
Resumen de Enero (Summary for January), AP Spanish diary.
'Never in my life', Una Wilson diary, 23 February 1937, cited in A. Inglis (1987), *Australians in the Spanish Civil War*, p. 150.
some posh outlying suburb, AP to parents ('Dear family'), 7 February 1937.
a curiously beautiful place, AP to NP ('Dear Angelface'), 7 June 1937.
there is no question, AP to parents ('Dear Fishes'), 23 March 1937.
'It's bewildering to think', NP to VP, SS *Moldavia*, 11 September 1936, NLA MS1174, 5126.
'They're making an old house', VP to NP, London, 23 September 1936, NLA MS1174, 5113.
'grimmish', NP to VP, Ardmore, 24 October 1936, NLA MS1174, 5151.
'Such a crowded, girlish letter', NP to VP, SS *Moldavia*, 13 September, NLA MS1174, 5127.
'If only she had sent me', NP to VP, Ardmore, 24 October 1936, NLA MS1174, 5150.
'It was very cheering to get that long letter', VP to NP, 'Waldorf', 89 Bayswater Rd, Darlinghurst, January 1937, NLA MS1174, 5200.
It seems a pity, AP to NP, 27 March 1937.
the dirty work, AP to parents ('Dear Wogs'), 4 am 20 May 1937.
'tiny snapshots of herself', NLA MS6759, Box 7, Folder 7/1.
'I feel a strong brotherly tie', M. Broggi, MML, IBMA, Box B-3: BRO.
ink, folders, whiskey, AP Spanish diary, 26 June 1937, NLA MS7162.
When the first shell came, AP to parents ('Dear Wogs'), 4 am [n.d. April/May 1937].
Shells crashing over as we waited, AP Spanish diary, 29 May 1937.
Yesterday we explored a large convent, AP to J. Fisher, 24 May 1937.
Somehow it is impossible to imagine, AP to NP ('Dear Angelface'), 7 June 1937.
One should be used to this sort of thing, AP to Glen Mills, 9 June 1937.
a wonderful experience, AP, 'Coming back to Chillbrook', 'Pilgrim's Way'.
Strange how one still goes on, AP Spanish diary, 5 June 1937.
And the fascists are in the streets, AP Spanish diary, 24 June 1937.
At moments I almost hate them, AP Spanish diary, Resumen de Junio.
I am growing battier, AP Spanish diary, 27 June 1937.
Writing again. T[hora]'s temper unbearable, AP Spanish diary, 2 July 1937.
Our last hospital was at Escorial, AP to NP, London, 29 July 1937.

Archie Cochrane, whose job it was, 'Witness to the death of Julian Bell', transcript of recording by Reggie Saxton in 2003, *International Brigade Memorial Trust Bulletin*, Issue 7, February 2004, p. 7.

Virginia Woolf wrote a short memoir, in Q. Bell, *Virginia Woolf*, Vol. 2, Appendix C, p. 258.

friendly & assuring, AP Spanish diary, 28 July 1937.

'Aileen's now in London', NP to LR, 10 June 1938, V. Smith (ed.), *Letters*, p. 157.

'I'm desperately concerned', VP to FDD, 9 February 1938, V. Smith (ed.), *Letters*, p. 155.

After four weeks of England, AP to parents ('Dear family'), 28 August 1937.

12. 'Call Aileen'

Craven As, shorthand book, AP to GM, 8 September 1937.

Huete is on one of the treeless, AP to parents ('Dear family'), 14 September 1937.

The conditions at Huete base hospital, see L. Palfreeman, *Salud!*, pp. 152–7.

There is butter and decent bread, AP to parents ('Dear family'), 14 September 1937.

a lovely story, AP to Thora Sinclair-Loutit [Silverthorne], 26 September 1937, MML, IBMA, Box D-1: G/2a.

and what a hell of a place it is, AP to 'Kenneth and Thora', 17 November 1937, MML, IBMA, Box D-1: G/2a.

'Here the sweet smell of blood', G. Green, cited in L. Palfreeman, p. 117.

Dear Loutits, You are a pair of shits, AP to Loutits, 2 December 1937, MML, IBMA, Box D-1: G/2a.

You have to learn to make the best, AP to HP ('Dear Mouse'), 23 October 1937.

nine big planes (Capronis), AP to G. Mills, 19 October 1937.

I started to write to you, AP to parents ('Dear family'), 8 November 1937.

The fascist radio stated, AP to parents, 17 January 1938.

'The untakable city is taken', Winifred Bates, 'With the British and American Medical Aid at Teruel', *Spanish Information Service Bulletin*, 11 February 1938, SLV MS10277, Saffin Collection.

'An ambulance driver goes in', Winifred Bates, 'With the British and American Medical Aid at Teruel'.

tall, genial, comforting figure, AP, 'Danger is never Danger', 'Pilgrim's Way'.

'a devastating irreverence for bureaucracy', N. Green, *A Chronicle of Small Beer*, p. 95.
extremely capable, AP to parents ('Dear family'), 8 November 1937.
quiet, capable, reliable sort of girls, AP to parents ('Dear family'), 14 September 1937.
She has developed a crush, AP to parents ('Dear family'), 8 November 1937.
'You kept me half-sane in Spain', Joan Gilchrist [Purser] to AP, 10 September 1945, NLA MS6759, Box 2, Folder 3/1.
Here one washes, AP to parents, 24 January 1938.
Her friend, Aurora Fernandez, cited in J. Fyrth and S. Alexander (eds), *Women's Voices in the Spanish Civil War*, p. 76.
The Nationalists and their allies, see A. Beevor, *The Battle for Spain*, p. 350, L. Palfreeman, p. 138.
A few days back, AP to parents ('Dear family'), 24 January 1938.
They came over, AP, 'Bury the Dead', 'Pilgrim's Way'.
One of the nurses, AP, 'Australians and Spain', Saffin Collection, VSL MS10277, Box 15.
safe and sound, AP to G. Mills, 19 March 1938.
Our front hospital is in tents now, AP, SMAC, Bulletin for June 1938, MML, IBMA, Box 29/B/4.
lofty mansion, AP to parents ('Dear family'), 3 April 1938.
After a very mobile existence, AP to parents ('Dear family'), 5 May 1938.

13. Prelude to a New War

'surrealistic production', cited in J. Baldwin, *Michel Saint-Denis and the Shaping of the Modern Actor*, p. 75.
Lorca's execution, see I. Gibson, *The Death of Lorca*, Chapters 7 and 8.
Suffering still, AP diary, NLA MS6759, Series 4/17, Box 6.
I have brought back, AP to parents, late May 1938, NLA MS6759, Box 1/1 [letters to family are all in this file until further notice].
'conducting the world', NP diary, 9 January 1940.
quite lively, AP to parents, 25 June 1938.
pedestrian, AP to HP, 21 June 1938.
would probably be still sitting, AP to VP, 11 September 1938.
Justice 'Bert' Evatt, Justice Evatt to VP, 6 August 1938, NLA MS1174, 1/5414.
I should perhaps have worked out, AP to NP, 12 October 1938.

'anxious', NP diary, 17 October 1938, NLA MS1174, Series 16, Box 25.

so I will do so, AP to parents, 16 July 1939.

'Death in the Olive Grove', AP to parents, 14 May 1939.

publish under a pseudonym, AP to HP, 11 June 1939.

'Last Mile to Huesca', AP Papers, NLA MS 6759, Series 4/19, Box 6. It seems other versions of the manuscript may have existed in Aileen and Helen Palmer's Papers but, after an extensive search, this is the only one that remains; see J. Keene, 'Aileen Palmer's Coming of Age' in B. Caine et al. (eds), *Crossing Boundaries*, pp. 186–7.

'Heart of the Heartless World', in P. Sloan (ed.), *John Cornford: A Memoir*, pp. 246–7.

I'd never want, AP, 'How Dutiful are Thy Feet?', 'Pilgrim's Way'.

'heavy local colour', AP to family, 10 March 1939.

suddenly saw the shape of the story, AP, 'The End and the Beginning', 'Pilgrim's Way'.

Thanks for M.U.M., AP to family, 20 December 1938.

more than anything else, AP to family, 21 February 1939.

Poetry and the People, see A. Caesar, *Dividing Lines*, pp. 211–12.

a book of Robert Capa's photographs, R. Capa, *Heart of Spain*, Aperture, New York, 1999; J. Jump (ed.), Poems from Spain, p. 66; http://www.youtube.com/watch?v=OtP1BHCRJTM

England has taken a firmer stand, AP to NP, 13 June 1938.

London has been in a state of jitters, AP to family, 16 September 1938.

The business of Czechoslovakia, AP to NP, 12 October 1938.

I see the fat's in the fire, AP to family 21 February, 1939; the story was published in Australia: *The Truth*, 3 February 1939; *Daily Telegraph*, 9 February 1939.

Don't think because I said, AP to 'Dear little family', n.d. August 1939 [posted 1 August].

'not the bits where you say', NP to AP, 14 August 1939, NLA MS1174, 1/5575.

seeing the Louvre, AP to parents, 13 August 1939.

'I haven't said yet how much it means', NP to AP, 16 August 1939, NLA MS1174, 1/5576–7.

You could see rows and rows, AP to parents ('Dearest darlings'), 29 August 1939.

'A Little Book of Gurs', AP, 'Australians and Spain', Saffin Collection, VSL MS 10277, Box 15; this book no longer survives.

She worried about sending it back, AP to family, 9 October 1939.
'The nasty barbed wire', letters from Gurs inmates to AP, 23 August 1939, Saffin Collection, VSL MS 10277, Box 15.
All the same, with all these elaborate preparations, AP to parents ('Dearest darlings'), 29 August 1939.
because I am going away from it, AP diary, NLA MS6759, Series 4/17, Box 6.
I left Perpignan on Friday evening, AP to parents, 4 September 1939.
I had been living in the expectation, AP diary, NLA MS6759, Serie 4/17, Box 6.

14. Love in the Blitz

a rather muddled sort of picnic, AP to parents ('Dearest family'), 14 September 1939.
carmine fingernails, AP to family, 21 February 1939.
who wore a black beret, D. Moore, *Survivors of Beauty*, p. 19; my thanks to Sharon Moore for donating this memoir by her mother.
I am sorry, darlings, AP to parents ('Dearest family), 29 September 1939.
'whatever turn the war takes', J. Metcalf to Australia ('Darlings'), n.d. September 1939, NLA MS6759, Box 1:1.
personally I don't feel nearly as depressed, AP to VP, 11 October 1939.
'says she's attractive-looking', NP diary, 4 June 1940.
'Joyce spoke about Aileen', NP diary, 29 October 1940.
The black-out certainly doesn't prevent me, AP to family, 9 October 1939.
I'm happy, oddly enough, AP to family, 23 June 1940.
Lord, dears, it's so near your birthdays, AP to family, 8 August 1940.
lovely, un-English weather, AP to family, 23 June 1940.
I looked from roof-tops, AP diary, 8 September 1940, NLA MS6759, Box 6, Folder 4/17 [subsequent mentions of AP diary from same source].
'Ambulance Station', AP, 'Pilgrim's Way'.
Apparently triggered by fear, explanation of writing 'Danger is never danger', AP, letter titled 'Dear Dr Morrison', NLA MS6759, Box 4, Folder 34.
'Danger is never danger', AP, *World Without Strangers?*, p. 20.
People re-act very differently to death, AP diary, 6 October 1940.
Life is all boredom, AP diary, 18 September 1940.
Sitting at home last night, AP diary, 19 September 1940.
I can't do anything with myself, AP diary, 18 September 1940.

Sometimes it's awful to be in love, AP diary, 9 November 1940.

There was a hole, AP to family ('Dear little family'), 20 January 1941 (wrongly dated 1940).

has a rather stabilising effect, AP to parents ('Darlings') 29 March 1941 (dated 1940).

very practical, AP to parents ('Darlings'), 30 April 1941.

laid up with a cold, AP to parents ('Darlings'), 30 April 1941.

I think that if ever I do have a child, AP to NP, n.d. 1941.

I have no intention of having one, AP to parents ('Dears'), 20 December 1941.

'Have you developed a Stepney accent?', NP to AP, February 1943, NLA MS1174, 1/6290.

'Says AY is more attractive', NP diary, 28 April 1942.

at one point some months ago, AP to VP ('Dear Vance'), 5 October 1941.

I'd rather like a wire from you, AP to family ('Dear little family'), 15 March 1942.

My job is roughly filing and research, AP to NP, ('Dear Nettie'), 19 January 1944.

15. Calling Aileen Home

'It's nearly a year (!)', HP to AP ('Dear Phace'), 30 March 1943, NLA MS 3044, Box 4 [subsequent references from this source].

the heavy stuff – the land-mines, AP to parents ('Darlings'), 30 April 1941.

I never wear head-gear, AP to VP, 5 October 1941.

'Long argument with V', NP diary, 1 September 1940.

'essentially a writer', NP to VP, 16 October 1942, NLA MS1174, 1/6217.

'toughness', NP to AP, 'End of April', 1942, NLA MS1174, 1/6108-9.

'heroic', I. Indyk, 'The ABC and Australian Literature: 1939–45', *Meanjin*, 49:3, 1990, p. 580.

'Vance is just becoming', HP to AP, 30 March 1943.

'Vance resigns on Monday', HP to AP, ('Dear Physsche'), 8 June 1944.

'I'm almost never home', HP to AP ('Dear Phace'), 27 March 1944.

'Darling AY', NP to AP, n.d. mid-1942, NLA MS1174, 1/6123–6.

'As a matter of fact, this illness', NP to AP, 3 July 1943, NLA MS1174, 1/6367–8.

'She had a pretty bad breakdown', VP to AP, 19 July 1943, NLA MS1174, 1/6377.

'As you've probably gathered', HP to AP, 23 July 1943.

'I want to ask you please', HP to AP, 21 October 1944.
'There'll be room for you', NP to AP, 8 October 1944, NLA MS1174, 1/6648.
'Dear old girl, we did hope', VP to AP, 2 December 1944, NLA MS1174, 1/6661.
'What a spiffing broadcast!', HP to AP, 21 October 1944.
'Vance was swollen with pride', NP to AP, n.d. November 1944, NLA MS1174, 1/6643. Transcript, NLA MS6759, Box 7.
an inconspicuous little woman of fifty-odd, AP transcript, NLA MS6083.
Aileen was *thrown into* the entourage, AP to HP, 17 April 1945.
elevated, AP diary, n.d. April 1945, NLA MS6759, Box 6/4/17 [subsequent mentions of AP diary 1945 from same source].
scared crazy, AP diary, n.d. April 1945.
For some inexplicable reason, AP diary, n.d. April 1945.
Today began well. You phoned, AP diary, 27 April 1945.
There's only a month or so left of my current life. AP diary, 27 April 1945.
Perhaps it's better all the same that I'm going, AP diary, 11 May 1945.
After I came back from Europe, AP, 'Novel (Rough)', NLA MS 6759, Box 5, Folder 4/14.
'I certify that this photograph', AP photograph, July 1940, NLA MS6759, Box 7/7/2.
(Leonard Crome's nickname from his childhood), Paul Preston, 'No Soldier', in Jim Jump (ed.), *Looking Back at the Spanish Civil War*, p. 33.
B's telephone voice always seems to come, AP diary, 9 November 1940.
Sometimes I'm seized with a terrible urge, AP diary, 11 May 1945.
Any lesbian incidents in my life, AP, 'Moon's Day', n.d. but on same yellow paper as notes to Helen dated 1971, NLA MS6759, Box 4/3.
And in London all sorts were easy to get on with, AP, 'The Moon and Sixpence', 'Pilgrim's Way'.
The purplish-white light in Piccadilly on Tuesday, AP diary, 11 May 1945.
foot-slogging, AP diary, 24 June 1945.
pegging away – excursions into Chinese dens, AP diary, 1 July 1945.
a little elevated from beer-drinking, AP diary, 15 July 1945.
It's been too pleasant in a way, AP diary, 23 August 1945.
So I emerge out of the oblivion, AP diary, 27 August 1945.
'I feel I want to touch wood', NP to AP, n.d. July 1945, NLA MS1174, 1/6795.

'darling old soul. I'm beginning to feel nervous', NP to AP, 19 July 1945, NLA MS1174, 1/6798.

'We hope you won't be disappointed', VP to AP, 15 July 1945, NLA MS 1174, 1/6797.

'I hope Aileen gets home pretty soon', Miles Franklin to NP, 24 May 1945, NLA MS 1174, 1/677.

'So glad to hear you are getting Aileen home', HHR to NP, 15 October 1945, NLA MS 1174, 1/6843.

Dad's brown hat, AP diary, 11 October 1945.

'Poets of Liberation', AP, NLA MS6759, Box 7/4/22. CEMA was the Council for the Encouragement of Music and the Arts, modelled on the council founded by John Maynard Keynes during World War II in Great Britain. This was the precursor of the Arts Council and the Australia Council.

Sorting out my impressions, AP diary, 27 October 1945.

Whether to write – to establish myself as a writer, AP diary, 27 October 1945.

Sitting on the veranda at Molly Bayne's shack, AP diary, 8 December 1945.

16. Mourning the Past

'Aileen's a blissful visitant', NP to Hugh McCrae, 13 January 1946, HM Papers, SLV MS12153, Box 2762/7; my thanks to Ralph Spaulding for this reference.

'on the side of the anti-Francoists', FDD to mother, 7 October 1945, NLA MSS1945, 1/359.

I don't remember much, AP, 'The Day of the Voyager', 1961, p. 5, NLA MS6083, Box 1/1. Aileen passed with 2nd-class Honours, NLA MS6759, Box 2/2/4.

her study of Russian features in her ASIO file, NAA A6119, item 111.

World of comfortable, cushioned people, AP, NLA MS6759, Series 4/4/21, Box 6.

In 1945 I was to all appearances, AP, 'Idiot's World', 'Dear Louise', part II, 1961, NLA MS6083, Box 1/1.

17. In Hospital

Of course, I didn't go quietly, AP, 'My Apprenticeship', 'DV/PW', Series 4/4/7, Box 5.

'those young and sensitive introverts', R. Ellery, *The cow jumped over the moon.*

'Aileen's "buffer" against the world', NP to E Higgins, 31 March 1948, ML MSS740/9.

'A spectator's legs were broken – just from merely looking on', from A. B. 'Banjo' Paterson's poem 'The Geebung Polo Club'.

fear of losing my effective self, AP to Dr Reed, 11 November 1960, NLA MS6083, Box 2/7.

'I dreamed waking and sleeping dreams', Michael King, *Wrestling with the Angel*.

'I was first given Insulin Shock Treatment', Olga Roncoroni to NP, 26 November 1948, NLA MS1174, 1/7540.

'written by Vance from memory for Aileen', MS6759, Box 1/7.

That I wrote, crying, AP, 'My Apprenticeship', 'DV/PW', Series 4/4/7, Box 5. A slightly different version of the poem, 'In Hospital', was published in her collection, *Dear Life*, by 'Caliban', Melbourne, Artprint, 1957.

18. Twentieth Century Pilgrim

This may be the title, AP, '20th Century Pilgrim', April 1948, MS6759, Box 7.

'irresponsible', NP to EH, 31 March 1948, ML MSS740/9.

a 1947 issue of *Meanjin*, P. H. Partridge, 'The Shape of Things to Come?, *Meanjin*, 6:4, summer 1947, pp. 251–2.

an article Christesen had reprinted in *Meanjin*, in 1945, Arthur Koestler, 'The Intelligentsia', *Meanjin*, 4:1, 1945, pp. 39–50.

Kurt Baier from the Philosophy department, Kurt Baier, 'The Changing Role of the Intelligentsia', *Meanjin*, 4:2, 1945.

'wonderful Louis Aragon and [Paul] Éluard poems', Deirdre Moore, 'Radical in the Making?'.

The university English department had always been dominated, see Lynne Strahan, *Just City and the Mirrors*.

supposedly 'unspeakable', see Brendan Stone, 'Towards a Writing without Power: Notes on the Narrative of Madness', *Auto/Biography*, 12, 2004, pp. 16–33.

19. Submerged Resentment

'Vance is much more hopeful', January 1948, cited in Robin Lucas, 'A Fine Ruddy Mess', p. 69.

which brought home to me the kind of worry, AP to Matron (Meyer), 4 April 1964, MS6759, Box 1/5.

'inspirational tribal elders', Geoffrey Serle, 'Palmer, Edward Vivian (Vance) (1885–1959)', *Australian Dictionary of Biography*, Volume 11, 1988.

'It's clearly a case of deferred shock, NP to E Higgins, 31 March 1948, ML MSS740/9.

'leaving Vance and the girls at home', NP to Bertram Higgins, Caloundra, end of June 1948, in V. Smith (ed.), *Letters*, p. 194.

'Poor child', Marjorie Barnard to NP, 21 April 1948, NLA MS1174, 1/7399.

'Aileen…I am most concerned about', KSP to NP, 9 May 1949, NLA MS1174, 1/7672.

'a brother whose nervous system' and 'submerged resentment', FDD to mother, 20 October 1948, NLA MSS1945, 1/1008.

'a reluctant immigrant', C. Lazar Geroe, 'A Reluctant Immigrant', *Meanjin*, 41:3, September 1982, pp. 352–7.

'Ferenczi also shifted analysis away', Joy Damousi, *Freud in the Antipodes*, p. 182.

'a very high Freudian', NP diary, 26 August 1940.

'Balkan embroideries', NP diary, 17 September 1940.

her qualifications were queried, see Stanley Gold, 'The Early History', *Meanjin*, 41:3, September 1982, pp. 342–51.

'Agitated by stringency of police', NP diary, 18 February 1942.

'the plot thickened', Deirdre Moore, 'A Memoir of my Psychoanalysis with Dr Clara Geroe', *Australian Journal of Psychotherapy*, 17:1&2, 1998, p. 183.

'She looks so alert and she's so free', NP to AP, end of July 1944, NLA MS1174, 1/6594.

We have both, in different ways, AP to KSP, 17 August 1963, NLA MS6083, Box 1.

the medical authorities, AP, '20th Century Pilgrim', April 1948, MS6759, Box 7.

which, according to a psychoanalyst, see P. McCallum, 'An interview with Frank Graham', *Australian Journal of Psychotherapy*, 3:1, 1984, pp. 76–81.

20. Psychoanalysis

'another small job by Dr Gero', VP to NP, 26 June 1948, NLA MS1174, 1/7431.

'Helen was telling me about her visit', VP to NP, 11 Sept 1949, NLA MS1174, 1/7738.

'Flora to dinner', NP diary, 1 May 1942 (entry written by Vance).

'It is lovely, Nettie', FE to NP, 18 March 1948, NLA MS1174, 1/7388.

Towards the end of 1947, AP, one page fragment, probably from 'Pilgrim's Way', from manuscripts in Deborah Jordan's possession.

M. Barnard Eldershaw, *Tomorrow and Tomorrow* (first published 1947); complete version published 1983 with full title. That year it was awarded the Patrick White prize for literature.

'Your darling daughter was the soul of goodness', FE to NP, 7 September 1953, NLA MS1174.

'a penetrating imaginative record', AP, 'Flora Sydney Eldershaw', *Overland*, November 1956, p. 9.

'emotional attachment', E. Young to VP, 23 October 1948, NLA MS1174, 1/7511.

'To Nina: whose understanding', VP to NC, n.d. 1948, University of Melbourne, Meanjin archive, U84/52. This correspondence has been organised by Nina Christesen, with comments in her handwriting. There are only letters by Vance as he says he destroyed hers. He asked her to destroy his, but she not only kept every little note as well as longer letters, she clearly wanted them put in her archive. See also Judith Armstrong, *The Christesen Romance*, pp. 92–5.

maintained that the writing in Vance's trilogy, see S. B. Clark's 1967 thesis: 'Vance Palmer: A consideration of his career in Australian Letters', p. 117, p. 163 & p. 239; copy in NLA MS6083, Box 4.

Your pa was in bed, AP to NP, 20 June 1948, NLA MS1174, 1/7425. At the top of the letter in Nettie's shaky handwriting: 'Look at DIARY 1948' (which no longer survives).

'A great surprise yesterday', VP to NP, 16 September 1949, NLA MS1174, 1/7744.

'Evening. Aileen at first rhetorical', NP diary, 30 December 1949.

'I've been reluctant to you', VP to NC, n.d. late 1950, MU Meanjin archive U84/52.

It would be very inconvenient, AP, 'Notes of a Convalescent', April 1961, NLA MS6083, Box 1.

'limped home sorely wounded', FDD to mother, 18 May 1947, NLA MSS 1945/1/797.

'To another writer he made more salacious comments', Vivian Smith, personal conversation with author.

'The Palmers – there is a family', D. Martin, *My Strange Friend*, p.269.

'drunk, manic and dishevelled', D. Hewett, 'Excerpt from "The Empty Room"', p. 8.

21. Peace Activist and Poet

'I feel that it is my duty', KSP press statement, cited in R. Throssell, *Wild Weeds and Windflowers,* p. 199.

a photograph from the conference, NLA MS6083, Box 4.

'Miss Palmer said she had seen the effects', newscutting, 'Kew woman reports on trip to Japan', no details, NLA MS6759, Box 7/5/1.

'Not only had cities been destroyed', AP press statement, NLA MS6759, Box 7/5/1.

'After 30 years of Japanese occupation', AP press statement, NLA MS6759, Box 7/5/1.

a poet of conscience, AP, 'Dear Louise', 28 January 1961, NLA MS6083, Box 2/2.

Kruschev's secret report, See D. Bridges (ed.), *Helen Palmer's Outlook*, intro. Robin Gollan, pp. 13–14.

'Here is a poet', review from *Overland*, no details, NLA MS6759, Box 3/11.

'Song from a Distant Epoch', *Meanjin*, 7:1, autumn 1958, p. 31; later published as 'The Silent Land' in AP, *World Without Strangers?*.

'Advice to Oneself', Ho Chi Minh, *Prison Diary*, p. 28.

I feel Vietnam, AP to KSP, 15 July 1965, NLA MS6083, Box 1.

To have done a really good job, AP to Lorraine and Malcolm Salmon, 12 August 1965, NLA MS6083, Box 2.

'If the recent stirring reception', D. Marr, 'Vietnamese Sources on Vietnam', *Bulletin of Concerned Asian Scholars*, 4:1, 1971, p. 119.

22. Family Discord

I was not under insulin treatment, AP, 'The Snakes and I', NLA MS6759, Box 5/4/7.

'because she no longer needed', HP to Dr Stubley, 15 April 1957, NLA MS6083, Box 2/9.

'She's very heavily on N[ettie]'s mind', VP to HP, 11 August 1957, NLA MS6083, Box 2/5.

a socialist journal called *Outlook*, for further information see D. Bridges (ed.), *Helen Palmer's Outlook*.

'Helen had an extremely logical mind', M. Tipping, 'Remembrance of Palmers Past', *Overland*, 100: 1985, p. 15.

'essential that we underline to her', HP to parents ('Dear N & V'), 25 May 1958, NLA MS6083, Box 2/1.

'The Ballad of 1891', HP, in D. Bridges (ed.), *Helen Palmer's Outlook*, p. 169.

'You might be able to help me', CC to AP, 3 March 1959, MU Meanjin Archive, U84/52.

far less photogenic than Vance, AP to CC, 15 February 1959, 15 Irymple Ave, East Kew, MU Meanjin Archive, U84/52.

Vance was at home, see J. Armstrong, *The Christesen Romance*, p. 131.

Vance died smoothly and painlessly, AP to Stephen Murray-Smith, 31 October 1964, NLA MS6759, Box 5/4/12.

Blake died as I'd like to die, AP, 'For Love or Money', 'Pilgrim's Way'.

I went along with her, AP, 'The Old Lady Takes Off', DV/PW', 1964, NLA MS6759, Box 5/4/12.

23. Aileen and Nettie

In a rare photograph from the early 1960s, NLA MS6759, Box 7/7/1.

Eurydike [sic] *was my mother*, AP to Dr Morrison, Cup Day 1970, NLA MS6759, Box 5/4/7.

Where I probably went wrong last November, AP, 'Dear Louise', January 1961, NLA MS6083, Box 2/2.

bringing into legible form, AP to KSP, 17 August 1963, NLA MS6083, Box 1/1.

This week I've been trying to prepare, AP, 'The Horses are Dead-Black', 1961, NLA MS6083, Box 1/1.

Festival Espagnol brochure, NLA MS6759, Box 7.

The festival included a display of arts, Report of the Festival, Saffin Collection, VSL MS 10277, Box 15.

Letters to Pablo Picasso, AP, 2 July and 12 August 1962, Saffin Collection.

write a few words, AP to Dr Bell, 11 March 1963, NLA MS6083, Box 1/1.

I feel very grateful, AP to KSP, 17 August 1963, NLA MS6083, Box 1/1.

'as if they were by a new poet', HP to NP, n.d. [January 1963], NLA MS6759, Box 1/5.

'Aileen is very well', HP to NP, n.d. [August 1963], NLA MS6759, Box 1/5.

'Lines Painted on the Wall of a Death-Cell', AP, *Vietnam Advances*, 8: 1963, NLA MS6759, Box 4/4/2.

'We seldom have the opportunity', HP to AP, 5 October 1963, NLA MS6759, Box 1/5.

I just need the words to write to my mother, AP, 'March 13th 1948', NLA MS6759, Box 7/4/22.

What I am trying to clarify, AP, 'Day of the Voyager', 1961, NLA MS6083, Box 1/1.

As a child, and often since, AP to HP, 22 November 1963, NLA MS6759, Box 1/5.

This I feel you cd more easily do, AP to HP, 19 September 1964, NLA MS6759, Box 5/4/12.

However, whatever her contribution, AP, 'Draft Note on N.P.', NLA MS6759, Box 5/4/12.

24. World without Strangers?

'Anything that didn't make sense', HP, 'Aileen', transcript of tape 27/3/79, NLA MS6083, Box 25/7.

I feel this is after all a foreign country, AP diary, 27 October 1945.

'Song from Planet 90', AP, *World Without Strangers?*, p. 12.

'A View of the Beach', AP, *World Without Strangers?*, p. 25.

'The Invisible Woman', AP, *World Without Strangers?*, p. 9.

'I was most delighted to read your poem', Eric Westbrook to AP, 11 October 1960, NLA MS6759, Box 3/3/11.

'The Wanderer', AP, *World Without Strangers?*, p. 22.

It is also a rejoinder to John Manifold's sonnet 'The Sirens', see *Hecate*, 36:1&2, J. Rodriguez, pp. 214–15, S. Martin, pp. 216–17.

'A Sort of Beauty', AP, *World Without Strangers?*, p. 18.

'Remembering Garcia Lorca', AP, *World Without Strangers?*, p. 29.

How far can I trust my good moods?, AP, 'Notes of a Convalescent', p. 23, April 1961, NLA MS6083, Box 1/1.

one of the bright bunch of intellectuals, AP, 'Day of the Voyager', pp. 13–14, 1961, NLA MS6083, Box 1/1.

Get away from Melbourne, AP, 'Notes of a Convalescent', p. 23, April 1961, NLA MS6083, Box 1/1.

alternating wish-fantasies, AP, 'Dear Louise' (DL/IV), p. 10, 1961, handwritten manuscript given to Deborah Jordan.

Mixed up in it was Moses, AP, 'Notes of a Convalescent', pp. 23–4, April 1961, NLA MS6083, Box 1/1.

'Treeless is the Land', 'Variations to a Legend', section VIII, AP, *World Without Strangers?*, p. 45.

'strange beauty', AP, 'The Orange Tree', 'Pilgrim's Way'.

'the competing narratives of mental illness', H. Lee, *Virginia Woolf*, p. 191.

'shudder', HP, 'Aileen', transcript of tape 27/3/79, NLA MS6083, Box 25/7.

25. No Words

but it doesn't take long, AP, 'Notes of a Convalescent', July 1961, NLA MS6083, Box 1.

the sisters started discussing whether their parents' papers, AP to HP, 15 March 1961, NLA MS3044, Box 4.

You visualise it as a posthumous collection, AP to HP, 30 June 1965, NLA MS6083, Box 2.

'the importance of being Ernest', for example, AP to HP, 2 June 1965, NLA MS6083, Box 2.

The key problem for me in months to come, AP to HP, 30 June 1966, NLA MS6759, Box 1/6.

In 1965 Clem Christesen inquired, AP to HP, 4 May 1965, NLA MS6083, Box 2.

'Nobody gave Heseltine permission', HP to AP, 15 December 1965, NLA MS3044, Box 4.

Vivian and I had long discussions, AP, 'The Wind and the Rain', 1967; manuscript courtesy of Deborah Jordan.

school story, AP to Jessie McLeod, 5 March 1980, NLA MS6759, Box 1/7.

'emotionally exhausted', Susan Sheridan, notes from visit, passed on from Sally Newman with Sheridan's permission.

Aileen received a rejection letter, CLF to AP, 25 October 1966, NLA MS6759, Box 3/4.

'archival jolt', T. Bishop, *Riding with Rilke*, p. 36.

Guido writes of the four 'moments', GB to AP, 7 November 1967, NLA MS6759, Box 3/6.

You told me to keep my brain occupied, AP to Matron Meyer, 1 April 1974, NLA MS6759, Box 3/11.

H darling, When I lie down, AP to HP, 25 October 1978, NLA MS6759, Box 1/7.

'For the first time I'll be able to help Aileen', HP, 'Being a Nothing', NLA MS6083, Box 25/7.

In a short piece simply called 'Aileen', HP, 'Aileen', 27 March 1979, NLA MS6083, Box 25/7.

Having spent large parts of thirty years, AP 1981; my thanks to Deborah Jordan for allowing me access to the tape recording.

should possibly be discarded altogether, AP to JM, 14 March 1980, NLA MS6759, Box 1/7.

'it was the "act of writing" itself', S. Newman in M. Dever, A. Vickery and S. Newman, *The Intimate Archive*, p. 163.

'When Aileen chose a life of action', NP to EH, 31 March 1948, ML MSS740/9.

Spain stands out in my own life, AP to Mulk Raj Annand, 15 December 1962, NLA MS6759, Box 3/11.

'I talked to her in a kind of visitor's room', Judith Keene, personal communication with author. See also J. Keene, 'Aileen Palmer's second coming of age', in Barbara Caine et al. (eds), *Crossing Boundaries*.

'No words', Colleen Burke, *Southerly*, 58:3, 1998, pp. 184–5; later published in *The odd pagan or two*, Kardoorair Press, Armidale, NSW 2007.

On a mild, sunny morning in Canberra: account of Spanish Civil War memorial on 11 December 1993, V. Deacon, 'History in the Making'. Donated by Vera Deacon to author.

Danger is never danger, AP, *World Without Strangers?*, p. 20.

There was a myth: Vera Deacon: 'I understand that Aileen, born 1915, was not well. She was traumatized by the death of her loved one during the Spanish Civil War and wrote a moving poem…I remember a few words "War is not war until your own love…"', VD to Peter Murphy, 27 October 2010. In possession of author.

Bibliography

Manuscripts

Australian National University Archives (ANU)

Amirah Inglis Papers

Marx Memorial Library, London (MML)

International Brigade Memorial Archive

Mitchell Library, State Library of New South Wales (ML)

Esmonde Higgins Papers
Malcolm and Lorraine Salmon Papers

National Library of Australia (NLA)

Aileen Palmer Papers
Aileen and Helen Palmer Papers
Helen Palmer Papers
Vance and Nettie Palmer Papers
Frank Dalby Davison Papers

State Library of Victoria (SLV)

Saffin Collection

University of Melbourne (MU)

Meanjin Archive

Other works consulted

Aarons, Mark (2010), *The Family File*, Melbourne, Black Inc.

Armstrong, Judith (1996), *The Christesen Romance*, Melbourne, Melbourne University Press

Baldwin, Jane (2003), *Michel Saint-Denis and the Shaping of the Modern Actor*, West Point, Connecticut: Praeger

Barnard Eldershaw, M. (1983), *Tomorrow and Tomorrow and Tomorrow*, London, Virago. First published in a censored version as *Tomorrow and Tomorrow*, Melbourne, Georgian House, 1947

Bell, Quentin (1972), *Virginia Woolf: A Biography*, London, The Hogarth Press

Bird, Delys (ed.) (2000), *Katharine Susannah Prichard: Stories, Journalism, Essays*, St Lucia, University of Queensland Press

Bishop, Ted (2005), *Riding with Rilke: Reflections on Motorcycles and Books*, New York/ London, W. W. Norton

Bomford, Janette (1993), *That Dangerous and Persuasive Woman: Vida Goldstein*, Melbourne, Melbourne University Press

Bridges, Doreen (ed.) (1982), *Helen Palmer's Outlook*, Sydney, Helen Palmer Memorial Committee

Buchanan, Tom (2007), *The Impact of the Spanish Civil War on Britain*, Brighton, Sussex Academic Press

Burke, Colleen Z. (2007), 'No words', *The Odd Pagan or Two*, Armidale, NSW, Kardoorair Press

Caesar, Adrian (1991), *Dividing Lines: Poetry, Class and Ideology in the 1930s*, Manchester, Manchester University Press

Campama, Eva (2001), 'Aileen Palmer: An Australian in the Spanish Civil War' in *Changing Geographies: Essays on Australia*, Susan Ballyn et al. (eds), Centre d'Estudis Australians, Universitat de Barcelona, pp. 299–304

Coleborne, Catherine and Dolly MacKinnon (eds) (2003), *'Madness' in Australia: Histories, Heritage and the Asylum*, St Lucia, University of Queensland Press

Cowles, Virginia (1941), *Looking for Trouble*, London, Hamish Hamilton

Damousi, Joy (1994), *Women Come Rally: Socialism, Communism and Gender in Australia 1890–1955*, Melbourne, Oxford University Press

—— (2005), *Freud in the Antipodes: A Cultural History of Psychoanalysis in Australia*, Sydney, University of New South Wales Press

Dever, Maryanne, Newman, Sally and Vickery, Ann (2009), *The Intimate Archive: Journey through Private Papers*, Canberra, National Library of Australia

Ellery, Reginald S. (1956), *The Cow Jumped over the Moon: Private Papers of a Psychiatrist*, Melbourne, F. W. Cheshire

Fitzpatrick, Kathleen (1975), *PLC Melbourne: The First Century 1875–1975*, Burwood, The Presbyterian Ladies' College

Fyrth, Jim (1986), *The Signal was Spain: The Spanish Aid Movement in Britain 1936–39*, London, Lawrence & Wishart

—— and Alexander, Sally (eds) (1991), *Women's Voices from the Spanish Civil War*, London, Lawrence & Wishart

Geroe, Clara Lazar (1982), 'A Reluctant Immigrant', *Meanjin*, 41:3, pp. 352–7

Gibson, Ian (1974), *The Death of Lorca*, Frogmore, Herts: Paladin

Gold, Stanley (1982), 'The Early History', *Meanjin*, 41:3, pp. 342–51

Golden, Jill (2006), *Inventing Beatrice*, South Australia, Wakefield Press

Green, Nan (2004), *A Chronicle of Small Beer: The Memoirs of Nan Green*, Nottingham, Trent Editions

Hemingway, Ernest (2005), *For Whom the Bell Tolls*, London, Vintage (First published 1941)

Heseltine, Harry (1970), *Vance Palmer*, St Lucia, University of Queensland Press

Hewett, Dorothy (2000), 'Excerpt from "The Empty Room"': an Autobiography in Progress', *Overland*, 160, pp. 4–10

Ho Chi Minh (1962), *Prison Diary*, trans. Aileen Palmer, Hanoi, Foreign Languages Publishing House. Republished Bantam Books, New York, 1971, with new introduction by Harrison E. Salisbury

Indyk, Ivor (1990), 'The ABC and Australian Literature: 1939–45', *Meanjin*, 49:3

Inglis, Amirah (1987), *Australians in the Spanish Civil War*, Sydney, Allen & Unwin

Jordan, Deborah (1999), *Nettie Palmer: Search for an Aesthetic*, Melbourne, History Department, University of Melbourne

—— (2007), 'Shaped on the Anvil of Mars: Vance and Nettie Palmer and the Great War, *Journal of Politics and History*, 53:3, pp. 375–91

Jump, Jim (ed.) (2006) *Poems from Spain: British and Irish International Brigaders on the Spanish Civil War*, London, Lawrence & Wishart

Keene, Judith (1987), 'A Spanish Springtime: Aileen Palmer and the Spanish Civil War', *Labour History*, 52, pp. 75–87

—— (1988), 'Aileen Palmer's second coming of age', in Barbara Caine et al. (eds), *Crossing Boundaries: Feminisms and the Critique of Knowledges*, Sydney, Allen & Unwin, pp. 180–92

—— (1988), *The Last Mile to Huesca: an Australian Nurse in the Spanish Civil War*, Sydney, New South Wales University Press

—— and Pardo Lancina, Victor (2005), *A una milla de Huesca*, Zaragoza, Prensas Universitarias

King, Michael (2000), *Wrestling with the Angel: A Life of Janet Frame*, New South Wales, Pan Macmillan

Leavitt, David (1993), *While England Sleeps*, New York, Viking. First published in Great Britain by Abacus, 1998

Lee, Hermione (1996), *Virginia Woolf*, London, Chatto & Windus

Long, R. H. (1954), *Poems*, Melbourne, Australasian Book Society

Lucas, Robin (2009), '"A Fine Ruddy Mess": the Publication of Nettie Palmer's *Fourteen Years*', *La Trobe Journal*, No. 83, May, pp. 69–76

Mangini, Shirley (1995), *Memories of Resistance: Women's Voices from the Spanish Civil War*, New Haven, Yale University Press

Manifold, J. S. (1978), *Collected Verse*, St Lucia, University of Queensland Press

Marr, David (1971), 'Vietnamese Sources on Vietnam', *Bulletin of Concerned Asian Scholars*, 4:1

Martin, David (1991), *My Strange Friend: an Autobiography*, New South Wales, Pan Macmillan

Martin, Sylvia (2009), 'Aileen Palmer – Twentieth Century Pilgrim: War, Poetry, Madness and Modernism', *Hecate*, 35:1-2, 94–107

—— (2010), 'Response to Judith Rodriguez's note', *Hecate*, 36:1&2, pp. 216–17

Modjeska, Drusilla (1981), *Exiles at Home: Australian Women Writers 1925–45*, Sydney, Angus & Robertson

Moore, Deirdre (1996), *Survivors of Beauty: Memoirs of Dora and Bert Birtles*, Sydney, Book Collectors' Society of Australia

—— (1998), 'A Memoir of my Psychoanalysis with Dr Clara Geroe', *Australian Journal of Psychotherapy*, 17:1&2, pp. 179–91

Newman, Sally (2000), 'Body of Evidence: Aileen Palmer's Textual Lives', *Hecate*, 26:1, pp. 10–38

—— (2002), 'Silent Witness? Aileen Palmer and the Problem of Evidence in Lesbian History', *Women's History Review*, 11:3, pp. 505–30

Orwell, George (1938), *Homage to Catalonia*, London, Secker & Warburg

Palfreeman, Linda (2011), *Salud! British Volunteers in the Republican Medical Service during the Spanish Civil War, 1936-1939*, Eastbourne, Sussex Academic Press

Palmer, Aileen (1957), *Dear Life*, by 'Caliban', mimeographed by Artprint, Melbourne.

—— (1964) *World without Strangers?* Melbourne, Overland

Palmer, Helen (1954), *Beneath the Southern Cross*, Melbourne, Cheshire

Palmer, Nettie (1914), *The South Wind*, London, J. G. Wilson

—— (1915), *Shadowy Paths*, London, Euston Press

—— (1924), *Modern Australian Literature 1900–1923*, Melbourne, Lothian

—— (1932), *Talking It Over*, Sydney, Angus & Robertson

—— (1937) *Australians in Spain*, Sydney, Spanish Relief Committee (new edition: enlarged by Nettie Palmer and Len Fox, Sydney, Current Books Distributors, 1948)

—— (1948), *Fourteen Years: Extracts from a Private Journal 1925–1939*, Melbourne, Meanjin Press

—— (1950), *Henry Handel Richardson: A Study*, Sydney, Angus & Robertson

—— (1952), *The Dandenongs*, Melbourne, National Press

Palmer, Vance (1915) *The World of Men*, London, Euston Press

—— (1930), *The Passage*, London, Stanley Paul

—— (1932), *Daybreak*, London, Stanley Paul

—— (1937), *Legend for Sanderson*, Sydney, Angus & Robertson

—— (1948), *Golconda*, Sydney, Angus & Robertson

Plath, Sylvia (1963), *The Bell Jar*, London, Faber & Faber

Preston, Paul (2010), 'No Soldier', in Jim Jump (ed.), *Looking Back at the Spanish Civil War*, London, Lawrence & Wishart

Probyn, Clive and Steele, Bruce (eds) (2000), *Henry Handel Richardson: the Letters*, Vols 1–3, Melbourne, Miegunyah Press

Richardson, Henry Handel (1964), *Myself When Young*, Melbourne, Heinemann

—— (1977), *The Getting of Wisdom*, Melbourne, Heinemann

Rodriguez, Judith (2010), 'A Note on Aileen Palmer's 'The Swans/The Wanderer', *Hecate*, 36:1&2, pp. 214–15

Sloan, Pat (ed.) (1978), *John Cornford: A Memoir*, Fife, Borderline Press

Smith, Vivian (1975), *Vance and Nettie Palmer*, Boston, Twayne Publishers

—— (ed.) (1977), *Letters of Vance and Nettie Palmer 1915-1963*, Canberra, National Library of Australia

—— (ed.) (1988), *Nettie Palmer: her Private Journal,* Fourteen Years, *Poems, Reviews and Literary Essays*, St Lucia, University of Queensland Press

Sparrow, Jeff (2007), *Communism: A Love Story*, Melbourne, Melbourne University Press

Spender, Stephen (1951), *World within World*, London, Hamish Hamilton

Stone, Brendan (2004), 'Towards a Writing without Power: Notes on the Narrative of Madness', *Auto/Biography*, 12, pp. 16–33

Strahan, Lynne (1984), *Just City and the Mirrors: Meanjin Quarterly and the Intellectual Front, 1940-1965*, Melbourne, Oxford University Press

Sullivan, Rosemary (2007), *Villa Air-Bel: the Second World War, Escape and a House in France*, London, John Murray

Throssell, Ric (1975), *Wild Weeds and Wind Flowers: The Life and Letters of Katharine Susannah Prichard*, Australia, Angus & Robertson

Tipping, Marjorie (1985), 'Remembrance of Palmers Past', *Overland*, 100, pp. 10–18

To Huu (1959), *Poems*, trans. Aileen Palmer, Hanoi, Foreign Languages Publishing House

Vickery, Anne (2007), *Stressing the Modern: Cultural Politics in Australian Women's Poetry*, Cambridge, Salt Publishing

Worsley, T. C. (1971), *Fellow Travellers*, London, London Magazine Editions. It was later republished by GMP Publishers, London, in their Gay Modern Classics series, 1984

Young, Edith (1971), *Inside Out*, London, Routledge & Kegan Paul

Acknowledgements

In a project as dependent on archives as this, my first thanks must go to the librarians and staff of the libraries I have consulted. The main Palmer archives are held in the National Library of Australia; there are also papers in the Mitchell Library, State Library of New South Wales; La Trobe Library, State Library of Victoria; Noel Butlin Achives Centre, Australian National University and the University of Melbourne Archives. For access to papers and photographs relating to the Spanish Civil War, I thank the Marx Memorial Library, London, and the Working Class Movement Library, Salford, UK.

I am grateful for the support I received to research and write this biography from the Australia Council in the form of a Literature Board Grant, a CAL Manning Clark House Residential Fellowship, a Varuna Publisher's Fellowship and assistance from the University of Tasmania.

I thank the people who have provided willing assistance in the form of research advice and personal knowledge or who have shared work of their own on the Palmer family. These include Judith Armstrong, John Barnes, Vera Deacon, Maryanne Dever, Carole Ferrier, Deborah Jordan, Sharon Moore, Sally Newman, Barbara Ramadge-Ross and Ralph Spaulding. Thanks too to my colleagues at the University of Tasmania: Ralph Crane, Lucy Frost and Hamish Maxwell-Stewart.

My research on Aileen Palmer's time serving in the Spanish Civil War involved travel to Spain. Mieke Mulder Scheffer and Jordi Matamoros were generous hosts in Barcelona and drove me around Spain to many of the battle sites. My knowledge would have been much the poorer without this experience and they have my heartfelt thanks. I am grateful to Susan Ballyn,

Tom Buchanan, Eva Campamà Pizarro, Amirah Inglis, Judith Keene and Stuart Walsh for their assistance on matters concerning the Spanish Civil War.

Thanks to readers who made valuable suggestions on parts of the manuscript – Helen Barnes-Bulley, Barbara Holloway and Matthew Stephens – and special thanks to Judith Keene, Susan Sheridan and Vivian Smith for their permission to include their memories of Aileen Palmer in the book. Thanks to Colleen Burke for allowing me to quote a section of her poem 'No Words'.

I would like to thank Terri-ann White and UWA Publishing for taking on the biography of a woman who has been best known as the 'tragic daughter' of writers, Vance and Nettie Palmer, thereby offering readers a more nuanced account of her life. Thanks to Suzannah Shwer for her meticulous copy-editing and to in-house publishing editor Kate Pickard for guiding the manuscript to its final form.

To my writer friends, Barbara Brooks, Sara Hardy, Miranda Morris and Sari Wawn, who have listened to my doubts as well as my enthusiasms over the years of this long project, thank you. Finally, my loving thanks go always to my extended family – Matt, Jamie, Astrid and Grant – and, above all, to my first reader and constant companion, Lizzie Mulder.

Index

www.ingramcontent.com/pod-product-compliance
Lightning Source LLC
Chambersburg PA
CBHW021134090426
42740CB00008B/783

* 9 7 8 1 7 4 2 5 8 8 2 5 4 *